Reading Art, Reading Irigaray

# Reading Art, Reading Irigaray

## The Politics of Art by Women

Hilary Robinson

I.B. TAURIS
LONDON · NEW YORK

Published in 2006 by I.B.Tauris & Co Ltd
6 Salem Road, London W2 4BU
175 Fifth Avenue, New York NY 10010
www.ibtauris.com

In the United States and Canada distributed by Palgrave Macmillan,
a division of St. Martin's Press, 175 Fifth Avenue, New York NY 10010



ISBN 10: 1 86064 953 X
ISBN 13: 978 1 86064 953 0

A full CIP record for this book is available from the British Library
A full CIP record for this book is available from the Library of Congress
Library of Congress catalog card: available

Typeset in Palatino by Dexter Haven Associates Ltd, London
Printed and bound in Great Britain by TJ International Ltd, Padstow, Cornwall.

# Contents

# Acknowledgements

Coming to the conclusion of this work it is a shock to look back and recognise exactly how many years I have lived with it in one form or another, and how many people have supported it and me along the way. While it has been gestating, my family has seen me through a PhD, two promotions and latterly a move to a different country: your differing gestures of support along the way have been warm, unconditional and, I know, crucial. Friends and work colleagues too have been wonderfully generous in their support while often bemused at my drive forward: I thank you all. But there are two people in particular I wish to name and thank here for their support and input. Professor Griselda Pollock was an exceptional teacher, mentor and example. Her love of intellectual engagement in the name of feminism and in pursuit of a culture appropriate for women is extraordinary and tireless: she has done so much and brought so many of us to find our own paths towards that goal. Dr Suzanna Chan was first my student, then my research assistant, helping hugely in preparing this text. She is now herself teaching and building a feminist intellectual culture: I learned certainly as much from her as I ever taught, and the future is bright in such hands. Generation to generation, becoming women: thank you.

# Introduction

> What I am going to try and talk about today, often in the form of questions, stands at the meeting point of the properties of *physical matter* and an elaboration of *sexualised subjective identity* that has still to be thought through and put into practice. (Irigaray 1987a: 167; 1993f: 153)

Art that has been made by women in recent years often challenges its audiences to think differently if we wish to understand it. To take just a few examples, work by senior artists such as Louise Bourgeois or Nancy Spero, by established mid-career artists such as Tracey Emin or Mona Hatoum and that of many emerging artists confounds the categories established for the discussion of art. Feminists have long argued that the art world's discourses are not sufficient for the women who engage with it. To take the four examples I have named, Bourgeois and Spero may be regarded as the 'grand old ladies' or as the doyennes of the American art world, and therefore are categorised as 'the exceptions'.[1] Hatoum's work is often marginalised into a category of 'black British art' or indexically linked to her racial identity as if it can speak of nothing other than that.[2] Tracey Emin's life and the events in it are the subject of investigation in the art press and tabloid newspapers alike, while her work is barely written about, analysed or evaluated.[3]

The work of these women also now confounds the established discourses – or the assumed discourses – of feminist criticism. The activism, the challenges to modes of representation from an overtly feminist standpoint and the investigation of the cultural structures that inform what it is to 'be a woman', all of these are not present in the work of women as we enter the new century in the same way that they were in the 1970s and 1980s. The work of women is challenging feminist discourse on cultural politics to respond to that work and to keep up with its developments. Spero's work is hugely informed by the feminist movement of the 1960s and the 1970s, and she was highly active in the radical movements in the USA at that time. But it appears to me that the politics of her work are now less immediately legible than they used to be. They are still there: there is a call to action in her work that is still palpable. However, her work is now also urging its viewers to develop their critical and political languages and their ways of reading her work. It asks us to rethink what feminist cultural politics might be today, and what a feminist approach to understanding the production of art by women might be. Louise Bourgeois has never embraced feminism as such, although she has never particularly distanced herself either. Her concerns, it could be argued, have always been gender specific, and as she has grown older they appear to become more so. Increasingly too, her art is augmented by the publication of many interviews or extracts from diaries and notebooks that draw our attention to woman-specific or girl-specific experience, be it from the particularities of her own life or from narratives that she weaves. In the 1970s such works as the *Femme-Maison* series found an enthusiastic response from within feminist criticism. Today her *Cell* works and stitched pieces speak in a more complex manner of being-female and of the relation between the specific experiences of one woman and the identifications that other women might make.

Tracey Emin too has never embraced feminism but she, like Bourgeois, has a breathtaking confidence in her ability to speak as a woman. Most of her work speaks of experiences in such a manner that the audience assumes they have come from the artist's own biography. They are usually emotional, often sexual, or have emotional and sexual connotations or contextual narratives. While the events or experiences in Emin's work may range from the everyday (going to the lavatory) to the exceptional and traumatic (an abortion procedure that went wrong), her sex and her sexuality are there, central, and where appropriate, celebrated, but otherwise simply matter of fact. While she may package her gender and sexuality in some of her activities outside of her art practice – modelling for Vivienne Westwood, for example – in her work her body and sexuality are not packaged according to dominant cultural representations (in describing it thus I am distinguishing between Emin and an artist like Pippilotte Rist whose representation of body-image, sexuality and persona in her video works seems to owe a lot to the packaging of those qualities of young women in film, music videos and advertising). Emin also is under no illusions about who has the best understanding of her work: not the art critics, but 17-year-old working-class school girls (Illuminations 2003).

Mona Hatoum's work from her time as a student in the 1970s has been informed very much by an engagement with radical politics, whether sexual politics, the politics of race or of national identity. This was quite explicit in many pieces through the 1980s such as *A Thousand Bullets for a Stone* (1988) which took as its starting point a news photograph of a Palestinian woman confronting an armed soldier, or the short video *So Much I Want to Say* (1983), which is a close-up shot of the artist's face with a man's hands over her mouth, which she repeatedly tries to pull away. A voice-over has her constantly repeating the phrase of the title. Another video, *Measures of Distance* (1985), is an exquisite exploration of the mother–daughter relationship, using photographs Hatoum took of her mother in the shower, audio recordings of the two women speaking in Arabic together and further recordings of Hatoum reading translations of letters her mother sent. The letters also hold the piece together visually, with the Arabic writing superimposed on a grid over the photographic images. Through the 1990s Hatoum's work has embraced a more minimalist aesthetic – sculptures using schematic furniture forms or the enlarged forms of kitchen implements, installations with wires with electrical currents running through them, or with individual strands of her hair knotted to form almost invisible lengths from ceiling to floor that brush the viewers as they walk through.

The work of all these artists asks its viewers to rethink what feminist politics of cultural criticism might be. Clearly, with each, the articulation of gendered identity and experience is a major part of the work; clearly also, this is manifested not simply through the content of the work, but also through the selection, manipulation and deployment of the materials to make that work. The challenge for feminist discourses around the production and reading of art is to find means to articulate the difference of artists who are women. Present art critical discourse being theoretically and structurally wanting, it is necessary to build feminist analyses and terminology which can not only be brought to bear upon present critical discourse but also facilitate the legibility of artworks by women in ways that have been rare to date. What has become politically interesting about the work of artists such as Spero, Bourgeois, Hatoum and Emin, as well as many others, is that it makes visible 'the meeting point of the properties of physical matter and an elaboration of sexualised subjective identity' (Irigaray 1987a: 167; 1993f: 153), to use Irigaray's thrilling and challenging phrase. At once with this statement we could be in a woman artist's studio. We could be contemplating her practices. We could be at a site – the meeting point of the properties of *physical matter* and an elaboration of *sexualised subjective identity* – which is the site of her enunciation through those practices. It is this meeting point that this book aims to elucidate, proposing that certain key concepts and arguments in the work of Irigaray are productive in the search for feminist critical analyses of contemporary art practices by women, not because they 'explain' the work, but because they can help make those practices legible. This book, then, is necessarily strategic and political: it is intended that some of the ideas which emerge from it will find their way back, as questions, into that possible place of a woman artist's studio, her practice and the site of her enunciation.

Two main impulses have shaped the focus for the book. The first was concern about the state of feminist art criticism and about the status of feminist art practice; the second was the conflict between my pleasure and interest in reading some of Irigaray's philosophical writings and my confusion when reading her essays on art. My initial concern was that artists such as Mona Hatoum, Rachel Whiteread, Louise Bourgeois, Jana Sterbak, Nancy Spero, Janine Antoni, Tracey Emin and many others – artists working in diverse media with diverse aims, but with clear recognition of themselves as gendered female – may have had critical appraisal by feminists, but they have not, by and large, seen deeper shifts within theories of art produced by feminism which can accommodate (or which have been provoked by) their practices. Additionally, a number of younger women artists in Britain have emerged onto the national and international art scene who appear to have nothing to say, in their work or beyond, about feminism – even though the surface style of much of this work may recall feminist work and concerns of the 1970s – and about whom feminist criticism has appeared to say nothing. A malaise begins to be delineated.

At least in part this malaise is a result of (and helps to perpetuate) very real problems. For example, the continuing low employment rates of women in art schools creates problems for feminist practitioners and critics, and perpetuates the isolation of women students (who are often in the majority) from knowledge, analyses and theories of their history and present context as women. Feminist activity among tutors in universities and art schools, possibly as a result of the pressure to publish, is increasingly focused on theoretical and academic production, apparently at the expense of activist and practical strategies to deal with these issues in day-to-day interaction with colleagues and students. Increasingly through the late 1980s and into the 1990s 'feminism' had become a misnomer for an academic approach, or one of a series of methodologies. Many of those searching for their PhD subjects lit upon gender or 'feminist' issues as a choice of academic subject, rather than having a set of feminist politics as the underlying driver for their research, whatever its subject might be. A 'feminism' developed that was essentially depoliticised, that drew in little from beyond the texts it studied, and which could barely intervene in actions and practices beyond the theoretical. Thus within the academy there was little coherent clarity about tasks and strategies for the coming years, while there was at the same time awareness that there was still so much work to be done.

Interestingly, and perhaps in response, a handful of major publications in the USA and Britain in recent years have insisted upon the importance of historicising feminist art practices, charting the movement's diverse activities primarily in those countries, its engagements and strategies (for example, de Zegher 1996; Fuller and Salvioni 2002; Jones 1996a; Reckitt and Phelan 2001; Robinson 2002). At the same time, key publications in other countries have responded to the same necessity to archive and historicise, but at the same time have interrogated the dominant theoretical positions emanating from the USA and Britain (for example, Datuin 2002; Huangfu 2000; Kerr and Holder 1999). Such publications provide a grounded, archival, evidence-based context for theoretical and strategic development at this crucial juncture, when the still-remembered experience of the artists active in the 1970s is being turned into Art History for today's students. Griselda Pollock's essay 'The Politics of Theory' (Pollock 1996c) was a timely reminder for writers on art to keep their political feet on the ground when doing this, and her book *Differencing the Canon* – as significant a book for art writers in the new century, I believe, as *Old Mistresses* (co-authored with Rozsika Parker) was in the 1980s – demonstrated the need for continuing intervention in the fundamental structures of the discipline, Art History (Pollock 1999; Parker and Pollock 1981).

As a result of the challenges to feminist discourses by artists, the new approaches to archiving and historicising work, the interrogation of the USA/British feminist hegemony by artists and art writers in different parts of the world, and the historical moment in the history of feminist interventions in art and art writing, it is a very rich time for turning to different ways of thinking about the making of art by women and how that work becomes legible – how we can reach understandings of it, how we can 'read' it. So turning to the writings of Irigaray is not a direct response to the malaise outlined above, and in making this turn I am not suggesting that her work contains in any transparent form the solution to these problems; nor am I suggesting that her work has a unifying theoretical 'glue' for pulling together the differing strands of activity at present. It is rather that there are elements in her thinking concerning women's subjectivity, the enunciation of that sexed subjectivity and of mediation between subjects, which are not only exciting philosophically, but are also important for theoretical and critical discussions of contemporary art. In addition, Irigaray's work is not generated from a solely theoretical framework. It is informed by, and feeds back into, a range of practices – for example, professional (her work as a psychoanalyst), party political (such as her work with the youth movement of the Communist Party of Italy), spiritual (her practice of meditation), and scientific (her collation of the uses of language). It is this return of practice to the acts of theorising, and of theory to the place and time of practice – allowing practice to be productive of theory – that to my mind is one reason why Irigaray's work is so attractive for artists. It is my contention that, although it barely engages with art directly, much of Irigaray's work cuts across many of the tired areas in present-day art criticism, and can help us to develop ways of reading the practices of contemporary women artists, and feed into the studios and related practices of those artists.

Such possibilities were not at all apparent to me in my initial reading of an article which is among the few where Irigaray discusses visual art. My reaction to 'A Natal Lacuna' (with a commentary by Margaret Whitford, 'Woman with Attitude') was one of disappointment and confusion (Irigaray 1994b; Whitford 1994b). In it Irigaray considers the work of artist Unica Zürn as a 'failure'. She says that Zürn, in her desire to produce a 'descriptive reality' of her 'psychic truth', has produced an art that is 'ugly', a symptom of her own fragmented psyche. This, argues Irigaray, is a result of Zürn's failure to 'give birth to herself' as a woman. She uses this 'failure' to argue that 'it is difficult for a woman to be born', and for the importance for women of producing wholeness and 'beauty', particularly through 'her own morphology'. Whitford's commentary concentrates on the aspects of Irigaray's essay which touch upon visual art, and includes an explanation of Irigaray's understanding of the death drives and their relationship to creativity. She suggests that Irigaray's concept of 'beauty' is woman's identity for herself, and reads Irigaray to be calling for women to create figurative, idealised representations of women. She then states that Irigaray has, therefore, a conservative approach to art.

This was confusing. I had certainly not thought of Irigaray as potentially conservative in her understanding of art; indeed, my initial reading of her work found that it would have much to offer artists in its discussion of language and representation. Key to this project was realising the difficulties of interdisciplinary work. Neither Irigaray nor Whitford have a background in the visual arts. Irigaray is a psychoanalyst and philosopher, and Whitford a philosopher. In her writings Irigaray, in particular, has worked in a richly interdisciplinary way, and, in writing about her, Whitford has had to follow suit. Yet the underlying problem of 'A Natal Lacuna' for an audience of artists and critics (a problem perpetuated by Whitford's article also) is precisely the failure to understand or show knowledge of the practices of visual art in general and the necessary corollary, feminist analyses and developments of visual art as manifested through practices, histories and theories. Thus neither of these articles provide the interdisciplinary reading necessary to facilitate access – and thus the construction of models of practice – for contemporary practitioners and critics. My initial readings of the two articles identified particular problem areas: the prioritising of the literary arts over the visual arts; the lack of attention to the specificities of visual art practices; and the stress upon the artwork as product only, without consideration of the processes involved in its making (Robinson 1994). In trying to follow up on this reading, it rapidly became apparent that Irigaray has written very little on art – other than the piece on Unica Zürn mentioned above, the main essay is 'How Can We Create Our Beauty?' (Irigaray 1990b, 1993h), which will be discussed in Chapter 5. In addition, while many artists and writers on art have made reference to Irigaray's work and influence, it is rare that they have done more than talk in very general terms that do little to elucidate how useful Irigaray's work could be in this context. Two exceptions are Griselda Pollock and Rosemary Betterton, in, for example, (Betterton 1996; Pollock 1996b). There are few others.

In trying to identify the threads in Irigaray's work which can help us rethink the political and cultural discourse of contemporary art practice and criticism, there are a number of things that this book will not do. Four in particular should be mentioned. First, it will not relate her work to that of other philosophers and psychoanalysts, nor map out her indebtedness to them. Second, it will not chart the detailed chronology of the development of her thinking. There are others who are far more qualified to do both of these jobs than I, and I acknowledge the importance of their work for my own.[4] The third thing it will not do is use Irigaray's work to 'explain' women's artwork and fourth, nor will it use artworks to 'illustrate' Irigaray's writing. I hope to avoid these two simplifications with two moves. On the one hand I will outline the analyses, structures and strategies that Irigaray teases out as conducive to the development of representational structures which are appropriate for women, rather than those which maintain the languages of patriarchy. Then, on the other hand, I will look for moments in the practices of artists and in contemporary artworks that can be read through an understanding of strategies that Irigaray identifies as manifested by women in patriarchal culture. In doing this I aim to avoid proscribing or prescribing particular practices (whether representational, contextual or of media); but rather to open up discourses of possibility of and for contemporary art practices.

One thing that emerged clearly (if negatively) from the existing work on Irigaray was how few of the commentators had read further than *This Sex* and *Speculum*, and how many relied upon the comments of others in a manner that was often more muddled than enlightening, with even basic terminology and concepts being misused. This approach is summed up in one book, whose author seems to make a virtue out of not reading Irigaray's actual work:

> In what follows I shall refer rather more to the writings of those feminists who see themselves as broadly propagating Irigaray's ideas than to her own works, which are generally found to be too obscure to interpret with confidence. It is, in any case, the kind of theoretical moves being made in feminist theory which are my concern more than the accuracy with which these may be attributed to certain theorists (Curthoys 1997: 143).

Because this approach seemed common (if seldom so explicitly stated), I resolved to read Irigaray's own works as closely as possible in order to fathom her meanings and use of terminology. Her work is 'a-academic' and highly resistant to academic procedures. I found it necessary to trace her use of particular terms as they are used in different books and essays in order to determine her use of them – not a project which would be feasible for writers of shorter articles as her writing is rarely indexed.

This has influenced the structure of the book, which is in three parts. Part 1, 'Structures of Visual Representation', aims to reach an understanding of Irigaray's philosophy of sexual difference in so far as it impacts upon the production of meaning in the realm of the visual, and, consequently, the visual aesthetic. Therefore it comprises a close reading of Irigaray's work as it relates to the practices and structures which inform the production and reception of visual representation. Mimesis and its related terms are crucial concepts for analysing how we learn to behave in a manner appropriate for our social structures, and how we create art. Chapter 1, 'Mimesis', begins by positing a series of questions concerning mimetic practices in contemporary work by women in order to focus on the widespread significance of such practices and the need to differentiate between their differing nuances and manifestations. The chapter identifies two aspects of mimesis: non-productive and productive. The first is discussed in relation to mimicry and mime, which maintain patriarchal structures as they are down through the generations. 'Masquerade' is identified as the practice of femininity as constructed by patriarchy. It maintains women as 'other of man's same' within patriarchal structures. Hysteria is discussed here also, as the mark of a site of resistance to the masquerade which is femininity; ultimately, however, it is identified as non-productive, as its strategy to achieve the power of self-determination is one of mimeticising femininity to the extreme of paralysis, muteness or even death. Sites of resistance or 'reserve' other than hysteria, mark what I call a 'productive mimesis'. In order to (re)gain the site of their subjectivity (which in a phallocentric economy can only yet be hypothesised), women have to retraverse the site of their exploitation knowingly and strategically. Irigaray's own work is identified here as both practice and analysis of productive mimesis. A model from Paul Ricoeur helps us to see how productive mimesis is a praxis, moving constantly between social prefiguration, textual configuration and (in the act of reading and interpreting) practical transfiguration. This retrieves Irigaray's work from being regarded in purely academic, textual terms, and repoliticises its analysis.

Chapter 2 follows Irigaray's analyses of the visual structures and representation in the visual. Phallocentric structures are predicated upon the visibility or non-visibility of the penis; phallocentric ways of seeing thus hinge on seeing it or not seeing it, not upon seeing it or seeing the vulva (seeing difference). Phallocentric representations are built upon the site of this partial sight and its blind spots. I argue that women are thus confirmed again, as other of the same, configured not as subjects, but as representations, with no access to appropriate significatory systems – a disaster for the legible articulation of subjectivity through art. Irigaray's use of the term 'syntax' is introduced. This enables the distinguishing of inflections, significations and sites of enunciation in a Symbolic which is not one, but is multiple. The possible reconfiguration of the structures informing our practices of sight and seeing are discussed. The notion of the reserve is reintroduced. The mirror has a silvery backing touching the glass – the reserve of the mirror. The movement through the surface of a flat mirror to its backing disrupts the illusion of the frozen surface and evokes the concave space of the mirror more suited to woman – the 'burning mirror' of the female mystics. The work of Anish Kapoor is discussed in this context.

I argue through this chapter that Irigaray is not anti-visual, but that she is anti-phallocentric, and as such wishes to restore a relationship of interdependence between sight and touch. She also stresses a revaluing of other senses. Listening becomes important in establishing relationships between subjects. Phallocentric structures allow men to look only for their same, and reduce all else to object status, to value sight-dependent subject–object relations. Insistence upon sexual difference means that subjects realise they cannot transcend other subjects: therefore, structures of intersubjective relationships are needed. For women, if they are not to remain in relationships of immediacy, gift-objects of communication and practices of listening have to be developed in order that these relationships may be mediated. This has great implications for the role and function of the art object, its presentation and for its consideration by an attentive audience of subjects. The mediation of subjectivity in performance work is discussed using the case of Janine Antoni's *Loving Care*. The status of the art object in the market, and intersubjectivity between artist and audience are explored through Buddhist models of attentiveness, drawn to our notice by Irigaray.

Through exploring some of the core practices involved in the making of art and in looking at art in relation to key elements of Irigaray's thinking, Part 1 establishes a theoretical framework from which to move forward. Part 2, 'Body and Legibility', focuses more upon the relation between practice and materiality in the relation between the body and the artwork. This is a site of interchange between the structural properties of formal procedures and the structural processes of subjectivity and offers greater focus on a resonance between, on the one hand, particular structures and arguments within Irigaray's writing, and on the other hand, particular art practices and artworks. Chapter 3 argues that a consideration of Irigaray's understanding of 'morphology' could help us renegotiate the functions of media in practices of art. I argue that some critics have misread this term as referring to anatomy, whereas it is a means of understanding the relationships between forms – for example, between subjectivity, body and language. Thus, although each subject will have her or his own morphology, each gender will also have a morphologic appropriate to it. I then offer a reading of Irigaray's use of the terms 'the lips' and 'the mucus' as an engagement with a morphologic of mediation appropriate to women. The emphasis in developing this as a theoretical structure for the analysis of art practices is not to employ any media as metaphors for mucus (this is discussed in relation to paint in particular), but to consider them as sites of mediation which could possibly reveal a morphologic appropriate to women. The legibility of work by different artists is considered in this context, and in particular how feminist writers have tried to make particular works legible, and how introducing the concept of morphology may assist legibility. Rosemary Betterton's reading of the work of Laura Godfrey-Isaacs through structures of fetishism is discussed in relation to this: it is seen to fall apart when the artist moves away from painting, whereas a morphologically aware approach may advance the understanding of Godfrey-Isaacs' work further. An article by Joan Key on works by Bridget Riley and Rachel Whiteread, and one by Alison Rowley focusing on Jenny Saville, are also identified as moments of present critical practice which demonstrate why such a theoretical development is timely. If their arguments are reconfigured in Irigarayan terms, Key and Rowley are seen to identify uses of media in works by the different artists which can be read as informed by a morphologic of the mucus, and other moments where instead the works collapse back into mimeticising a phallic morphology.

Chapter 4 attends to the practices of gesture in the making of artworks. The focus is upon Louise Bourgeois's recent work and the way in which her processes have been accounted for by critics. Many critics have read into her work the influence of her childhood experience of emotional betrayal by her father and her continuing anger about this into her old age. Irigaray's paper 'Gesture in Psychoanalysis' outlines the suppressed, but gendered, practices of gesture in the practice of psychoanalysis, before moving on to consider Freud's main analysis of gesture in childhood, which was of a boy trying to master the absence of his mother – little Ernst playing with a cotton reel. Irigaray argues that girls make different gestures when they miss their mothers: not the throwing and retrieving of an object like little Ernst, but inter-subjective games with dolls, or the marking out of subjective space with their bodies, with whirling or spinning 'dances'. I argue that in Bourgeois's work we may see, as well as anger at her father, grief at the trauma of her mother's displacement. This can be read in her interest in spinning and her gestural delineation of space in the *Cell* series of the 1990s and 2000s, and in her creation of the stitched and stuffed figurative works of the late 1990s onwards.

Part 3 of the book, 'Women's Genealogies', moves into a discussion of how it is possible to represent, read and partake of women's structures of knowledge and being, both in the realm of the divine and of the familial. Chapter 5, 'Divine Beauty', discusses the aspirational models of the divine that have been provided for women, and attends to Irigaray's argument that we will only fully 'become women' – attain our subjectivity – once we have a 'transcendent', including notions of a female 'divine' and of a 'universal' appropriate to the morphologic informing it. Once again, the subject 'woman' that one might become is distinct from the representation 'woman' constructed by phallocentrism. For women, a phallocentric prioritising of sight deprives them of a sense of their own beauty, replacing it with the 'beauty' supplied by the representation, 'woman'. Women do not have their own sense of a divine beauty, a corresponding ideal representation that is theirs. Irigaray's conception of the beautiful for women is not arbitrarily abstract, but rooted in the body and bodily experience, even when it pertains to the divine. This is discussed in the context of representations of the goddess. Irigaray identifies a crucial historical shift in how the genitals of goddesses were represented, from showing the lips of the vulva, to smoothing them over and sealing them. Representations of goddesses, both ancient works and recent ones by artists such as Cynthia Mailman and Yolanda López, will be discussed in this context. So too will what Irigaray calls 'hysteroscopy' – a fetishising of male desire in the discourses of representation, whether in pornographic imagery or in the work of artists such as Kitaj or Courbet. Beauty, argues Irigaray, is not to be found in such fetishising, but in forms of representation that allow women fully to become the subjects, women.

The final chapter, 'Mother–Daughter Genealogies', takes this argument and grounds it in the representation of the mother–daughter relationship. Irigaray not only argues that patriarchy is founded upon a symbolic matricide, but also that until women can imagine their own mothers partaking of the divine then they will have no divine of their own. She makes very practical suggestions for the creation of an appropriate symbolic between mothers and daughters that will help work towards this. The representation of St Anne and Saint Mary, as a mother–daughter couple that is also a divine couple, is a rich source for exploration of this in the Christian cultural context, as they are often shown with Anne teaching Mary to read – a passing on of knowledge that does not appear in the Bible. Adélaïde Labille-Guiard's *Self-Portrait with Two Pupils* (1785) is also an interesting depiction of a woman as teacher, passing knowledge to a younger generation – a potentially subversive activity. When searching for models of representation among women of earlier generations, the thorny question of essentialism has to be tackled. I argue that in searching for morphological resonance, many women artists are discovering productive sites of genealogy and syntax: a productive mimesis rather than a maintenance mimesis. This is discussed particularly in reference to the work of Hannah Wilke and Frances Hegarty both of whom have explicitly represented their relation to their mothers. These works, I argue, produce a morphologically coherent space for a productive mimesis.

Throughout the book terminology will be developed from an understanding of Irigaray's use of language. These terms will then be carried forward in subsequent chapters to be used in the development of other terms or further refined. A key example of this is the term 'woman', use of which will be explicitly developed throughout the first part of the book. 'Feminine' has been avoided for two reasons. Firstly, the lack of equivalent usage in French and in English means that to use it as understood in English would complicate rather than clarify – see for example Margaret Whitford's glossary note for 'féminin': 'translated as feminine or female, depending on the translator. [...] The question of nature or culture is an interpretive one, and accordingly the interpretation has been left to the reader' (Whitford 1991a: 17). My second reason for avoiding the term explains why I find this degree of openness unhelpful. 'Feminine' has frequently been used to name qualities which are not only constructs, but which can be adopted by both sexes. Thus for example, Hélène Cixous's exemplars of writers of the 'feminine' include James Joyce and Jean Genet (Cixous 1981). In avoiding the term I am also following the example of most of Irigaray's translators after *Speculum* and *This Sex*. To reconfigure the gap left, Irigaray's use of the term 'syntax' is introduced in Chapter 2. This accounts not only for uses of language, but indeed for the production and understanding of all significatory systems in the Symbolic (gestural, political, visual…). At present the dominant syntax is phallocentric, but there is the potential for the development of a syntax appropriate for women. Additionally (as will be described in the main body of the text) I have restricted use of the term 'femininity': its use by Freud is outlined by Irigaray as a product of a phallocentric syntax, and is not a quality of women's making.

As I have just indicated, translation is a politically and culturally creative practice, and one which may be constructive and destructive to the textual intention of the writer whose work is being translated.[5] Irigaray's work with its significant and diverse textual strategies 'represents difficulties of translation', as she has said, both of its thinking and also of its use of language.[6] Anyone who is not fluently (bi-culturally) bi-lingual is at the mercy of/indebted to the translators of the texts almost as much as to Irigaray herself: the translation can affect to a huge extent the reception of a work, and thus the development of thinking in the second language.

In this book I have depended upon the standard translations of Irigaray's work. Where I have felt unsure about the translation, I have either included the French in brackets, or modified the translation. The aim in modification has always been to provide the more literal translation, rather than an interpretive version; and/or to honour Irigaray's repetition, echoing or fidelity to particular terminology. Modification is always footnoted.

Irigaray's own writing is full of particularities of punctuation which add to the text, including ellipses, parentheses and italics. Because of this, in quoted passages, my own ellipses are marked thus: […] leaving her ellipses as: …; and insertions of the original French are bracketed thus: […]. I have ensured that all words in italics in the translated passages correspond to Irigaray's own italicising. For clarity's sake I have sacrificed these stresses in any French language insertions, placing all French in italics.

# PART 1

# Structures of Visual Representation

# 1

# Mimesis

> I search for myself, as if I had been assimilated into maleness. I ought to reconstitute myself on the basis of a disassimilation... Rise again from the traces of a culture, of works already produced by the other. Searching through what is in them – for what is not there. What allowed them to be, for what is not there. Their conditions of possibility, for what is not there.
>
> Woman ought to be able to find herself, among other things, through the images of herself already deposited in history and the conditions of production of the work of man, and not on the basis of his work, his genealogy. (Irigaray 1984: 17; 1993c: 9–10)

Working with what is already there as a given, searching through it painstakingly for what is not there, disaggregating a subjectivity from the objects provided and the conditions of their production – this is what lies at the basis of Luce Irigaray's utterly pragmatic politics and philosophy of culture. This book will trace through her writings to discern how she does this in relation to the visible, to visuality and to representation. From that, with the help of other structures within Irigaray's writings, it will model ways of reading the practices of and works by artists who are women.

Within Irigaray's writing a cluster of terms implying some form of repetition are used: mime, masquerade, mask, mimicry, hysterical mimeticism, mimesis, reproduction, representation and the phrase 'as if' (usually placed in quotation marks or in italics) are among the most prominent. They appear strongly in *This Sex Which Is Not One* (Irigaray 1977a, 1985d) and *Speculum: Of the Other Woman* (Irigaray 1974, 1985b) and are scattered through other publications such as *Je, Tu, Nous* (Irigaray 1990a, 1993i). These concepts are of the utmost importance for visual art, not only for the languages *of* art (making of resemblances, images and representations within the art object) but also for the discourses *around* art (art as a set of practices with traditions, histories and theories from which practitioners learn and within which they situate themselves).

This book is concerned throughout with the interdependence of these two aspects of art. I will use Irigaray's work to expand the present discourses around art and to increase the legibility of artworks by women. Irigaray's writing can be used in ways that help us understand new, or other, or different legibilities of artworks, ways of understanding that allow women (as artists and viewers of art) to recognise their subjectivity as women. As the quote at the top of this chapter implies, this has to be done while acknowledging the traditions and languages of art in which we (artists and art-writers) are situated. As feminist art historians have argued, it is a tradition that has historically and structurally excluded women from fully being artists precisely because it has excluded them from having full access to its discourses and practices. At the heart of this dubiously gendered structure of the art world, and intimately connected to these notions of access to language, are also constructs of appropriate subjectivity, and of the nature of culture and reproduction.

## MIMETIC PRACTICES IN ARTWORKS BY WOMEN

It is common sense that artists use various mimetic practices in the work. The much prized quality of 'originality' is all but non-existent other than in relatively incremental terms. Overwhelmingly, artworks can be categorised according to period and country, demonstrating how much artists owe to those around them from whom they have learned their skills. What is also obvious is that in recent decades, mimetic practices have been used by women in their work in a manner that is overt, that is strategic, and that comments upon those practices and/or upon the works being mimeticised, in ways that have little to do with the usual mimetic processes of learning. Thus, when we look at the recent art practices of women we are often looking at two differing but related sets of mimetic practices. First, how the artist has learned to look, to select, to craft, to compose and to offer forward – how she has learned her visual language – and how she has sought to advance and make that language her own. Second, we are looking at her knowing interrogation and critique of practices that have gone before, her exposure of elements within those practices, her use of them to comment on them, her acknowledgement of them. In this second category at least – and quite possibly in the first – are works that raise theoretical questions about visual culture in general (not just that part of it called 'art'), its gendered nature, its generation and germination, the structures of looking that it inculcates, and how these are passed through the culture and through the generations. The methods that artists use – the nature of the mimetic practices – also vary, ranging from mimicry and mime to masquerade and the excessive mimeticism of hysteria. What such works question is the production and reading of visual languages and their part in creating and articulating subjectivity. What we as viewers should also be asking is 'why is so much work using these methodologies and raising these questions being made by women in recent years? How can we read these practices? What is the relation between the articulation of sexual politics, the articulation of women's subjectivities, and the production of visual art? What are the strategies these artists are using and why?'

Since the 1970s Nancy Spero has been making work that has as its main representational element images of women that she has appropriated from elsewhere. There are goddesses, dancers, peasant women, athletes, women who are pregnant or giving birth and many others far less easy to categorise. They come from Europe, Asia, Africa, Australasia, the Americas. They are taken from sources ranging from the pre-historic through others such as ancient Egyptian tombs and Greek vases to contemporary newsprint. Generally, Spero has made prints from these images, re-drawing them in a linear style with little detailing. The same figures may appear again and again in the same works and in different works. What are the mimetic practices at work here? Why? How can we look afresh at these images, read them differently? What does such repetition upon repetition do? What subjectivity is being articulated here? How is it legible?

In her 1987–1988 series *Ain't Jokin'*, Carrie Mae Weems took various North American racist riddles, rhymes and stereotypes and made literal photographic interpretations of them, with the text of the riddle or rhyme under the image or on the label. For example, in one we see a black woman from the back, her shoulder and profile, her head turned, eyes cast downwards. She is wearing a dress or top with spaghetti straps that leaves her upper back all but naked. She holds up a frame, within which we see the face of a white woman, wearing a white hat and veiling. She in turn is holding a glittered star, as if she were the Snow Queen. Her look is directed at the face of the black woman. Under the photograph is the text: 'Looking into the mirror, the black woman asked, "mirror, mirror on the wall, who's the finest of them all?" The mirror says, "Snow White you black bitch, and don't you forget it!!!".' What are the mimetic practices that Weems is using, and why? What is at stake for a black woman to repeat such a riddle and give it further visual articulation? What is the relation between repeating the riddle and creating the image? What subjectivity is being articulated here? How is it legible?

Yoko Ono performed *Cut Piece* in Kyoto (1964), New York (1965) and London (1966). It was then repeated several times by Charlotte Moorman during the 1960s and by Jon Hendricks in 1968. The performer sat on a stage motionless with a pair of scissors at her side. Members of the audience were invited to come up one at a time and, using the scissors, to cut off bits of her clothing.

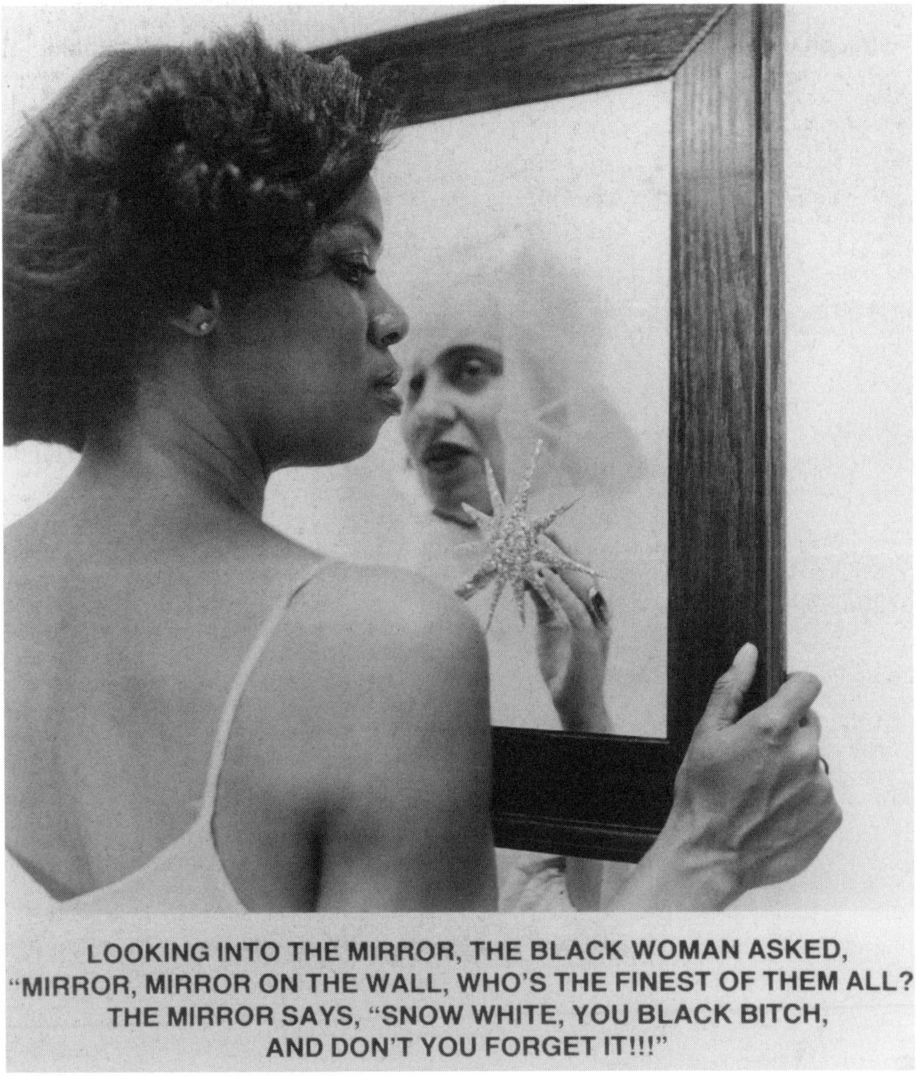


Carrie Mae Weems, *Mirror, Mirror*: from the *Ain't Jokin'* series, 1987–1988. Silver print, 20″ x 16″. Courtesy of the artist.

While passivity and aggression are not the prerogative of one sex rather than the other, these are qualities that socially carry strong connotations of appropriately or inappropriately gendered behaviour for each sex. A man has performed this work, and from the film evidence many women audience members came and cut off Ono's clothing, but the work was created by a woman, Ono, and is particularly charged when a woman performs it. Notions of sexual aggression are under the surface, and at times to the fore. In the film of the work as Ono

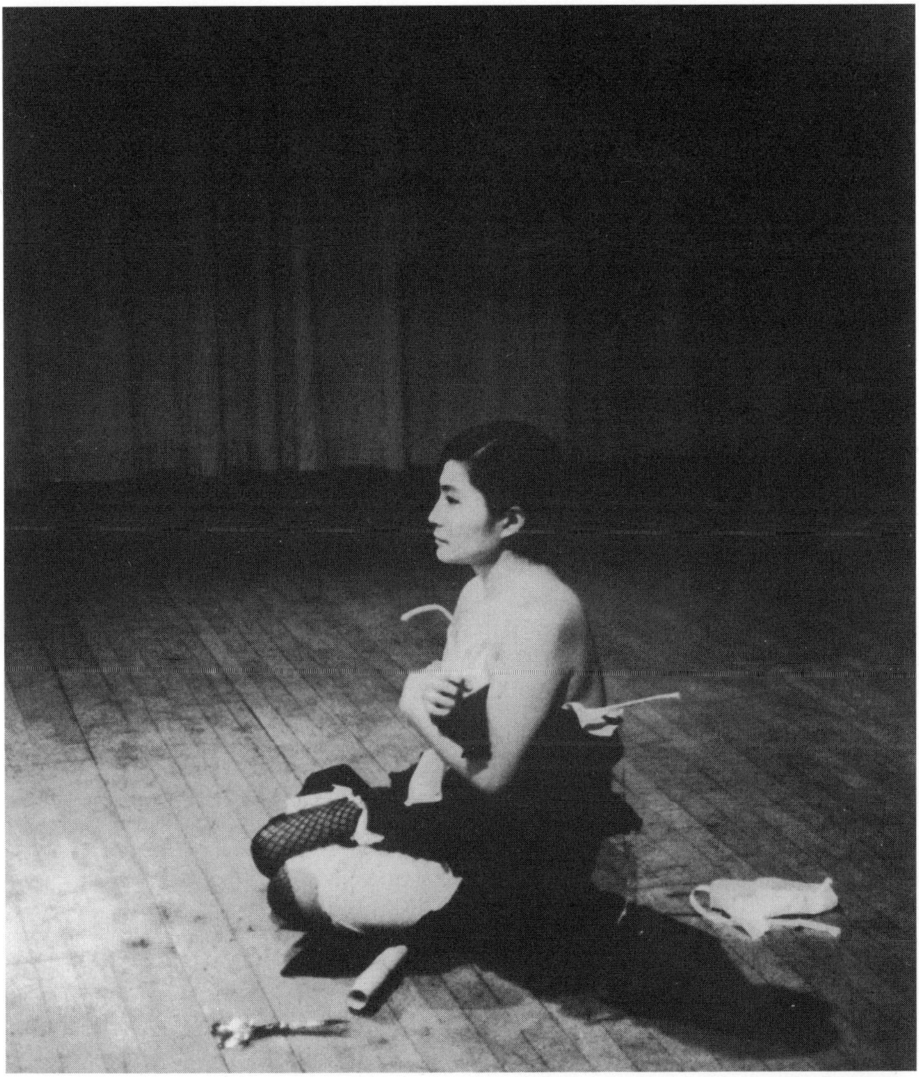

Yoko Ono performing *Cut Piece* 1965 at Carnegie Recital Hall, New York City. Photo by Minoru Niizuma/© Yoko Ono.

performed it in New York, for example, one man cuts a hole through her sweater over her nipple. Towards the end, another man spends far more time cutting and cuts far more off than anyone else, in a manner that can only be described as increasingly aggressive. Eventually he snips both bra straps, in such a way that Ono's breasts are exposed. Ono is clearly shaken by this particular intervention, and the film stops at this point.

Ten years after Ono first performed *Cut Piece,* Marina Abramovic performed *Rhythm O* (1974) in Naples. Abramovic stood next to a table with objects on it, including a gun, a bullet, a whip, an axe, a fork, a bottle of perfume, needles, scissors, a pen, grapes, olive oil, a rose, a saw, water, matches and other items. A label on the wall stated: 'There are seventy-two objects on the table that can be used on me as desired. I am the object.' After three hours Abramovic had been stripped, her clothes cut off. Documentary photographs show that her skin had been cut with a razor blade, she had liquids poured over her, she had the loaded gun put into her hand, the muzzle against her own neck. One photograph shows another woman wiping Abramovic's face clean. After six hours the performance was ended by some concerned people in the audience. In *Cut Piece* and in *Rhythm O,* what are the mimetic practices? Can such gestures of passivity be mimeticised so excessively that they become something other? Whose subjectivity is being articulated here? Where? How is it legible?

Rita Duffy's painting *Territory* (1996) consists of 15 panels, each 24" x 30". On each one paint is layered and sanded. Upon the top layer is drawn in graphite a detailed map, like an aerial photograph, of the 15 so-called 'peacelines' in Belfast – walls built to keep separate particular areas of Catholic and Protestant working-class housing, understood as flashpoints of Loyalist and Republican violence. Over the images in her painting Duffy has stencilled the words 'his heart beneath your heart / is a wardrum / and ignorant little fists already beat at your / borders / your tracked and stretchmarked body / the big pain.' The 'you' evoked can be read as a pregnant woman. Duffy leaves the words in an indirect and tense relation with the images. Neither is sufficient as metaphor for the other but the two are constantly deferring to each other in the meanings they produce. In this work (an unusual one for her) Duffy echoes the words of Seamus Heaney's poem 'Act of Union', in which Heaney plays on the sexual-political pun of the title, and speaks as the various male occupiers of the land. The second stanza reads:

> And I am still imperially
> Male, leaving you with the pain,
> The rending process in the colony,
> The battering ram, the boom burst from within.

The act sprouted an obstinate fifth column
Whose stance is growing unilateral.
His heart beneath your heart is a wardrum
Mustering force. His parasitical
And ignorant little fists already
Beat at your borders and I know they're cocked
At me across the water. No treaty
I forsee will salve completely your tracked
And stretchmarked body, the big pain
that leaves you raw, like opened ground, again.

Here the 'you' is a victimised, raped and occupied woman, metaphor for the land and state of Ireland. Eschewing the voice 'imperially male', disrupting the sonnet rhythm and rhyme, and dissecting the poem, Duffy aims to confound spaces of identity, and with them any possibility of identification. What are the mimetic practices in text and image? Can a female subjectivity be articulated through selective mimicry of a male voice? Is a new subjectivity being articulated here? And if so, how is it legible?

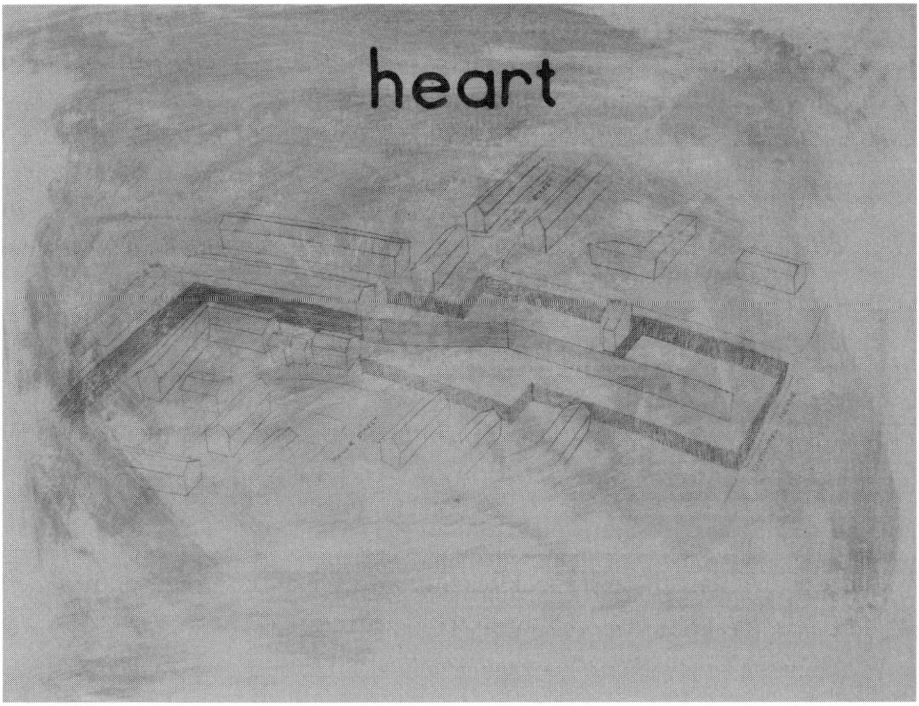


Rita Duffy, *Territory*: (detail), 1996. Graphite, pigment and gesso on board, 15 panels, 24″ x 30″ each. Courtesy of the artist.

Lucy Gunning's video *The Horse Impressionists* (1994) shows five women imitating horse sounds and movements. Having heard the sound of a woman imitating a horse neighing at the end of a night in a London club, but having been unable to locate her, Gunning advertised in the press for women who had these skills as girls and who had kept them as adult women. Over a period of months, she interviewed for and selected the five women in the video (Bush 2004). They are filmed in a static, documentary style, in parks and back yards. The women appear to be of differing ages, social class and milieu. They have varying degrees of self-consciousness, but for much of the time they focus fully on becoming horse. One mimics the movements of both horse and rider; another concentrates on the noises rather than the movements; but with all five, the moments of transcendence into horse remove feelings of embarrassment or humour in the viewer. What are the differing mimetic practices here? How and what does the moment of masquerade communicate between artist and audience? Whose subjectivity is at stake here, and whose is in a state of becoming? How is it legible?

In *Documenta IX* (Kassel, Germany) in 1992 Zoe Leonard exhibited an untitled work in the Neue Galerie. A series of seven elegant rooms in the museum feed into each other. They have jacquard-style wall coverings, and the paintings they contain are eighteenth and nineteenth century, domestic in scale, many portraits and family groups, some landscapes and still lives. Leonard removed the paintings that did not have women at the centre of their subject matter or narrative, leaving only portraits of women, with an occasional couple or family group where the woman was central. A still life with a fish was also left. In the gaps that were thus created, Leonard hung nineteen black and white photographs, 10″ x 8″, modestly mounted in portrait format with glass and clips. The images were of women's genitals in close up, about life-sized on the paper. What was created was a exhibition of paintings that were mainly formal portraits of women, of different character, age and emotional disposition, with formalist photographic portraits of women's genitals. The juxtaposition created an imaginative space for unexpected readings. In this apparently simple act of re-curating the rooms, Leonard made interventions in the common practices of museology, of the representation of sex, sexuality and sexual desire, of the representation of women, and of the role and function of women in ensuring the continuation of the bourgeois family line. What are the differing mimetic practices here? What mimeticisms are being exceeded, displaced or exposed? Whose subjectivity is in a state of becoming here? How is it legible?

These are a sample of the differing ways in which mimetic practices have been brought to the fore in works of art by women. They are outlined here not because I will be offering any simple or direct readings of such works, nor because any answers are transparent within the writings of Irigaray. Rather, I have wished to indicate the kinds of questions that are raised by such artworks and the differing ways in which they are raised. What they suggest is that there is a different type of legibility that is being worked for in many practices by women artists, and different languages that are being developed, indicative of a developing sense of how the visual is adequate or appropriate for articulating subjectivity. What is necessary is to understand how these developments within visual languages are legible, and how they make legible women's subjectivities.

These matters of subjectivity in relation to cultural production have been central to Irigaray's work. This chapter will consider her delineation of the terms surrounding mimesis, and the ways in which she discerns women's practices of cultural reproduction. It will sift through this varied terminology and her deployment of it as investigation and as practice. The aim will be to begin to equip us with some of the analytical tools necessary to begin to restructure our methods of reading works like those outlined above.

## MIMESIS

Some commentators on Irigaray have attended to her use of the terms surrounding mimicry and mimesis; however, they frequently use these words as if they had different meanings, leading to confusion about what the terms mean and how they might be used. For example, Elizabeth Grosz comments 'Irigaray mimics the hysteric's mimicry. She mimes mime itself' (Grosz 1989: 136); Margaret Whitford says 'Irigaray adopts the strategy of mimicry or mimesis' (Whitford 1991c: 70); and Naomi Schor talks of 'the old mimesis, sometimes referred to as masquerade' (Schor 1994b: 67; 1994a: 51). It is clearly important to establish what this cluster of terms mean, the differences between them and to establish how Irigaray is using them.

The concept of 'mimesis' is polysemic; it has multiple meanings and has been used to multiple ends. Gebauer and Wulf refer to 'the vagueness of the concept' which 'has been turned to advantage' by writers such as Benjamin, Adorno and Derrida. However, they state that:

> It is not arbitrariness that has characterised the use of the concept, but a peculiar intuition, which often appears in the form of an adaptation to broader historical changes. There is less a lack of conceptual discipline in the history of mimesis than a resistance to theory building. As a concept, mimesis betrays a distrust of

> the instrumentalities and procedures of theory kept 'pure' of the contamination of human practice. (Gebauer and Wulf 1995: 2)

So mimesis is a fluid concept, resistant to theorisation. It is not an hermetic philosophical theory with a discrete history and development, but an activity where theory and practice are in such proximity as to be virtually inextricable. Thus, not only is it problematic to provide a theoretical definition of mimesis, but also each philosopher to whom Gebauer and Wulf grant substantive space in their book on the subject can be seen as using mimesis strategically – towards particular ends. While they do not mention Irigaray's work (indeed, they do not focus upon any women philosophers – let alone feminist ones), a close examination of Irigaray's work shows that this is an appropriate framework through which to begin understanding her use of mimesis, both as a category for investigation, and as a practice in her own writing. The practice and theory of mimesis in Irigaray's work are linked, and cannot be independently defined or understood.

In the space of four pages of *This Sex*, Irigaray offers her contrasting understandings of 'mimesis' and 'masquerade'. For mimesis she draws her understanding from Plato, stating quite clearly that in his work mimesis is (at least) two:

> In Plato, there are two mimeses. To simplify: there is mimesis as production, which would lie more in the realm of music, and there is the mimesis that would be already caught up in a process of imitation, specularization, adequation, and reproduction. It is the second form that is privileged throughout the history of philosophy and whose effects/symptoms, such as latency, suffering, paralysis of desire, are encountered in hysteria. The first form seems always to have been repressed, if only because it was constituted as an enclave within a 'dominant' discourse. Yet it is doubtless in the direction of, and on the basis of, that first mimesis that the possibility of a woman's writing [une écriture de femme] may come about. (Irigaray 1977a: 129–130; 1985d: 131)

The first form of mimesis – which I shall call *productive mimesis* – involves a subtle double movement, which Irigaray touches upon in her reference to 'the realm of music': just as musicians read the piece of music they play, so too they will give their reading of that piece of music: their interpretation of it, imbued with particular nuances (this is precisely the area of the BBC Radio 3 series *Building a Library*, where differing interpretations of 'the same' piece of music are painstakingly compared). New meanings emerge from this process; and indeed it is here that Irigaray locates 'the possibility of a woman's writing'. Irigaray does not expand upon this Platonic model of mimesis as a model, but she does, as I shall show below, expand (upon) it through her practice. The second form of mimesis – for which I shall coin the terms *non-productive mimesis* or *maintenance mimesis* – is conversely bound up with verisimilitude, investigation of original truth, repetition, replication – maintenance of what has gone before.

Gebauer and Wulf situate Plato's model within cultural history, at the point of 'transition from oral to literary culture. [Plato's] assessment, in that context, is ambivalent: on the one hand, he recognizes its significance; on the other, he fears its power, which is difficult to calculate' (Gebauer and Wulf 1995: 6). Plato's fear of the power of mimesis is also a fear of the power of the writer to change an original meaning: for him, mimetic practices are also aesthetic practices, and both have what we might understand today as a political function.

Irigaray also marks this transitional cultural moment, the moment of shift from oral to literary culture, as being crucial. She links it to three related transitions: first, to our present differentiation of history (i.e., that which is recorded in writing) from pre-history (understood as that which was transmitted orally); second, to the separations of the realms of body from mind, nature from culture; and third, to the imposition of patriarchy upon cultures where female genealogies had integrity (Irigaray 1989: 30–31; 1994c: 12–13); (Irigaray 1990a: 24; 1993i: 24). She exposes the workings of the Platonic model, and its aim of maintaining a patriarchal ideal through a culture of non-productive mimesis. In such a culture:

> One need never pay off the debt, either in the past or in the future, if one can only attain the ideal of sameness, which of course defies deterioration of any kind. [...]
>
> And no shame is attached to being an employee of the head of the family, or even his slave, for 'working the land' is already to do as he does. [...] Miming the father's attributes is achieved here and now. And is the triumph of his logos alone. [...] It is at best the inscription of his eternal truths that he revives by repeating (them). Thus, man is swindled of the price of his own work. For he is now and always nothing but the more or less effective doubling of an omnipotent Phallus. Nonetheless, he submits to this fate and is even ready to die in order to perpetuate such an empire. The important thing is that history goes on. (Irigaray 1974: 440–442; 1985c: 351–353)

Thus, social and cultural relations are maintained as normative within patriarchy through maintenance and policing of a non-productive mimesis – a mimesis that perpetuates a state of stasis. This is managed through generations (father–son), across class divides (master–slave, employer–worker) and in religion (god–man), copying faithfully in order to replicate 'truth'. This structure resonates through Irigaray's writings in her term '*hom(m)o-sexualité*' (usually translated 'hom(m)o-sexuality'); a word play referring to 'man/same-sexuality', or same-sex relationships in the broadest sense: men, in recognising other men as the same as themselves, will seek to maintain power in a between-men culture: a culture of patriarchal stasis and sameness. This should not be confused with homosexuality as sexual relationship, sexual desire for the same sex being distinct from the identificatory processes involved in desire to be 'the same as'.

The structures of this maintenance mimesis can be compared to those central to child development and the learning of skills: the child has to be able to recognise another person as being of the same general type, desire to 'be as', and to evaluate the extent to which his or her own actions are a successful imitation (Grosz 1995: 90). It is, however, a structure of assimilation to the cultural environment against which Irigaray chafes:

> At the level of *culture*, it seems that we are brought up (whether consciously or not) to be trained in repetition, to adapt to a society's systems, and educated to do like, to be like, without any decisive innovations or discoveries of our own. [...] Can we free ourselves from [...] almost fatal repetition at the cultural level? (Irigaray 1990a: 41; 1993i: 37)

Maintenance mimesis is 'almost fatal' for women because, with 'man/same-sexuality' as both dominative and normative – man being the 'same of the same' – woman is elsewhere. Not as 'woman', but as what Irigaray calls 'otherness of sameness' or 'other of the same' [*autre du même*] (Irigaray 1977a: 148; 1985d: 152). She cannot be 'the same as'; nor, in a patriarchal culture, can she securely identify with a genealogy of women. Her function in patriarchy is that of the mirror, as a result of her 'otherness' reflecting back to man his 'sameness'. She has to adopt – and assimilate to – femininity. The 'almost fatal' nature of this move is therefore twofold: firstly, it requires her adaption and assimilation to a hom(m)o-sexual culture; and secondly, as the necessary corollary (because she is not 'the same as'), it requires her to replicate a 'femininity' that is not of her making. This is a 'femininity' erected by 'the same' to be its 'other' – an 'other' that is needed in order to recognise sameness. It is because of this function that I have dubbed it maintenance mimesis or non-productive mimesis. It maintains the given cultural structure; and while it is productive of an identity appropriate for the woman assimilated to a patriarchal culture, it does not produce a horizon of possibilities where women can become women, attaining their full subjectivities. The levels of repression required in this maintenance mimesis are enormous. It is here, in reference to woman's relation to this 'femininity', that Irigaray begins to use the terms mimicry, mime, masquerade, and hysteria in distinction from each other and from mimesis.

## MIMICRY

Irigaray uses the term 'mimicry' at two key moments in *This Sex*. In the interrelation of these passages and the way in which they echo each other she appears to be performing a self-mimicry; each passage, however, indicates in a differing direction. The first reads:

> There is, in an initial phase, perhaps only one 'path', the one historically assigned to the feminine: that of *mimicry* [*le mimétisme*]. One must assume the feminine role deliberately. Which means already to convert a form of subordination into an affirmation, and thus to begin to thwart it. Whereas a direct feminine challenge to this condition means demanding to speak as a (masculine) 'subject', that is it means to postulate a relation to the intelligible that would maintain sexual indifference.
>
> To play with mimesis is thus, for a woman, to try to recover the place of her exploitation by discourse, without allowing herself to be simply reduced to it. (Irigaray 1977a: 73–74; 1985d: 76)

This passage carries resonances of childhood mimicry and its impertinent assertion in the face of authority: 'form of subordination', 'a direct feminine challenge', 'demanding', 'to play' ... and leads toward an understanding of productive mimesis. (I shall return to this process later in the chapter.)

The second passage takes a slightly different direction:

> In a first phase, there is perhaps only one path, and in any case it is the one to which the female condition is assigned: that of *mimicry* [*le mimétisme*]. But the mimetic role itself is complex, for it presupposes that one can lend oneself to everything, if not to everyone. That one can copy anything at all, anyone at all, can receive all impressions, *without appropriating them to oneself,* and *without adding any*. That is, can be nothing but a possibility that the philosopher may exploit for (self-) reflection. [...] If she ['the philosopher's wife / woman'] can play that role so well, if it does not kill her, quite, it is because she keeps something in reserve with respect to this function. Because she still subsists, otherwise and elsewhere than there where she mimes so well what is asked of her. Because her own 'self' remains foreign to the whole staging. But she doubtless needs to reenact it in order to remember what that staging has probably metabolized so thoroughly that she has forgotten it: her own sex. (Irigaray 1977a: 147–148; 1985d: 151–152)

This appears initially more passive: 'the female condition is assigned', 'presupposes that one can lend oneself', 'receive all impressions, *without appropriating them*', '*without adding*', 'be nothing but a possibility that the philosopher may exploit'... This process is then named as 'mime'. Mime's difference from non-productive mimesis (being the same as, or, of the same) is that the femininity that woman mimes is *not of her own making* – and thus that, even as she mimes, she is always elsewhere, with something in reserve.

So, mimicry is identified by Irigaray as perhaps the only option for women within patriarchy, but one that is double-edged. It offers the opportunity for strategies of resistance. These strategies have to be undertaken with great delicacy and deliberation, because on the other hand mimicry involves the almost fatal repression of 'becoming woman'. Indeed, Dianne Chisholm calls Irigaray's concept of 'a symptomatic mimicry of patriarchy's fetishes and projections [...] potentially both terroristic and terrorized' (Chisholm 1994: 269).

One current usage of the term 'mimicry' is found in biology, where it means visual camouflage, or having the colouring of the environment. This usage also refers to the assimilation of an individual to its environment, which happens in a number of ways. The first is the use of camouflage for protection. Margaret Whitford indicates that this may add to our understanding of Irigaray's use of the term: 'Irigaray may be arguing, I think, that women also need to protect themselves against (re)assimilation and destruction by the masculine economy' (Whitford 1991c: 72). However, camouflage is not only used by the preyed-upon for protection, but also by the predators (tigers, armies, etc) as an aid to predation. Roger Callois (surrealist writer and friend of Lacan) identified other, psychotic, aspects of camouflage in the relation of the subject to space. In order to be confirmed in its identity, a subject or organism has to be secure in its perspective upon its body's relationship to the space it occupies (this is in distinction from the assimilation to the cultural environment that occurs in learning processes, but is a necessary aspect of the development of identity). In some psychotics there is no ability to locate themselves in space. Callois finds an analogy to this in the mimicry of insects. Their mimicry may produce the opposite of protection: Callois cites one insect whose resemblance to leaves makes it prey to zealous hedge-clippers, and another whose resemblance to the leaves it feeds upon makes it often prey to cannibalism. Also, he indicates, mimicry in insects can be surplus to requirements: it is visual, while many predators rely upon smell; and some insects practice mimicry even though they are not vulnerable to predators at all (Callois 1984: 24–25). Mimicry is an excess to strategies of survival, a product of a dislocation of identity and, says Elizabeth

Grosz, 'a captivation of a creature by its representations of and as space [...]. The mimicking insect lives its camouflaged existence as not quite itself, as another' (Grosz 1995: 190).

This seems closer to Irigaray's use of the term mimicry with a component aspect of mime. The subject compromises, represses or adapts its perspective on its own identity in favour of an *apparent* (literally, in its appearance, visible, perceivable) assimilation to its environment – in this case, assimilation to the virtual world of 'femininity' as erected by the structures of patriarchy. There is a close analogy with the visual performance of the mime artist. The audience does not actually see the wall that the mime artist walks into, the door he or she opens, nor do they actually see the dog that the mime artist is miming, but through his or her stylised movements of exaggerated gesture, it is as *if* the wall or the door or the dog were there. Those in the audience marvel because it is as *if* they can see the wall or door or a dog instead of a person. What is demonstrated is indeed a captivation of the mime by his or her representations of and as space.[1]

Irigaray's work demonstrates to us that when a woman is seen in our present culture it is not as the sexuate subject who is able to become woman because of the horizon of possibilities that are hers (in divinity, in civil rights, in the Symbolic...). Rather she is seen 'as' 'a' 'woman', *already miming* the 'femininity' of our culture. Mimicry, and particularly its component aspect of mime, is a strategy fraught with risk. Irigaray identifies this as a risk of hysteria, a condition that is itself contiguous with mime:

> Hysteria is silent and at the same time it mimes. And – how could it be otherwise – miming/reproducing a language that is not its own, masculine language, it caricatures and deforms that language: it 'lies', it 'deceives', as women have always been reputed to do (Irigaray 1977a: 138; 1985d: 137).

But Irigaray moves her account of mime in a circular motion back closer to the more resistant and impertinent structures of mimicry. In the movement of the woman always already miming femininity there is a possibility of deflecting away from a collapse into hysteria, what we can think of as a place of reserve: 'she still subsists, otherwise and elsewhere than there where she mimes. [...] Her own "self" remains foreign...' But (and this is crucial): 'She doubtless needs to reenact it in order to remember what that staging has probably metabolized so thoroughly that she has forgotten it: her own sex' (Irigaray 1977a: 147–148; 1985d: 152). This 'forgotten' does not speak of an unmediated truth or an authentic self, but of a painstaking (re)building. Irigaray is not suggesting that either a unified subjectivity or an eternal feminine can be uncovered by a simplistic stepping into and out of character. Her writing the term 'self' in this passage remains in quotation marks, up for question: '"self"'.

## MASQUERADE

The discussion of mimicry has been in the realm of the political, as determined by terms such as 'patriarchy'. Irigaray also thinks through related concerns in the realm of the psychoanalytical through the concept of 'masquerade'. The term is best recognised in feminist theory through its incorporation into critical theory (particularly within film theory) since the mid-1980s. Here, it is found as a developing set of readings of Joan Riviere's essay 'Womanliness as Masquerade', first published in 1929 (Riviere 1986). In this, Riviere (a psychoanalyst and translator of Freud) discusses a particular case history, where the analysand was a professional woman 'engaged in work of a propagandist nature, which consisted principally in speaking and writing'. Despite her success in her job, this woman experienced anxiety after each public appointment, and sought reassurance from father figures among her colleagues, primarily through inappropriate flirting and seductive behaviour (Riviere 1986: 36). Through the dreams and analysis of this woman, Riviere deduced:

> Womanliness therefore could be assumed and worn as a mask, both to hide the possession of masculinity and to avert the reprisals expected if she was found to possess it – much as a thief will turn out his pockets and ask to be searched to prove that he has not the stolen goods. The reader may now ask how I define womanliness or where I draw the line between genuine womanliness and the 'masquerade'. My suggestion is not, however, that there is any such difference; whether radical or superficial, they are the same thing. The capacity for womanliness was there in this woman – and one might even say it exists in the most completely homosexual woman – but owing to her conflicts it did not represent her main development and was used far more as a device for avoiding anxiety than as a primary mode of sexual enjoyment. (Riviere 1986: 38)

This paragraph (particularly the first three sentences), overlaid with Lacan's understanding of masquerade, has prompted interest to the extent that it has become part of the canon of contemporary critical theory.

The prime commentators upon Riviere's and Lacan's concepts of masquerade include Jacqueline Rose (Rose 1982), Judith Butler (Butler 1990), Stephen Heath (Heath 1986) and John Fletcher (Fletcher 1988).[2] Rose suggests that for Lacan 'Sexuality belongs [...] in the realm of masquerade' and 'masquerade is the very definition of "femininity" precisely because it is constructed with reference to a male sign' (Rose 1982: 43). It is a unified concept of 'femininity', behind which is nothing but lack. Lacan incorporated the masquerade into his structures of fetishism and castration, and particularly the distinction between 'being' and 'having' the phallus – the former being the prerogative of women, and the latter, of men. Fletcher states that for Lacan: 'The masquerade comes to signify the alienation involved in the substitution of "appearing" for "being"' (Fletcher 1988: 53), while Butler is more emphatic: 'the "appearing as being" the Phallus that women are compelled to do is inevitably *masquerade*' (Butler 1990: 77).[3] She suggests that there are two understandings of Lacan's 'masquerade', and offers an 'either/or' option: 'the question here is whether masquerade conceals a femininity that might be understood as genuine or authentic, or whether masquerade is the means by which femininity and the contests over its "authenticity" are produced' (Butler 1990: 159). She links Irigaray firmly to the second position.

Heath's paper 'Joan Riviere and the Masquerade' was published as a commentary for the re-publication of Riviere (Heath 1986). It thus provided an indicative focus for many subsequent readings of Riviere's paper. Taking his cue from the first section of the key paragraph, he holds that 'In the masquerade the woman mimics an authentic – genuine – womanliness, but then authentic womanliness is such a mimicry, is the masquerade [...]; to be a woman is to dissimulate a fundamental masculinity, femininity is that dissimulation' (Heath 1986: 49). This is critiqued by Fletcher who is centrally concerned, he says, to 'retrieve the distinctive scenario of the masquerade, as first formulated by Joan Riviere' (Fletcher 1988: 53). He suggests that Heath in his reading of Riviere's pivotal paragraph:

> ...ignores the crucial opposition maintained [...] between 'a device for avoiding anxiety' and 'a primary mode of enjoyment,' which frames and regulates her apparent equation of femininity with the masquerade tout court. The force of the equation, I take it, is to indicate that the same attributes and behaviours are involved in each, but that they are caught up in and serve a different psychic economy. (Fletcher 1988: 54)

Fletcher's account of Riviere thus has some level of initial correspondence with the two strands of Irigaray's 'mimicry' outlined above, which could indeed be understood in turn as 'a primary mode of enjoyment' and 'a device for avoiding anxiety'.

Irigaray's understanding of masquerade, however, maintains a crucial difference from that of Lacan or Riviere. It is a difference rooted in her conception of 'femininity'. For Irigaray, 'femininity' is erected by men in both patriarchal and phallocentric structures to mark the other of their same. It is neither an essential aspect of woman's identity (even when taken to be so by those patriarchal or phallocentric structures), nor is it structured *by* women as reaction to/against patriarchy or phallocentricity. She links the masquerade explicitly at one point to Freud's concept of femininity:

> What do I mean by masquerade? In particular, what Freud calls 'femininity'. The belief, for example, that it is necessary to become a woman, a 'normal' one at that, whereas a man is a man from the outset. He has only to effect his being-a-man, whereas a woman has to become a normal woman, that is, has to enter into the *masquerade of femininity*. (Irigaray 1977a: 131–132; 1985d: 133–134)

And during her commentary on Freud's theory of castration she notes: 'In other words, the "fact of castration" will leave woman with only one option – the semblance, the masquerade (of) femininity, which will always already have been to "act like" the value recognized by/for the male' (Irigaray 1974: 55; 1985c: 49).

These passages place Irigaray's concept of femininity – and thus masquerade – at a step removed from Heath's reading of Riviere (that 'to be a woman is to dissimulate a fundamental masculinity, femininity is that dissimulation'). Although the masquerade of femininity will always already have been to 'act like' the value *recognized* by/for the male, it is important to note that this 'femininity' was *assigned* to woman as an inferior copy of man's relation to his origin. The masquerade is woman's playing of the script of femininity provided by man; and the script provides what Irigaray calls 'all the masquerades of "femininity" that are expected of her' (Irigaray 1977a: 26; 1985d: 27). 'The masquerade of femininity' is contiguous with 'the masquerade: femininity', and both are constructed through masculinity. She will always already be acting out the masquerade (of) femininity; and as we have seen above, she will always already be elsewhere. Irigaray does not suggest that one is prior to the other.

All this leaves hanging the question 'why?' If woman is always already elsewhere than enacting the masquerade (of) femininity, and inscribed into this is the possibility of resistance, then why is woman always already masquerading? Within the dominance of phallocentrism it is an inevitability:

> Psychoanalysts say that masquerading corresponds to woman's desire. That seems wrong to me. I think the masquerade has to be understood as what women do in order to recuperate some element of desire, to participate in man's desire, but at the price of renouncing their own. In the masquerade, they submit to the dominant economy of desire in an attempt to remain 'on the market' in spite of everything. But they are there as objects for sexual enjoyment, not as those who enjoy. (Irigaray 1977a: 131–132; 1985d: 133–134)

Masquerade is not woman's desire. Passing through the Oedipal phase, woman enters a value system which requires that she renounce the possibility of her own desire. In order to recoup desire – albeit a participation in man's desire – woman enacts the masquerade required of her. At least in this way she will have some pleasure from remaining 'on the market'. With this last phrase Irigaray leads us back into the realm of the political; she discerns corresponding structures of masquerade in patriarchy. The liberal aim of modifying current social structures to allow women the same economic, social and political rights of men without attending to the structuring of women's desire by the masquerade of femininity provided for them will provide no pleasure 'unless her pleasure comes simply from being chosen as an object of consumption or of desire by masculine "subjects"' (Irigaray 1977a: 80; 1985d: 84).

It is interesting to reflect Irigaray's conception of the masquerade back upon Fletcher's discussion of Riviere. He writes:

> There is no essence of 'womanliness'. In Riviere's argument it must be produced out of something very like its opposite. Riviere's distinction comes down to one between the mask of femininity as reaction-formation, renouncing and reversing wishes, and the mask of femininity covering the refusal to renounce them. In both cases it is the same mask. [...] This is not the Lacanian conception of a lack or a non-identity. Behind Riviere's mask there is always something else.
>
> The importance of Riviere's conception of the masquerade is that it constitutes a transgressive doubleness, an inscription of alternative wishes. The potential for a critical distance from the mythemes of femininity (passivity, responsiveness, deference, flattery, etc) is lodged already within it and the narratives it might generate. (Fletcher 1988: 55)

This echoes Irigaray. For Irigaray there is no essence of 'womanliness'. It is produced from something very like its opposite – the 'femininity' constructed by patriarchy and phallocentrism. Woman has no choice but to respond to these structures by enacting the masquerade. A renunciation of her desire is involved; so too is the fact that she is already elsewhere – she is neither lacking, nor subject either to the 'eternal feminine'. In what seems initially like a bleak scenario, the possibility for resistant strategies are in fact embedded within the structure – even if masked by the masquerade itself. For Irigaray, once again, the strategies for resistance can follow differing paths: hysterical mimicry, or productive mimesis.

## HYSTERIA

If woman's adoption and adaption of 'femininity' is a mimetic process, in which women masquerade that which they are required to be, then hysteria is a strategic redoubling of that mime, taking it to the nth degree in order to attempt to wrest back some control over destiny, identity and sexuality. Hysteria can be understood as a calculated continuum of the masquerade 'femininity'.

In the devastating essay 'And the One Doesn't Stir Without the Other' Irigaray lays bare the structure of phallocentrism that demands the disruption of female genealogies and of mother–daughter relationships (Irigaray 1979, 1981). What she writes is not the voice of the hysteric; rather she indicates through the daughter's voice the immanence of hysteria in this structure, the not-yet-hysteria that is the result of phallocentrism and 'normalisation' through psychoanalysis. It is worth quoting a substantial passage:

> And if you lead me back again and again to this blind assimilation of you – but who are you? – if you turn your face from me, giving yourself to me only in an already inanimate form, abandoning me to competent men to undo my/your paralysis, I'll turn to my father. [...]
>
> He leaves the house, I follow in his steps. Farewell, Mother, I shall never become your likeness.
>
> I do gymnastics. I practice the body exercises suited to my disorder. I'll become a schooled robot. I move my body, completely unmoved. I advance and move about to the rhythm prescribed for my cure. Will, not love, regulates my gestures, my leaps, my dancing about. Each hour of the day finds me applying myself: trying to obey the doctors' orders. I concur totally with their diagnosis of my condition. I give them my complete attention, all my energy. I'll be the living demonstration of the correctness of their principles. Animated, reanimated by their understanding.
>
> See from afar how I move with measured steps, me, once frozen in anger? Aren't I good now? A nearly perfect girl? I lack only a few garments, a little jewelry, some makeup, a disguise [*travestissement*], some ways of being or doing to appear perfect. I'm beginning to look like what's expected of me. One more effort, a little more anger against you who want me to remain little, you who want me to eat what you bring me rather than to see me dress like you, and I'll step out of the [*ton*] dream. Out of my disorder. Out of you in me, me in you. I'll leave us. I'll go into another home. I'll live my life, my story.
>
> Look at how healthy I am now. I don't even have to run after a man, he comes toward me. He approaches me. I await him, immobile, rooted. He's very near.

> I'm paralyzed with emotion. My blood no longer circulated very well. I hardly breathe. I leave.
>
> I can't tell you where I am going. Forget me, Mother. Forget you in me, me in you. Let's just forget us. Life continues… (Irigaray 1979: 12–13; 1981: 62–63)

The mother that the little girl wants to be like is already inanimate, causing the little girl to turn to her father and the fathers of psychoanalysis. She schools herself in the gestures required of her, desiring their approval, concurring with their opinion. This makes her womanly – all she needs in addition are the appropriate accoutrements of dress and make-up.[4] Her desire to be like the mother has turned to anger that the mother wished to feed her, rather than wanting her daughter visibly to mimic, to masquerade, 'femininity'. The daughter's sexuality has become passive to the extent that she actively masquerades, but then waits to be chosen by a man. The separation from the mother is complete…but of course the daughter ends up repeating the same masquerade as her mother. The phenomenon of hysteria is shown by Irigaray as an inevitability in the structuring of 'femininity': 'Hysteria is all she has left. […] And hysterical miming will be the little girl's or the woman's effort to save her sexuality from total repression and destruction' (Irigaray 1974: 85–86; 1985c: 71–72). Mimicry, 'femininity' and hysteria, are so closely related and intertwined as to be almost contiguous. Where two are found, the third will not be too far distant.

Elizabeth Grosz has indicated anorexia as a contemporary example of hysteria as a strategic choice: 'a defiant taking-to-extremes of these ideals […] a not always successful attempt at self determination' (Grosz 1989: 136). Certainly the anorexic determines to become the perfectly thin body, maintaining an absolute control over diet and exercise in a mimetic parody of the effort required of young (white) Western women.[5] Hysterical mimicry might underlie other eating disorders, such as bulimia and bingeing (sugar and spice and all things nice, that's what little girls are made of).

Lynda Nead has reaffirmed the placing of this discussion in the realms of the visible, the aesthetic and of mimicry. Writing of the absolute control required in our culture of the borders and orifices of the female body and the representations of it, she describes it as 'an aesthetic that has structured the representation of the female body in western art since antiquity' (Nead 1992: 5–6). Drawing upon Kenneth Clarke, Jacques Derrida and Mary Douglas, Nead shows how, across the breadth of activity in Western culture: 'the female body is defined as lacking containment and issuing filth and pollution from its faltering outlines and broken surface' and how art constantly (re)submits it to regulation and 'repair' (Nead 1992: 7). Irigaray too has confirmed the hysteric's bodily relation to a dominative aesthetic:[6]

> Enigmatic 'somatizations', hysterical 'dreams' in which we are supposed to see 'the caricature of a work of art', as Freud puts it in *Totem and Taboo*. Woman's special form of neurosis would be to 'mimic' a work of art, to be a *bad (copy of a) work of art*. Her neurosis would be recognized as a counterfeit or parody of an artistic process. It is transformed into an aesthetic object, but one without value, which has to be condemned because it is a *forgery*. (Irigaray 1974: 156; 1985c: 125)

After outlining 'the primacy of boundaries in social configurations of the female body' Nead turns also to the anorexic body. The woman see her anorexic body as an image that is subject to a set of conventions and judges it accordingly:

> Here again the body is seen as image, according to a set of conventions, and woman acts both as judge and executioner. But rather than anorexia being seen as a distortion of physical needs, it can be posed instead as a confusion of psychical perceptions and, more exactly, as a confusion of form and its boundaries. For the anorectic, there is always excess matter deposited over the surface, the form of the body. The goal is to get rid of that surplus and to reveal the essential, core self – to get back to the original boundaries. (Nead 1992: 10–11)

This echoes Callois's identification of the dislocation of the insect's visual identity. In the case of hysteria, however, the intention, desire and will of the hysteric are important. Hysteria is the location of a 'reserve' of the masquerade of femininity: it exceeds the femininity that vouchsafes man his identity. Irigaray locates in this 'a revolutionary potential in hysteria' (Irigaray 1991f: 47); a potential which Grosz summarises as:

> a mode of defiance of patriarchy, not the site of its frustration. In this sense, the hysteric is a proto-feminist, or at least an isolated individual who, if she had access to the experiences of other women, may locate the problem in cultural expectations of femininity rather than in femininity itself. The hysteric's defiance through excess, through *overcompliance*, is a parody of the expected. (Grosz 1989: 135)

It is for this reason that the phallocentric response of attempting to 'cure' the hysteric by training her in a more appropriate adaptation to 'femininity' is itself a false 'cure', treating 'the wrong subject, the woman, her repressed (recuperable) desire, as if "she," not the symbolic relation, were the locus of illness' (Chisholm 1994: 272). The woman is thus not returned to her 'self', her genealogies; the cause of her resistance is ignored. Irigaray's response as an analyst to hysteria is to attempt to work through it, at least in part, in the realm of the aesthetic:

> Hysteria must not be destroyed but allowed access to the imagination and to creativeness. For the hysteric access to such an identity is effected through a sexualised art, a colored and sonorous art, an art whose libidinal resources blossom in duality and reconciliation, within one woman, between mother and woman, and among women. Thanks to such an art, the hysteric should be able to regain her perceptions – her virginity, her gender – and keep hold of them. (Irigaray 1987a: 179. Translated modified; 1993f: 164)

## PRODUCTIVE MIMESIS

While she recognises a revolutionary potential in hysteria, Irigaray has no wish to valorise the hysteric, to maintain her condition or to move all women towards a state of hysteria. Instead, through identifying both mimicry and a place of resistance within hysteria she models the strategies used by the hysteric into a productive mimesis. Gebauer and Wulf point towards some striking correlations between hysteria and mimesis, which can help clarify how it is possible for Irigaray to make a political and resistant move from one to the other:

> It becomes evident that the concept of mimesis necessarily loses its intellectual centrality with the rise of rational thought. [...] The change [to rational thought] itself allows us to recognize a second characteristic of mimesis: while modern rational thought refers to the single isolated cognitive subject, mimesis is always concerned with a relational network of more than one person. (Gebauer and Wulf 1995: 3)

While Gebauer and Wulf do not here define 'rational thought', in the context of their book this phrase could imply both the historical rise of 'rationality' in ancient Greece, subsequently reaffirmed in the Enlightenment, and the acquisition of 'rationality' in the individual. Thus it can be related, through the moment of cultural transition from oral to written histories, to Irigaray's location of the development of patriarchy, and also to the accession of the subject to the Law of the Father or the phallocentric Symbolic. Both hysteria and mimesis are grounded in the social, and have elements of desire for approval/love: the person performing the mimesis desires to continue, and fit into, particular social patterns; the hysteric is adopting the gestures of 'femininity'. Both have elements of resistance: in productive mimesis (such as the musician), the aim is to develop, add to or exceed a given situation that has been found insufficient to allow for the articulation of subjectivity; and the hysteric wishes to regain and retain her subjectivity through absolute control of that 'femininity', exceeding it through becoming the best at it (for example, the slimmest, in the case of anorexia). Both, then, will maintain a critical distance from established logic and rationality – in the case of hysteria, a critical distance that is increased by the linking of men, masculinity and rationality on the one hand, and women, femininity and irrationality on the other. (Maybe in this positioning of mimesis, we can begin to see why some male artists feel able, structurally, to call upon aspects of 'femininity' while declining the compromised subjectivity and relation to the Symbolic allowed women.)

Gebauer and Wulf explain the links between the social and the political that can be discerned in practices of mimesis:

> The mimetic production of a symbolic world refers to other worlds and to their creators and draws other persons into one's own world. As is apparent in this constellation, mimesis implies the recognition of mediation between worlds and people; it does not designate a subjection to received models, but rather an acceptance of traditions and the work of predecessors. It also implies a recognition of power: the inclusion of others introduces power, if only in symbolic terms, into one's own personal world, into the interpretive and perspectival modes developed there. The history of mimesis is a history of disputes over the power to make symbolic worlds, that is, the power to represent the self and others and interpret the world. To this extent mimesis possesses a political dimension and is part of the history of power relations. (Gebauer and Wulf 1995: 3)

While the move from the social to the political is useful, this paragraph also contains the limits of Gebauer and Wulf's gender-free ('universal') understanding of mimesis. Implied here is an unproblematic relation to a Symbolic – an unproblematic access to it and *representation in* it. But the mimesis of the hysteric is doomed to be a mimesis of powerlessness, mimicry of a 'femininity' that was never 'hers'. This then calls into question Gebauer and Wulf's 'mediation between worlds and people'. Without wishing to designate all women as hysterics, but remembering the embeddedness of hysteria in the structures of 'femininity', the questions for women are: is this a mimicry of mediation? And if women have no mediation between themselves, then what is the mediation they mimic? If, as Irigaray argues, women's genealogies are utterly disrupted, then there *are* no (cultural) traditions or predecessors. Women mimic either men, or their disempowered, hysterical 'predecessors' – 'predecessors' in inverted commas, because these women were always already (what else could they do?) mimicking something not 'theirs'.

Through her work Irigaray argues for the development of structures that will allow for the reaffirming and integrity of female genealogies, and the related development of structures of mediation and the Symbolic. At present the majority options are either to mimic a 'femininity' not of our making, or to mimic men and the phallic Symbolic – which are, of course, (two sides of) the same (coin). To get out of this bleak spot, we must pass through the resistant moment of hysteria and through productive mimesis. The way to achieve this is found in a passage of Irigaray's quoted earlier concerning mimicry, and its subsequent discussion of mimesis. This passage breaks down into three paragraphs, which will be taken in turn.

> 1. There is, in an initial phase, perhaps only one 'path', the one historically assigned to the feminine: that of *mimicry*. One must assume the feminine role deliberately. Which means already to convert a form of subordination into an affirmation, and thus to begin to thwart it. Whereas a direct feminine challenge to this condition means demanding to speak as a (masculine) 'subject', that is, it means to postulate a relation to the intelligible that would maintain sexual indifference. (Irigaray 1977a: 73–74; 1985d: 76)

Irigaray is suggesting that women have two strategies of response to their subordination. One, maintaining 'sexual indifference', evokes an 'equal rights feminism'. It is an approach that would be akin to desiring a bigger slice of a poisonous pie (Lippard 1995: 81) or to denying that gender is of any cultural importance. The other option is the strategy Irigaray has learned from the hysteric. She notes elsewhere that 'there is always, in hysteria, both a reserve power and a paralyzed power [...], the possibility of another mode of "production", notably gestural and lingual; but this is maintained in its latency. Perhaps as a cultural reserve yet to come?' (Irigaray 1977a: 136; 1985d: 138). As the hysteric mimics 'femininity', so too Irigaray suggests that there is a possibility of tapping into this reserve cultural power through a deliberate mimicry of the role allotted women. This would be a knife-edge strategy, with a danger of falling into the self-defeating paralysis of the hysteric.

> 2. To play with mimesis is thus, for a woman, to try to recover the place of her exploitation by discourse, without allowing herself to be simply reduced to it. It means to resubmit herself – inasmuch as she is on the side of the 'perceptible', of 'matter' – to 'ideas', in particular to ideas about herself, that are elaborated in/by a masculine logic, but so as to make 'visible', by an effect of playful repetition, what was supposed to remain invisible: the cover-up of a possible operation of the feminine in language. It also means 'to unveil' the fact that, if

> women are such good mimics, it is because they are not simply resorbed in this function. *They also remain elsewhere*: another case of the persistence of 'matter', but also of sexual pleasure. (Irigaray 1977a: 73–74; 1985d: 76)

The suggestion here is that the difference between the woman playing with mimesis and the hysteric's self-defeating mimicry is that the hysteric, in attempting to wrest control of the production of her 'feminine' subjectivity, also allows herself to be reduced to it. Instead, mimesis has to occur in the realm of the playful, and can do so for two reasons. Firstly, women undertaking mimesis understand it in political terms ('trying to recover the place of their exploitation'); and, secondly, because the 'cultural reserve yet to come' remains embedded in their strategy, they therefore always remain/retain it elsewhere than in the 'feminine'. The hysteric's strategy, on the other hand, is one of an isolated individual, rather than collectively political (feminist); her stubborn reserve is 'resorbed' into her perfection of her act of mimicry.

It is also significant that Irigaray uses the analogy of visibility – mimesis making visible that which was meant to be invisible – even if the visible here remains cited as 'visible'. Following on from her thorough critique of what she terms phallocentric 'specul(ariz)ation' in *Speculum*, it tells us that Irigaray is not leaving the realm of the visible, visual languages and metaphors of visibility to phallocentrism: they are to be worked through using the strategy of productive mimesis as much as speech and writing. Indeed, the visible is far too urgent a matter within Irigaray's critiques to be left to the old specul(ariz)ation. Its blind spots, its dreams of symmetry, its representations of woman as the other of the same, are all areas where women can enact a productive mimesis, exposing the lacunae in its texts. And if this working of the visual is at best parallel to Irigaray's '*parler-femme*' (Irigaray 1977a: 133), with its indication of verbal speech, then I would like to suggest that maybe it develops something more like a witnessing-woman. This phrase carries a multiplicity of appropriate and contiguous evocations. 'Witness', like 'perceive', combines the visual and the intellectual, and the phrase can also indicate the woman and women who witness(es), an active witnessing of the construct 'woman', and the performative mode of a woman bearing witness.

> 3. Elsewhere of 'matter': if women can play with mimesis it is because they are capable of bringing new nourishment to its operation. Because they have always nourished this operation? Is not the 'first' stake in mimesis that of re-producing (from) nature? Of giving it form in order to appropriate it for oneself? As guardians of 'nature', are not women the ones who maintain, thus who make possible, the resource of mimesis for men? For the logos? (Irigaray 1977a: 74; 1985d: 76–77)

As Rosi Braidotti suggests, Irigaray's productive mimesis 'allows women to revisit and repossess the discursive and material sites where "woman" was essentialized, disqualified or quite simply excluded' (Braidotti 1992: 187). The site of the mothering body is surely the most poignant of all of these. Irigaray's return to the body and to reproduction is the move that has raised the hackles of her critics most of all. In 1985 Toril Moi, for example, argued that Irigaray 'falls for the temptation to produce her own positive theory of femininity. But [...] to define "woman" is necessarily to essentialize her' (Moi 1985: 139). But in conflating 'femininity' and 'woman' Moi seems to be making an essentialising move herself in order to construct her argument (indicating the slippery elusiveness of the whole problematic). Rosi Braidotti, however, follows her own comment on Irigaray's outline of mimesis by insisting that 'working through the networks of discursive definitions of "woman"' produces processes of female subjectivity and of a 'gendered female feminist community'. It forms an 'ontological leap forward' where the collective 'we, women' can empower the subjective becoming of 'I, woman':

> This leap is forward, not backwards towards the glorification of an authentic archaic feminine power or of a well-hidden 'true' essence. It does not aim at recovering a lost origin or a forgotten land, but rather to bring about here and now a mode of representation that would take the fact of being a woman as a positive, self-affirming political force. It is an act of self-legitimation whereby the 'she-self' blends her ontological desire to be with the conscious willed becoming of a collective political movement. This distinction between the will and desire marks a separation of register, of levels of experience, which must be underlined and never confused. [...] The distinction between identity and subjectivity is to be related to that between will and desire. (Braidotti 1992: 186)

This is a productive framework through which to approach Irigaray's comments on mimesis and reproduction. Irigaray consistently refuses to reduce women to mothers, and therefore refuses to construct either 'woman' or 'mother' as a site of origin for women. Such a reduction would be a displacement of woman's subjectivity and her relation to origin. As Alys Eve Weinbaum points out, 'reproduction ventriloquizes mimetic repetition on the biological level. [... The term] "reproduction" signifies [...] the biological process that both Western metaphysics and capitalism use to reduce women to mothers' (Weinbaum 1994: 112). Irigaray's use of rhetorical-ironic questions and her citing/siting of the terms 'matter', 'first', and 'nature' begin to prove the possible productivity of mimesis in relation to reproduction. It also *performs* mimesis in relation to that same reproduction. In other words, Irigaray is invoking, in this use of the term 'reproduction', what Braidotti calls the 'female embodied self' in order to sustain 'the project of redefining female subjectivity' (Braidotti 1992: 186). If 'woman' is not reduced to 'mother', then the act of reproduction (as mimesis) cannot provide her 'essence', nor can its representation show us her relation to origin: she is always already elsewhere. The problem is located in the reduction of 'woman' to 'mother'.[7]

## IRIGARAY'S MIMETIC PRACTICE

As we can now see, Irigaray does not use mimesis as a purely theoretical tool; rather, it is embedded in her practice, and not always easily identifiable, available for study or amenable to academic modelling. Indeed, the mimesis we detect in her writing is likely to be only the tip of the iceberg, and, I would guess, provokes much of the exasperation felt by her critics. As noted early in this chapter, mimesis is rooted in practice, and is irreducible to theory: it 'eludes theory formation. It is a product of human practice and must always be regarded as the issue of a deed, as a part of practice' (Gebauer and Wulf 1995: 316). Further, the practice of a productive mimesis is never purely cerebral, but can always be found, either substantively or as a trace, in the body:

> The aspect of production expresses the nature of mimesis as activity undertaken by actors, as a deed. This [...] is articulated variously with the passage of time: as an act of painting or writing, as a making with one's own hands, as a generation of sounds with the voice or with musical instrument, or in reading aloud, or, ultimately, in reading silently, which retains scarcely any physical component at all. But there remains always a physical residue, which makes its presence felt in typically physical processes of depletion, such as fatigue [...] Mimesis brings into play a practical knowledge, a sens pratique. (Gebauer and Wulf 1995: 315–316)

This aspect of mimesis can be found threaded through Irigaray's writing, for example in her antipathy towards, and refusal to adopt, the cerebrally abstract, and her refusal also to produce or use clearly extricable theoretical or academic models.[8]

During the defence of her PhD thesis (later published as *Speculum*), Irigaray was asked what method she had used for her research:

> A delicate question. For isn't it the method, the path to knowledge, that has always led us away, led us astray, by fraud and artifice, from woman's path, and to the point of consecrating its oblivion? [...] In order to reopen woman's path, in particular in and through language, it was therefore necessary to note the way in which the method is never as simple as it purports to be, the way in which

> the teleological project [...] the method takes on is always a project, conscious or not, of turning away, of deviation, and of reduction, in the artifice of sameness, of otherness. In other words, speaking at the greatest level of generality so far as philosophical methods are concerned: of the feminine. (Irigaray 1977a: 146–147; 1985d: 150)

So academic methodologies in themselves distract from 'woman's path', enacting a form of fraud and artifice for women. The 'teleological project' (of academic 'objectivity'?) in posing as a straightforward path is in fact embroiled in the complications of 'the same' and 'the other'. Thus the teleological project is a masquerade, is 'feminine'.

> Thus it was necessary to destroy, but as René Char wrote, with nuptial tools. The tool is not a feminine attribute. But woman may re-utilize its marks on her, in her. To put it another way: the option left to me was to have a *fling with the philosophers,* which is easier said than done... for what path can one take to get back inside their ever so coherent systems? (Irigaray 1977a: 147; 1985d: 150)

In this event, the only thing possible is to use the attributes of 'femininity' (which are given to woman, and are almost all that she has); to explore the marks they have left upon her, and to use them to party with the philosophers. This is in parallel with Audre Lourde's assertion 'For the master's tools will never dismantle the master's house. They may allow us temporarily to beat him at his own game, but they will never enable us to bring about genuine change. And this fact is only threatening to those women who still define the master's house as their only source of support' (Lourde 1984: 112). At first sight, Lourde's statement may indicate separatism, while Irigaray's may indicate capitulation. However, to attempt a teleological project would be to 'speak (as a) man', request the support of the master's house, and ignore any potential *parler-femme*; to use a separatist strategy would be to leave the meta-discourse of our culture intact. If the patriarchy requires mime of women, and phallocentrism requires masquerade, then, says Irigaray, that is what they will get with a vengeance, utilising the reserves of those practices and structures – the aspects beyond the cognisance of the 'master' and the reach of his 'tools'. It has been suggested that Irigaray not only *writes on* the philosophers, but that she *writes* the philosophers (Weed 1994: 84). There is a danger in this of underestimating her project. Irigaray appears to have taken to heart Virginia Woolf's analysis that 'women have served all these centuries as looking glasses possessing the magic and delicious power of reflecting the figure of man at twice its natural size' (Woolf 1949: 53): that is, she does it to such excess that the *gaps and blind spots* are revealed at 'twice their natural size'. The reason that mimesis, rather than miming, can do this is that element of reserve which has been noted at various points through this chapter: 'having a fling with the philosophers also entails safeguarding *those components of the mirror that cannot reflect themselves*: its backing, its brilliancy, thus its dazzlements, its ecstasies' (Irigaray 1977a: 147; 1985d: 151). As she says elsewhere, 'marks and masks are different [*hétérogène*] in their relations with signs' (Irigaray 1980: 86; 1991b: 80): through utilising the marks of 'femininity' Irigaray enacts a mimesis of the *representation* of 'femininity' – in order to undo it... in order to begin the opening of some space for a developing woman's Symbolic, the '*parler-femme*', the 'witnessing-woman'.

Irigaray presents herself as mimeticising 'the philosopher's wife / woman' [*la femme du philosophe*] (Irigaray 1977: 148) (translated as 'wife' in Irigaray 1985a: 151). Dianne Chisholm describes Irigaray here as having 'acted the part of the cultural terrorist' (Chisholm 1994: 270), before continuing:

> I read this voice as a trope, a parody-mime, that voices woman's silencing or exposes woman's being overspoken by men's logic of the Same. Such a 'voice' does not emanate directly from the repressed female body but functions as a metaphorical disease in a body of male discourse, riddling it with hints, allusions, parables of women's sexual difference. (Chisholm 1994: 272)

She will inhabit the phallocentric texts of the philosophers, fulfil her role of the other of the same, reflecting the same back to himself: 'Reproductive material and duplicating mirror, the philosopher's wife / woman [*femme*] also has to underwrite that narcissism which often extends onto a transcendental dimension' (Irigaray 1977a: 147. Translated modified; 1985d: 151). The rhetorical / ironic questioning found in *Speculum* and elsewhere is but a prominent aspect of this.

It is at the point not only of realising that 'Irigaray's mimesis is a way of retracing backwards the multilayered levels of signification, or representation, of women' (Braidotti 1994: 124), but of realising the extent of the convolution of forms of this risk, that many of Irigaray's commentators – and supporters – such as Weed, Chisholm, Xu and Berg appear to experience a hiatus (I say this while acknowledging my indebtedness to their insights). There is an inevitable tension between the academic teleological project of their texts (and mine) and Irigaray's project; a tension exacerbated, I feel, if the discussion of Irigaray's strategy is restricted to analyses of her texts that are most immediately 'on' the philosophers. The productivity of her texts is then restricted to an academic endeavour, and (despite occasional word play)[9] her mimesis becomes containable as an abstract methodology, '*parler-femme*' becomes an '*épater les académiciens*'. 'Femininity' is deconstructed, displaced; 'woman' is de-essentialised; 'essentialism' rebutted or strategised ...but a gap remains, a 'hole' in the academic lens, which is not (yet) canny enough to be a mimesis of the 'hole' in the scoptophilic lens of the dominant economy (Irigaray 1977a: 25–26; 1985d: 26). The gap is that *'parler-femme' is practice* – and concomitantly, mimesis *is* practice; a developing Symbolic *is* practice; 'her' subjectivity *is* practice; Irigaray's oeuvre *is* practice. As such, it is irreducible to theory; which returns us to the earlier characterisation of mimesis as being irreducible to theory.

Equally, as practice, it is a web of *strategic* practices. While Irigaray has warned that 'philosophical discourse [...] constitutes the discourse on discourse' and is thus precisely the area which should be challenged (Irigaray 1977a: 72; 1985d: 47), this does not mean that the discourses for which philosophy sets the agenda are unworthy of attention. Indeed, their inclusion is crucial if the investigation of philosophical discourse is not to remain abstract. While it would be naive to concentrate on these, leaving the meta-discourse of philosophy untouched, says Irigaray, focus on the 'limited or marginal issue' (Irigaray 1977a: 72; 1985d: 74) is also strategic, and from *Speculum* onwards is included in her work. The two main strands that emerge are ethics, folding back onto women's political collectivity, women's rights and civil rights; and Irigaray's own struggle towards a Symbolic, an articulation of subjectivity and mediation through the *'parler-femme'*, the practice of (the) witnessing-woman. The gap in the present academic lens can only be articulated if one understands Irigaray's oeuvre *as/is* mimesis, rather than taking mimesis as academic methodology, of relevance only to her work 'on' the philosophers.

Paul Ricoeur has developed an analysis of mimesis which can be used to rescue Irigaray's practice of mimesis from any reductive understanding of it as being a methodology. His paper 'Mimesis and Representation' aims to disentangle mimesis from its quite general understanding as a closed and limited form of representation – to ensure it is 'removed from the enchanted precincts of re-presented presence' (Ricoeur 1981: 16). It allows for a reading of Irigaray's poetics – her oeuvre – not as an object for study, but as productive of an horizon of possibilities within which the reader is implicated.

Ricoeur follows two paths. The first is to move from Platonic mimesis which is 'interpreted in terms of a redoubled presence, works of art and of language being taken for weakened copies of things, whereas the things themselves borrow whatever tenor of meaning they have from their intelligible models, the Ideas' (Ricoeur 1981: 15–16). He concentrates instead upon Aristotle's development of what I have termed above productive mimesis, found primarily in his *Poetics*. Here, mimesis 'only takes place within the area of human action, or production, or *poiesis*'. Thus mimesis does not seek to maintain something already given, but it is 'an augmentation of meaning in the field of action' (Ricoeur 1981: 16).

Ricoeur's second move is away from a semiotic understanding, which works upon abstracted texts, towards one based upon hermeneutics, which situates texts in a concrete process with practices of life that surround reading and writing and understanding:

> ...[semiotic] theoreticians build upon an abstraction [...] by considering only the internal laws of the literary work. It is the task of hermeneutics, on the contrary, to reconstruct the set of operations by means of which a work arises from the opaque depths of living, acting, and suffering, to be given by an author to readers who receive it and thereby change their own action. For a semiotic theory that abstracts from this whole span of meaning, the work is constituted as an interior that alone is relevant. [...] For hermeneutics [...] there is neither an inside nor an outside to the work – the distinction of inside and outside being a methodological artifact – instead there is a concrete process in which the textual configuration conjoins the practical prefiguration and the practical transfiguration. (Ricoeur 1981: 17–18)

This immediately warns us away from seeing our task as readers of texts as an abstraction, but rather to look for continuities between the text and that which is exterior to it. Ricoeur develops his three categories of practical prefiguration, textual configuration and practical transfiguration from three of Aristotle's terms: *poiesis* (making, action), *sustasis* or *mythos* (the synthesis of incidents into a story) and *mimesis* (the imitation of an action), which 'thus form a chain that has to do with *praxis*, where each term must be understood in terms of its relations to the others' (Ricoeur 1981: 16–17). He names these mimesis$_1$, mimesis$_2$ and mimesis$_3$.

These categories may go some way towards explaining the gaps in many of the commentaries on Irigaray's use of mimesis. A semiotically influenced reader (according to Ricoeur) will place texts (in this case, Irigaray's) in the category of *sustasis*, or textual configuration, and will feel most at home when they assume that this is also what Irigaray is doing: hence the over-attention given to those of Irigaray's texts where she deals directly with texts by others. Modern semiotics isolates the text by constructing textual autonomy:

> Thanks to writing, and also thanks to emplotment, the narrative text acquires a semantic autonomy that cuts it off in three ways. First, from the presumed intention of its author; second, from the capacity of its first audience to receive it; third, from the socio-cultural conditions of its genesis. Mimesis$_2$ is the emblem of this triple autonomy. (Ricoeur 1981: 21)

Far from decrying mimesis$_2$ (referred to here as 'emplotment'), Ricoeur is arguing for it to be seen as a mediation between mimesis$_1$ and mimesis$_3$, rather than in isolation. Ricoeur also indicates the historicity of mimesis$_2$, which is 'governed by a schematization that is historically structured in a tradition or traditions, and it is expressed in individual works which stand in varying relations to the constraints generated by this schematism' (Ricoeur 1981: 25). His further descriptions and analyses of it make one wonder if those who focus on Irigaray's texts 'on' other philosophers in their discussions of her mimesis are seriously mis-focusing attention within her work, and also mis-focused in their understanding of mimesis. Ricoeur's comment, for example, that 'the poetic function suspends this concern for an external reference and turns language back on itself in order to celebrate itself' (Ricoeur 1981: 21) is redolent of Irigaray's use of language in the texts where she is expressly working towards the articulation of the *'parler-femme'*, the articulation of subjectivity.

A further encouragement towards the integrative understanding provided by Ricoeur's mimesis$_2$ (emplotment, configuration of action or textual configuration) is provided by Irigaray's comments on her use of 'inversion', which can be understood in this context as mimesis. Referring to it as a method used by Marx on the works of Hegel, and by Nietzsche upon Plato – i.e., their inversion of something exterior to themselves – she says that for her it was more complex:

> In my case, it was more a question of inverting myself. I was the other of/for man, I attempted to define the objective alterity of myself for myself as belonging to the female gender. I carried out an inversion of the femininity imposed upon me in order to try to define the female corresponding to my gender: the in-and-for-itself of my female nature. This process is extremely difficult to carry out and explains most of the misunderstandings about my work and thought. (Irigaray 1992b: 108; 1996: 63)

If we consider this 'femininity' and the female body[10] as texts in the Symbolic *as well as*, and *at the same time* as they operate in the real, then the full play of Ricoeur's three strands of mimesis can be woven through the complexities of Irigaray's project. The 'texts' on which she works – those by Levinas, Merleau-Ponty, Freud, etc – are then placed as components of the wider text of 'femininity' in mimesis$_2$, while practice (Ricoeur's 'practical') and women are still present in the discussion of mimesis$_1$ and mimesis$_3$. The full understanding of mimesis$_2$ within Irigaray's oeuvre, then, will be her project to write her subjectivity ('define the objective alterity of myself for myself as belonging to the female gender'), part of which process entails writing through the 'femininity imposed upon [her]'. It is thus not restricted to her work upon other philosophers.

We can begin to see that Ricoeur's three strands of mimesis move laterally through Irigaray's work, rather than delineate discrete aspects of it. Indeed, to take just one aspect of her mimetic practice: if her working through of the texts of others in order to write her subjectivity can be located within mimesis$_2$, then the texts themselves are substantively within mimesis1 and her comprehension of their nature and her politicised response to them are within mimesis$_3$.

For Ricoeur, as I have said, mimesis$_2$ is a mediation between mimesis$_1$ and mimesis$_3$. Mimesis$_2$ cannot occur without some form of intelligibility, born of wider, specific, cultural understandings:

> Mimesis$_1$ is this pre-understanding of what human action is, of its semantics, its symbolism, its temporality. From this pre-understanding which is common to poets and their readers arises fiction, and with fiction comes the second form of mimesis which is textual and literary. [...] Fiction would never be understandable if it did not configurate what is already figured in human action. (Ricoeur 1981: 20)

It is possible to see that this is the aspect of mimesis wherein lies the embeddedness of 'femininity' in our culture. Related to this is not only Irigaray's identification of philosophy as the key field of investigation, but also an aspect of her work which I feel is under-valued by her commentators: her development of possible structures of ethics and civil rights – in Ricoeur's terms, the necessary 'practical prefiguration' to the 'textual configuration' of mimesis2. This does not function as a simple cause and effect – this structure produces those texts. Rather, the interplay of structure and texts means that the productivity of textual configuration actively requires and provokes productivity in the realm of practical prefiguration in order to guarantee its intelligibility. In this case, women's subjectivity articulated through an appropriate Symbolic (a '*parler-femme*' or 'witnessing-woman') would be meaningless without attention to the structures of civil rights and ethics.

Ricoeur's final strand concerns practical transfiguration: 'Generalizing beyond Aristotle, I shall say that mimesis$_3$ marks the intersection of the world of the text and the world of the hearer or reader. Therefore it is the intersection of the world unfolded by fiction and the world wherein actual action unfolds' (Ricoeur 1981: 26).

Underlying this is an acceptance of 'the problematic of the reception of a work as an integral part of the constitution of its meaning' (Ricoeur 1981: 27).

Here, then, we find not only the reader herself (Irigaray in her act of reading), but also, in her reading, the spur towards the feminist project, which becomes manifest in mimesis1 and mimesis2. Ricoeur argues that this demands a re-thinking of representation as 'imitation copy': 'It is no longer what is accidental to action that is re-presented or made present anew but what is essential' (Ricoeur 1981: 27). In seeing mimesis2 as 'configurating act', and keeping the flow between the three in the realm of praxis, this third strand is available as an 'action about action'. Thus the world is not so much re-described through mimesis, as re-signified. Once again, this helps us understand the practice of mimesis in Irigaray's work as not only not restricted to her reinvestigation of the philosophers, but also as productive effect. I am thinking here particularly of an image evoked (in for example *Je, Tu, Nous, Sexes and Genealogies*, and *I Love To You*) of the woman reader (listener, viewer) making sense of what she is reading (hearing, seeing) through an active sense of female genealogies, and its concomitant on the horizon, a sense of the universal for women as half of humanity, rather than subsisting as the 'other' of the whole. This image of the woman reader (listener, viewer) is of course not only Irigaray, but also a possible 'myself' that Irigaray evokes in me, as her reader.

Ricoeur ends his paper with a 'modest conclusion'. It is 'the wish that the concept of representation, upon which converge philosophy's most serious attempts to question itself, rediscovers the polysemy and mobility that will make it available for new adventures of thinking' (Ricoeur 1981: 31). This is a prompt for us to look at Irigaray's consideration of representation and the ways in which her broader work is productive of new considerations *for* representation, in a way which is not reductive to illustration, positive images or the discourse of hysteria. Instead we should recognise three strands of Irigaray's new adventures of rethinking representation through mimetic praxis or productive mimesis: civil rights and ethics for women, the Symbolic for women and the universal for women.

# 2

# The Visible

Irigaray has been described, most prominently by Martin Jay, as being anti visual or anti-ocular (Jay 1993: 526–542). His treatment of 'oculocentrism' and 'anti-oculocentrism' as quasi-essentialist categories turn Irigaray's political project and its political, social and cultural implications into her 'nothing-to-see' in his 'blind spot'. Cathryn Vasseleu has responded to this, insisting that Irigaray's critique of the visual or the ocular is contingent upon her critique of phallocentrism and patriarchy. Rather than being anti-ocular per se, Irigaray critiques the overvaluation of particular structures of sight which are in intimate relation with structures of phallocentrism and supportive of the patriarchy. Vasseleu asserts that 'Irigaray addresses illumination as an ineradicable passion', and argues that in naming Western philosophy as 'photology' the weight of Irigaray's argument does not fall on the elaboration of 'light as the founding metaphor of metaphysics' but that 'her argument is instead directed toward the figuration of a complicity between photology and phallocentrism' (Vasseleu 1996: 130-131). Vasseleu returns Jay's comments to gendered political structures, with the effect that his comments can then be seen as symptomatic of aspects of those structures. Her analysis indicates that Irigaray has identified links between phallocentric and patriarchal structures and the threaded areas of light, illumination, visibility, representation, the Symbolic and sexuality, and that to collapse an anti-oculocentric critique into an anti-ocular position is as reductive as collapsing an anti-phallocentric critique into an anti-male position. Irigaray's argument is not against visuality as such, but against the phallocentric Symbolic structures informing our culture including structures of how we understand the legibility of what is visible in structures of the Symbolic order. In these, the phallic gaze and structures appropriate to man are over-valued at the expense not only of other senses (in particular, touch) but also of Symbolic structures appropriate to woman. The implications for both making and looking at art are far-reaching.

## PHALLOCULOCENTRISM

Irigaray's project has consistently had at its heart the problematic of woman's access to the Symbolic, and the need to create the conditions wherein a Symbolic syntax appropriate to women can develop, not only in speech, but also in visual systems of gesture and representation. She argues strongly that phallocentrism is based upon its established activity and understandings in the realm of the visual – what is or is not seen allows for the construction of castration anxiety and of woman as 'other of man's same'. This then determines the representation of women and the construction of 'femininity' in the Symbolic order. However, Irigaray's concept and structuring of the Symbolic differs from the more widely understood and utilised Lacanian version. It is important to recognise that throughout Irigaray's thought, patriarchal and phallocentric monolithic conceptions (be they social, divine, philosophical or cultural) are resolutely and delicately rethought as (at least) dual in nature. The same is true of the Symbolic.

Lacan's concept of the Symbolic order is 'a mediative function [...] which separates the Imaginary from the Real, creates loss and forms the necessary distance from the other's *jouissance*' (Ragland-Sullivan 1992: 423); it does not, however, have any gender specificity in and of itself. For Irigaray, critiquing a patriarchal culture and its structures, the present syntax in the Symbolic order is a mediation function of a phallic Imaginary in its interaction with the Real. What she works towards, in distinction from this, is a dually structured Symbolic order: a Symbolic that is structured through difference, and is productive of – and can accommodate – a 'double syntax':

> Might we not say that it is because it has produced and continues to 'hold' syntax that the masculine maintains mastery over discourse? [...] This syntax of discourse, of discursive logic – more generally, too, the syntax of social organization, 'political' syntax – isn't this syntax always [...] a means of masculine self-affection, or masculine self-production or reproduction? [...] The 'other' syntax, the one that would make feminine 'self-affection' possible, is lacking, repressed, censured: the feminine is never affected except by and for the masculine. What we would want to put into play, then, is a syntax that would make women's 'self-affection' possible. A 'self affection' that would certainly

> not be reducible to the economy of sameness of the One, and for which the syntax and the meaning remain to be found. (Irigaray 1977a: 130–131; 1985d: 132)

This possibility of shifting the syntactical structure of the Symbolic marks an important difference between Irigaray and Lacan (Minsky 1996: 198). Developing the concept of syntax within the structure of the Symbolic enables the distinguishing of inflections, significations and sites of enunciation. These are presently phallocentric; but Irigaray's term 'syntax' marks the possibility of appropriate significatory structures for women. Her argument is that women should develop an appropriate syntax through the sites of reserve identified in the last chapter. If phallocentric discourse is analysed as one syntax among others within the gender-neutral concept of the Symbolic, then the Symbolic is (at least) dual and not in and of itself monolithic or phallic. Change is possible. It is important to note that Irigaray does not propose two Symbolics, one for men and one for women: such a binary does not appear in her work. Instead, she elaborates a structure which is not one, and which cannot be counted in ones (one + one), but which is always already plural. This is endorsed by comments in a later interview, where she says: 'I suggest starting again from an initial definition of the symbol: an object-sign divided in two to indicate a meeting between two people, linked to each other through this division, both out of faithfulness to themselves and to the entire object-sign' (Irigaray and Lotringer 2000: 60). While she is here talking about the symbol as object-sign, and not about the Symbolic, it would be untenable to have 'an object-sign divided in two' which is the product of two Symbolics, rather than produced by a Symbolic which is (at least) two.

Fundamental to phallocentrism is a dependence upon sight and the visual before all other senses, and the siting, through sight, of woman as 'other of the same': '*The gaze is at stake from the outset*. Don't forget, in fact, what "castration", or the knowledge of castration, owes to the gaze, at least for Freud. The gaze has always been involved' (Irigaray 1974: 53; 1985c: 47). In *Speculum* Irigaray dissects the relationship between classic psychoanalysis and the phallocentric gaze, and the embeddedness of the seeing/not seeing dichotomy in the theory and the practice of psychoanalysis. The phallocentric gaze (Freud's gaze) sees the presence or absence of the penis before all else, and upon this (mis)sight builds its justificatory theory of castration. In addition, the phallic gaze (Freud's gaze) is not to be gazed upon, and thus remains unquestioned – not only potent, but in this way invested with omnipotence. Sitting behind the analysand, Freud sees that she does not have a gaze: this is a conceptual structure for psychoanalytic practice which echoes the establishment of the 'fact' of woman's castration in the structure of psychoanalytic theory. According to

Freudian psychoanalysis, because woman has 'nothing that is penis-shaped', woman has nothing:

> Woman's castration is defined as her having nothing you can see [*rien à donner à voir*], and her having nothing. In her having nothing penile, in seeing that she has No Thing. Nothing *like* man. That is to say, *no sex/organ* that shows itself in a form capable of founding its reality, reproducing its truth. *Nothing to be seen is equivalent to having no thing. No being* and *no truth*. The contract, the collusion between one sex/organ and the victory won by visual dominance [*la maîtrise par le regard*] therefore leaves woman with her sexual void, with an 'actual castration' carried out in actual fact. She has the option of a 'neutral' libido or of sustaining herself by 'penis-envy'. (Irigaray 1974: 53–54; 1985c: 47–48)

Woman is deemed to have no thing of her own, no being or truth of her own, no ontology; instead, she is deemed simply not to have the ontology of man. Thus she is 'other of the same', rather than accepted in and respected for her difference. The phallocentric gaze 'discovers' all this, and can account for it and confirm her as 'other of the same' through the structures of castration theory and penis-envy. Thus also the omnipotence of the phallocentric gaze is confirmed. The 'blind spots' of psychoanalysis and of phallocentrism are woman's body and woman's sexuality. This, then, is the location of essentialism in relation to sex in the phallocentric economy: that the whole edifice of phallocentrism is built upon whether the penis can or cannot be seen and what is deduced from that, not upon whether the genitals seen are male or female. Phallocentric desire thus turns upon the sight of the penis: phall-oculo-centrism.

## THE PHALLOCENTRIC SYNTAX

Writing this becomes a struggle. Words fail. Within phallocentric thinking there is no space, no comprehension, no air or water or warmth for a syntax that is appropriate to women. For phallocentrism the man's ontology is the only one which signifies, hingeing on the metaphor of having or not having the penis (verifiable through sight). The formulation 'woman' is produced only in negative relation to this possession. So too will be her entry into the phallic syntax in the Symbolic order: what has come to be known as 'phallologocentrism'. Here, the penis is raised in the Imaginary to a relationship with the phallus as a signifier in the Symbolic. What is crucial is that identification with the word, the structure and use of the word, is developed on *visual investigation* of having/not having the penis: what could be called phall-oculo-logo-centrism.[1]

Irigaray mimeticises Freud in order to expose his 'blind spot':

> The little girl does not submit to the 'facts' easily, she keeps waiting for 'it to grow', and 'believes in that possibility for improbably long years'. Which means that no attempt will be made by the little girl – nor by the mother? Nor by the woman? – to find symbols for the state of 'this nothing to be seen', to defend its goals, or to lay claim to its rewards. *Here again no economy would be possible whereby sexual reality can be represented by/for the woman.* (Irigaray 1974: 55–56; 1985c: 49)

Once again the woman reader of this interrogation of Freud swings wildly between despair at the bleakness of the scenario given, and a grim laugh that Freud thought such a scenario credible, desirable and the only one possible. Irigaray repeatedly critiques the phallocular syntax and its representation to itself of a concept of 'woman' which is dependent upon the seen/not seen of the penis, each time coming at it with slightly different emphasis, or another twist. If phalloculologocentrism 'sees' woman as other to man's sameness, she argues, then it follows that its concept 'woman' is representation of this. As such, 'she' ('woman') does not represent her own ontology, and has no Symbolic syntax. As such, 'she' *does* represent (though he cannot see it) his 'blind spot': she 'remains the place for the inscription of repressions' (Irigaray 1974: 63–64; 1985c: 55). Inscribed into *his* conception of her/of her body are *his* repressions, *his* 'horrors of nothing to see'; they are written into the visible of representations of her/of her body; written into *his* visuality; *his* representations. Buoyed up by this, patriarchy denies her access to symbolic structures; or, in 'liberal' regimes, permits limited access only insofar as she denies difference and aspires instead only to equality, *masquerades* as 'the same as', masquerades herself as 'other of the same' ('A man minus the possibility of (re)presenting oneself as a man = a woman' (Irigaray 1974: 27; 1985c: 27)). All else is either unseen or unsee-able, denied visibility or accorded only the space of latent or actual 'hysteria'. Hence Rosi Braidotti: 'To sum up Irigaray's theory of sexual difference as a political and epistemological project, I would emphasize […] the belief that the subject Woman is that which has been excluded in the masculine system of representation, because she is in excess of it and as such she is unrepresentable' (Braidotti 1994: 123).

Denied her ontology and an appropriate syntax in the Symbolic, woman's subjecthood is also deniable: *the subjects, women,* are elsewhere from the representation 'woman' constructed by and represented in phalloculologocentrism (this echoes the concept of 'reserve' in the last chapter). Irigaray warns us away from proposing a universal female subject: 'the feminine is diverse, as I believe, because subjectivity is diverse [...] I don't know if it's possible to talk about a concrete subject, a feminine subject' (Irigaray in Hirsh and Olson 1995: 151). From now on I will use the terminology 'the representation, "woman"', where it is necessary to distinguish between the construct 'woman' (as a series of phalloculologocentric representations) and the potential of 'the subjects, women'. In our present patriarchal culture the two intersect. Actual women act out and live through these representations – become these representations – in their everyday lives through the structures of mimesis. This is policed in the everyday by patriarchal implementation of phalloculologocentrism.

Irigaray's overall project aims to disentangle the intersection of the representation, 'woman' and being the subjects, women, in the lives and languages – the self-representations and self-articulations – of actual women. The problem remains in the phallic syntax insofar as the phallic gaze cannot see the subjects, women, and as a result can only construct representations of 'her' – 'woman'. The subjects, women, therefore are nothing in the flaw that is its blind spot, unrepresentable:

> A fault, a flaw, a lack, an absence, outside the system of representations and autorepresentations. Which are man's. By a *hole* in men's signifying economy. A nothing that might cause the ultimate destruction, the splintering, the break in their systems of 'presence', of 're-presentation' and 'representation'. A nothing threatening the process of production, reproduction, mastery, and profitability, of meaning, dominated by the phallus. (Irigaray 1974: 57; 1985c: 50)

On the back of this 'nothing' that is the representation, 'woman', is the reserve of the subjects, women; always already elsewhere, the subjects, women, are the danger in his blind spot, the danger of the 'mystery' that he has made. Placing this problem in the Symbolic is not a theoretical ruse for avoiding the messy, awkward, glorious world of the practical, the material, the empirical; but rather to attend to the function of the Symbolic as a mediation between the Imaginary and the Real. How can women (including women artists) begin to articulate their experience – for example, through political, collective, strategic activity, and through the making of art – if the symbolic means available and comprehensible to them are not fully appropriate? It is politically urgent to identify where and why this may be the case, in order to develop strategies to counter the situation. The mimetic structures identified in the first chapter enable us to seek consciously that place of reserve in order to develop structures for a syntax in the Symbolic which is more appropriate. This is why Irigaray is able to name the danger that the subjects, women, are to phallocentric 'systems of "presence", of "re-presentation" and "representation"' while appropriating terminology descriptive of the realm of the Symbolic order.

For phallocentrism, man's birth is birth into the realm of the visual (for the 'subject'), birth into visibility (of the 'subject' and his penis to others), birth into victory over maternal power, and birth from that place which he can see marks the otherness of his sameness (Irigaray 1987c: 71; 1993b: 59). Therefore, in the patriarchal structures informed by the phallocentric gaze woman/women will always already be mother; the female other will always be (m)otherness of his sameness, in his hom(m)osexual economy. The effect of this upon current understandings of women's relation to origin is important for mapping the difference between the representation 'woman' and the subjects, women. Irigaray describes how, in phallocentric structures, once the little boy enters the phallic stage he desires to return to the place of origin – the mother – 'in order to reestablish continuity with it and to see and know what happens there' and reproduce himself (Irigaray 1974: 45; 1985c: 41). The structures of male heterosexuality, to reiterate, depend upon desire *to be* the same (hom(m)osexuality), not upon desire *for* difference; and subsequently upon the sight of the other of the same. Woman cannot have the same relation to origin as man because, within the phallic economy, she is always already (m)other of the same: that is, she is the site of origin for man. She is site of his maintenance mimesis, his reproduction of the same. She, who has not got one and is not one, cannot be counted in the economy of one + one + one +...except by playing her role in maintaining man's genealogy (Irigaray 1974: 45; 1985c: 41).

If woman's relation to origin is discounted, then there will be discernible effects within phalloculologocentric representational systems:

> Freud is still party to a certain logos and therefore to a certain economy of 'presence', and he will be able to picture [*se représenter*] the little girl becoming a woman only in terms of *lack, absence, default*, etc. To take an example or paradigm, Freud can discuss the little girl's relation to the place of origin only as a vacancy, a taking leave of the mother: as rejection, or hatred of the mother. That is to say, as a fault in the re-presentation of origin. (Irigaray 1974: 45–46; 1985c: 41–42)

Just as there is no symmetry between the two sexes in their relation to origin, so too there is no reciprocal arrangement in their relation to the present economy of representation. If woman is 'seen' as 'castrated', as not having something (and thus as having no ontology of her own, and no signifiers in the phallic Symbolic), then her relation to origin and her representation of and to self will be seen as negative. How can she love the fact that she is like something that has nothing, that is nothing but the gap where something should be? Margaret Whitford points out the devastating effect of this:

> *All* relations between women, and particularly the most intense and intimate ones, are affected by the patriarchal rupture of the primitive mother-daughter bond. One can only identify with a phallic or castrated mother, i.e., with a mother as defined by the patriarchal economy. To become a woman in patriarchy means in effect abandoning the mother. (Whitford 1994a: 28)

Irigaray has described this eloquently and even more forcefully as not being a *displacement* of the woman's origin-desire, nor an *abandonment*, but 'an exile, and extradition, an expatriation, from this/her economy of desire. [...] Woman would thus find no possible way to represent or *tell the story of the economy of her libido*' (Irigaray 1974: 47. Translation modified; 1985c: 43).

With no syntax appropriate to her in the Symbolic, and with a total disruption of her genealogies, woman is in a state of dereliction. Hysteria – actual or latent – is once again a structural inevitability: in attempting to wrest control of her subjectivity, her womanliness, her sexuality (as outlined in the chapter on mimesis), the hysteric finds herself in a non-symbolised space – the space of hysterical paralysis, hysterical muteness, hysterical babbling, incomprehensible in the present Symbolic order, incomprehensible as it has no syntax appropriate to it, and without any collectivity of action lending potential mediation among women, to women, and in response to which phallocentrism has no 'cure' other than a re-training in the syntax and languages of the phallic economy:

> But this fault, this deficiency, this 'hole', inevitably affords woman too few figurations, images, or representations by which to represent herself. It is not that she lacks some 'master signifier' or that none is imposed upon her, but rather that access to a signifying economy, to the coining of signifiers, to their exchange, is difficult or even impossible for her because she remains an outsider, herself (a) subject to their norms. She borrows signifiers but cannot make her mark, or re-mark upon them. Which all surely keeps her deficient, empty, lacking, in a way that could be labelled 'psychotic': a *latent* but not actual psychosis, for want of a practical signifying system. (Irigaray 1974: 85; 1985c: 71)
>
> Instead, there is a distanceless proximity between the woman and her utterance, and thus between women: 'this distanceless proximity between women – between mother and daughter? – distanceless because no symbolic process allows us to account for it'. (Irigaray 1985a: 295–296; 1991a: 107)

This is obviously of great relevance when women's ability to make meaning through visual arts is under consideration. Within Western economies of representation, we have patriarchal structures, accountable under the strict regime of phalloculologocentrism. As a sub-section, in 'Fine Art' we have the seemingly mutable languages of representation within the art markets (including the art schools, the journals, etc) of modernity. But as the slightest examination reveals, these structures, while feigning a liberating openness and multiplicity, are unforgivingly patriarchal at all levels – from their structural organisation through to the visible and material symbols of the works they trade. They are riven with father–son power struggles dressed in the clothes of the market's desire for novelty (the avant-garde), which mask the fundamental maintenance mimesis through which continuity is ensured. The sons are taught; stars validated; markets guaranteed. The position of women attempting to make meaning – develop an appropriate syntax – comprehensible within these structures is compromised to an extent hard to underestimate. The art world requires that its artists produce work that can be accounted for within the structures of maintenance mimesis, and at the same time be seen as developing a visual language unique to the individual artist. It is this surface appearance of symbolic openness that appears both seductive and terrifying to the young women who are the majority of art students; it is the structure of maintenance mimesis that ensures them restricted success, whether in real terms (recognition) or in producing an appropriate syntax: as Irigaray says, 'she borrows signifiers but cannot make her mark, or re-mark upon them'.

## DISRUPTING PHALLOCULOLOGOCENTRISM

There are points of utter, unflinching bleakness in Irigaray's analysis of the situation in which women find themselves in relation to the Symbolic order as constructed through phallocentrism. However, as with mimesis, Irigaray analyses in order to identify places for resistance, moments of reserve – 'the cultural reserve yet to come' (Irigaray 1977a: 136; 1985d: 138); far from performing what might be called a 'victim feminism', 'she is envisaging the most far-reaching sociosymbolic reconstruction' (Whitford 1994: 30). Some of the complexities of this in relation to the phallic Symbolic are already clear: a woman's negative relation to phalloculologocentrism being a negative which is not simply a symmetrical opposite; her genealogies and relation to origin being utterly disrupted; her body, her sexuality, her ontology being unseen and unspoken; the strategy of productive mimesis being one of the few open to her; her 'cultural reserve yet to come' being literally unspeakable, lacking an appropriate syntax.

Women's strategies within the realm of representation will need to be multi-layered, multi-threaded:

> For what is important is to disconcert the staging of representation according to exclusively 'masculine' parameters, that is, according to a phallocratic order. It is not a matter of toppling that order so as to replace it – that amounts to the same thing in the end – but of disrupting and modifying it, starting from an 'outside' that is exempt, in part, from phallocratic law. (Irigaray 1977a: 67; 1985d: 68)

'Disconcert', 'disrupt', 'modify': these are terms found in this passage from *This Sex* that prefigure the tone of the later book *I Love to You* (1992), with its aim of creating a dialogic space for both genders, an accommodation between a syntax in the Symbolic appropriate to men and a syntax in the Symbolic appropriate to women, and a space of attentiveness for the male/female couple. Irigaray did not, even in her earlier works, envisage a world without men, without a syntax appropriate to men. A world without patriarchy, yes; a world where the economies of representation are not the dominion of phallocentrism, yes; but still a world where women and men would, at some level, have to reach some accommodation with each other. (Equally her distrust of what has become known as 'feminism' in France never detracts from her rigorous anti-patriarchal stance, and her insistence that men have to change.) As she says 'It is vital that a culture of the sexual, as yet nonexistent, be elaborated, with each sex respected' (Irigaray 1990a: 11; 1993i: 12). However, it is clear that, for Irigaray, respecting women includes respecting love between women, be that social, familial, sexual or in the realm of the 'divine'.

'Disconcert[ing] the staging of representation according to exclusively "masculine" parameters' should not be confused with substituting 'feminine' representations for 'masculine'. To do so, even in the name of a matriarchy or a sorority, would be to use the same structure of domination as those found in phallocratic orders – indeed, could perform a maintenance mimesis of phallocentrism. Instead, Irigaray has here placed the term 'masculine' in citation marks, implying that the term is as available for scrutiny and reordering as is the term 'feminine'. The phallocratic order, then, is not a monolith, but contingent upon its own representational orders. But the job has to start 'from an "outside" that is exempt, in part, from phallocratic law'. I would take this 'outside' to refer to the 'cultural reserve yet to come'; it remains within citation marks because phallocratic law does not recognise anything (as being) beyond its control, and because the 'cultural reserve yet to come' is as yet virtually unsymbolised in an appropriate way.

It is is important to recall Rosi Braidotti's identification of the subject, woman, 'excluded in the masculine system of representation' as she is 'in excess of it and [...] unrepresentable. This Woman, revindicated as the rallying point of feminist-minded women, also opens the possibility of elaborating an-other system of representation' (Braidotti 1994: 123–124). Irigaray's strategy of productive mimesis is at the heart of growing a syntax of the subjects, women. As Braidotti says:

> [it] amounts to a collective repossession by women of the images and representations of 'Woman' as they have been coded in language, culture, science, knowledge, and discourse and consequently internalized in the heart, mind, body, and lived experience of women. Mimetic repetition as a textual and political strategy is the active subversion of established modes of the representation and expression of women's experience. In this respect the redefinition of the subject Woman / women as both representation and experience amounts to no less than a change of civilization, of genealogy, of a sense of history. Feminist countergenealogies are the inroads to a new symbolic system by women. (Braidotti 1994: 120–121)

This collective repossession by women of the representations of 'Woman' requires, according to Braidotti, a moment of 'a strategic form of essentialism', which she defines as 'the temporary strategy that defines as Woman the stock of cumulated knowledge about the female, sexed subject – whose traits, qualities, and representation affect every woman' (Braidotti 1994: 124). Once again, this is not a simple act of reversal. As Irigaray says 'there is no simple manageable way to leap to the outside of phallogocentrism, *nor any way to situate oneself there, that would result from the simple fact of being a woman*' (Irigaray 1977a: 157; 1985d: 162). As we have seen earlier, the moment of phalloculocentric 'essentialism' of sexual difference is dependent upon the sight of the penis, not upon the possession or otherwise of male or female genitals. Repossessing representations in order to perform a productive mimesis upon them thus entails taking the risk of passing through this phalloculologocentric moment of 'essentialist' categorisation.

Irigaray points out that the deductions made by the phallic gaze upon seeing woman's genitals – even upon mis-seeing them as 'nothing' – are not inevitable (Irigaray 1974: 54; 1985c: 48). Oculocentrism could itself have been 'castrated' – had its position of centrality and dominance removed – had the sight of the 'missing penis' been seen not as the sight / site of something missing, of nothing, and thus as the site of the other of the same, but instead seen as the sight / site of difference, a site of man's difference and woman's difference. Woman's genitals would be seen, as are man's also; they would not be seen merely as not-man's, not-penis, no-thing. What is at stake here (despite Jay's comments cited at the start of the chapter) is not sight, not the ocular, but its *structural function* at the centre of the phallic economy of representation.

Some commentators on Irigaray's work suggest that she wishes to replace the visual with touch (Braidotti 1991: 148). While there is no evidence that she wishes to replace the phallic structures of seeing with similar structures for touch, she does, however, disrupt the position of sight as the originating sense:

> We regress and we progress, way beyond all sense of sight, from the most primitive to the subtlest realm of the tactile. Everything is given to us by means of touch, a mediation that is continually forgotten. Anything that emerges into the visible realm, the images of man and the world, remains for a while in history, but this visual birth [*une naissance*] does not fulfil all our native potentialities. (Irigaray 1987c: 71; 1993b: 59)

Man sets up the visual as primary in order to differentiate himself from a pre-natal and pre-Symbolic maternal context. Equally, touch is literally the 'unseen' of sight, insofar as sight is dependent upon the interrelation through touch of the component parts of the eyeball and eye socket. In this, touch can be understood as the 'reserve' of sight, unsymbolised. As women begin constructing a syntax appropriate for their subjectivity – or rather, as such a syntax becomes legible beyond a phallocular framework – so the relative importance of sight and touch will inevitably shift, although how exactly cannot be known. Also fundamental to the primacy of the phallic gaze is a continuation and exaggeration of the move from the empirical experience of matter (as in the experience of touch) towards the differentiation of form (which is what the phallic economy requires of sight) (Irigaray 1974: 97; 1985c: 80). Vasseleu locates this in the phallic economy of representation: 'The exclusion [of women from representation] is achieved in the differentiation between form and matter, in which matter remains the site of an unthematizable materiality. Though masculine identity is formulated in opposition to matter, the feminine as matter cannot be thought' (Vasseleu 1996: 130). (This discussion will inform later consideration of process and materiality of artworks.)

While Irigaray does indeed disrupt the relative valuation of sight and touch, she suggests also that things and experience in the realm of the visual can be seen and interpreted differently. In order to make her point she uses the visual representational analogies of the rebus and the pictograph in a discussion of dreams:

> Yet the fact that the dream can be interpreted only as a 'rebus' should have persuaded the 'reader' to turn it in all directions and positions, and not favor

> one type of inscription that would already prescribe a meaning to it: a linear, teleologically horizontal or vertical displacement, over a surface as yet unwritten, which it brands by cutting it up according to rules of repetition and recurrence, obeying processes that already paralyze the 'body's' system of gestures within a given graphic order, etc. Why not rather have recalled those 'pictures' ['*images*'] made for children, pictographs in which the hunter and hunted [*chassé(e)*], and their dramatic relationships, are to be discovered between the branches, *made out* from *between* the trees. From the spaces between the figures, or stand-in figures. Spaces that organize the scene, blanks that sub-tend the scene's structuration and that will yet not be read as such. Or not read at all? Nor seen at all? Never in truth represented or representable, though this is not to say that they have no effect upon the present scenography. (Irigaray 1974: 170–171; 1985c: 137–138)

Through this visual analogy Irigaray provides a thumbnail sketch of many strands of her thought: phallic dominance; the '*parler-femme*' yet to come; maintenance mimesis; hysteric paralysis; the unseen of the visible; the 'nothing-to-see' that is 'woman'. Thus she reminds us not to throw the baby of the visual out with the bath-water of the phallic economy; but rather to disrupt the phallic economy *within* the visual: to disrupt phall-oculo-logocentrism.[2] The effects of disrupting the phallocular will of course not be found only among women, nor in an essentialist, separatist 'woman's Symbolic'. The syntax appropriate to women and that appropriate to men, and the representation of men and women in their difference, will not occur with one syntax in isolation from the other (Irigaray 1990a: 34; 1993i: 32). Thus, there will be a resultant crisis of ontology for man: '*Exquisite/ex-schiziod crises of ontico-ontological difference.* What manner of recasting all economy will ensue? To tell the truth, no one knows' (Irigaray 1974: 180–181; 1985c: 145). Structures will change as the present values crumble.

Women's attempts to construct an appropriate syntax through visible representations have qualities verging on the poignant and the heroic, but with deeply political potential. The phalloculologocentric order, structured as it is upon a primacy of sight, is productive of an apparent ease of mediation through visual languages. This results from its projection of qualities of transparency onto the image, rather than treating as problematic both that which images might represent, and methods of seeing and reading those images. Seeing is believing (as discernible in the founding metaphor of phallogocentrism: castration theory); thus images are endowed with a commonsense non-questionability, a claim to verity. In particular, the brutality towards women often represented by images (including the brutality of denying women's ontology and subjectivity) frequently remains unquestioned; or, if it is questioned from within the women's movement, the response elsewhere (from men or women) can be one of incredulity. But the 'real', the 'truth', the 'norm', and the 'inevitability' of visual images are of course those traits as *developed within* and defined by phallocentrism; women's relation to them is determined by their production in and relation to a phallic syntax. Hence, the psychic brutality towards women frequently represented by, or produced by, visual imagery is an inevitable result of woman's excision from her genealogies and her lack of an appropriate Symbolic syntax. Thus it is also more far-reaching than might be expected by those who discuss only particular categories of images, and (ironically) only in terms of them being transparent representations, 'offensive to' or 'degrading of' women. This position is significant politically; but the picture is (pictures are) more complex.

## MIRROR

Irigaray uses the analogy of a mirror in various forms – particularly flat, concave and convex – to expose phalloculocentric structures and their determining of phallogocentric structures. She does this in order to undo those structures while asserting a potential ecstatic relationship with light in the realm of the spiritual for women; a prerequisite on the horizon of possibilities to enable the becoming of the subjects, women. Light, of course, is a prerequisite of the visual; and Irigaray draws several distinctions between patriarchal understandings of light, dark, shadow and so forth (particularly within philosophy) and anti-patriarchal ways of looking at these phenomena. Ultimately these lead towards an undoing of the phallocentric gaze of the 'subject' at the 'object' as the determinant of their relationship, and suggest instead intersubjective relationships where listening is as important as looking, but, crucially, both have qualities of attentiveness.

As we have seen, within Eurocentric culture 'woman' functions as 'other of the same' for man; and thus, bereft of her subjecthood, she can only do so as a representation. Irigaray says, 'Of course, a mirror is needed. But this can be "interiorized", *put inside*. Representation can dispense with and supplant the role played in the real life of the senses by the mirror' (Irigaray 1974: 116; 1985c: 95). As man is confirmed in his 'sameness' by her 'otherness', the representation, 'woman' (which he has constructed) functions for his subjectivity as a mirror. The paradox of the reflection in the mirror is that it indeed is not the *reproduction* of 'the same', but it is a *representation* which fixes the 'other of the same' as the device through which 'the same' knows itself:

> And even if, conceptually, my right hand and my left hand, or my hand and its image in the mirror, are rigorously the same, or the same thing, this would not be true for the intuitive character of space in which the *paradox of symmetry* was taken into account. Thus already a mirror turns out to support the apprehension of objects. [...] Does the subject derive his power from the appropriation of this non-place of the mirror? (Irigaray 1974: 256; 1985c: 205)

The construction of the representation, 'woman', as not-man, as other, is also a construction of 'woman' as always already (m)other for man. Here is the paradox of the mirror's symmetry: that the representation, 'woman', is not the same as him, but, as his place of origin, 'she' has to be defined by him in terms of 'her' relation to his sameness – the-same-but-other, other-of-the-same, the-same-back-to-front, inverted: mirror-image, rather than the same; mirror-image, rather than different. If she were to be recognised as different (as the subject, woman), then the structures of his 'subjectivity' would be in crisis.

The structures of castration theory are impossible to disentangle from the construction of the representation, 'woman' which makes her 'only the path, the method, the theory, the "*mirror*" for the "subject"' (Irigaray 1974: 297; 1985c: 239). In turn this investment of the one in the other is utterly dependent upon phallocentric ways of seeing, in particular the over-valuing of aspects of sight while ignoring sight's interaction with other senses – significantly, touch. The representation, 'woman', functions within phalloculocentrism as a *flat* mirror, 'a faithful, polished mirror, empty of altering reflections' (Irigaray 1974: 168; 1985c: 136), two dimensional, lacking any form of its own: 'the flat mirror reflects the greater part of women's sexual organs only as a hole' (Irigaray 1974: 109; 1985c: 89), confirming the male subject in his singular position, disallowing any play of couples, whether woman/man or mother/daughter (Irigaray 1974: 92; 1985c: 77). Instead it allows only the play of the paradox of symmetry. Woman as a desiring subject would expose the flat mirror as a fiction: 'in the advent of a "feminine" desire, this flat mirror cannot be privileged and symmetry cannot function as it does in the logic and discourse of a masculine subject' (Irigaray 1977a: 127; 1985d: 129).

This idealised reflecting of the male subject back to himself is a closed circuit within the phallocentric gaze. But then, as we have seen, the phallocentric gaze, phalloculocentric in its auto-eroticism, occupies the site of sight, ignoring other senses. It sees that woman is the other of its same; it sees she has nothing to see; it sees only the symmetrical paradox. It does not see that the/his representation, 'woman' (like the letter, the logos, which will be developed as a result of this 'seeing') is a phenomenon dependent upon the structures of the / his flat mirror. It does not see that the mirror does not reflect itself, that the mirror has its own form, that the mirror does not reflect its own silvery backing. This silvery backing is the 'reserve' of the mirror – a part of the mirror reserved from the phallocentric gaze: 'The backside of (self) representation, of the visual plane where he gazes upon himself' (Irigaray 1974: 167–168; 1985c: 135). As with the hysteric, and as with the implementation of productive mimesis, so too in the structure of the flat mirror which bears the phallocentric gaze upon the / his reflection-image of the representation, 'woman', there is a reserve that can be deployed strategically in order to disconcert the economy of representation, disrupt the unity of the male subject: 'This silvering at the back of the mirror might, at least, retain *the being* – which we have been perhaps and which perhaps we will be again – though our mirage has failed at present or has been covered over by alien speculations' (Irigaray 1974: 245; 1985c: 197). While phallocentric man does not see this reserve, he structures the 'absence of its presence' and its effects in order to sustain his subjectivity.

Irigaray suggests that we need to break through the two dimensionality of the flat mirror, in order to find the more appropriate mirror and achieve recognition of the silvery backing. In other words, the task is to disrupt the phalloculologocentric gaze, the dominance of its syntax in the Symbolic, and its creation, the representation, 'woman', in order to develop recognition of the subjects, women, and an appropriate syntax in the Symbolic; and also, importantly, to recognise the necessary discursivity that (inter)subjectivity and such a syntax entail (Irigaray 1977a: 130–133; 1985d: 132–135).

Irigaray shifts her terminology subtly to expose the implications of 'breaking (with) a certain mode of specula(riza)tion'. She presents a vision of what might be found upon disrupting the two dimensional surface of the mirror – 'this plan / e of representation' (Irigaray 1974: 178; 1985c: 143) – and with it, the representation, 'woman'. Breaking (with) a two dimensional plan / e of representation necessitates a breaking *through*; which brings us into contact with the brilliance of the reserve of the mirror as the result of a movement that evokes concavity:

> But perhaps through this specular surface which sustains discourse is found not the void of nothingness but the dazzle of multifaceted speleology. A scintillating and incandescent concavity, of language also, that threatens to set fire to fetish-objects and eyes plugged with gold [*les yeux aurifiés*]. The recasting of their truth value is already at hand. We need only press on a little further into the depths, into that so-called dark cave which serves as hidden foundation to their speculations. For there where we expect to find the opaque and silent

> matrix of a logos immutable in the certainty of its own light, fires and mirrors are beginning to radiate, sapping the evidence of reason at its base! Not so much by anything stored in the cave – which would still be a claim based on the notion of the closed volume – but again and yet again by their indefinitely re-kindled hearths. (Irigaray 1974: 178–179; 1985c: 143–144)[3]

The concavity – the space through and behind the flat mirror's surface – scintillates and burns infinitely. This is not the dark continent, the dark cave, the yawning gap or the vagina dentata. Each of these terms – and others related – are products of phallocentric fear of multiplicity and difference; phallocentric in nature, they are immutable notions stored in the fixity – 'the closed volume' – that is created by phallocentric man as the fearsome flipside to the/his beautiful object of contemplation.

This makes inevitable the rhetoric of Irigaray's following questions:

> But which 'subject' up till now has investigated the fact that a *concave mirror* concentrates the light and, specifically, that this is not wholly irrelevant to woman's sexuality [*le sexe de la femme*]? Any more than is a man's sexuality [*le sexe de l'homme*] to the convex mirror? Which 'subject' has taken an interest in the anamorphoses produced by the conjunction of such curvatures? What impossible reflected images, maddening reflections, parodic transformations took place at each of their articulations? (Irigaray 1974: 179; 1985c: 144)[4]

One must assume that Irigaray is aware of such paintings as Hans Holbein's *The Ambassadors* (1533) with its anamorphic skull in the foreground.[5] Other anamorphic paintings rely upon an even more phallic cylindrical mirror to provide, in the reflection, the 'correct' reading of the image. It could be argued, of course, that both of these forms of anamorphic image – reliant upon a fixed viewing position, and in the second instance, upon the phallic convex mirror – reassert the primacy of single-point perspective (the visual structure of phalloculocentric representation par excellence) as the only means by which confusion can be righted. Thus again the 'subject' is affirmed in his subjecthood and its worldly and transcendental structures. While these anamorphic representations do indeed claim to be metaphysical while re-centring the 'subject' through demanding a fixed viewing point, Irigaray here is discussing the fixity enforced upon the potentiality of a concave mirror. In this respect two artworks by Anish Kapoor come into mind.

The first was *Descent into Limbo* exhibited in *Documenta*, Kassel, Germany, in 1992. Carefully regulated numbers of viewers were allowed into a room, a windowless cubic space with diffused top light. In the centre of the floor was a round, dense matt black disk or rug, three metres in diameter. Kapoor's work at this time was known for his use of powdered pigments in saturated colours in his sculpture. This achieved such an absolute density of colour that the effect was sometimes paradoxically twofold: to enhance the viewer's perception of form, solidity and surface, while also disconcerting the viewer's perception of space. Initially, the assumption was that the same thing was happening in this work in *Documenta*, through the placing of black pigment on the floor. If a certain perceptual shift happened, however, viewers at *Documenta* realised that what they were walking around was not pigment on the floor, but in fact a substantial hole. Once the perceptual shift had happened it was impossible to revert to seeing the blackness only as a floor-level disk. Vision oscillated. Kapoor had created a sphere-shaped hollow under floor level, with a narrow slice of it cut off where it intersected with the floor. The walls of the sphere were then covered with the black pigment. Such works are physically vulnerable: a related work exhibited in the Venice Biennale of 1990, which was set vertically into a wall, did not survive the viewers' curiosity and their insertion of hands into the space and fingers around the rim. The delicate powdered pigment, once disturbed, betrayed the form it was covering, and destroyed the intended perceptual challenge. In *Documenta*, the sphere was much larger, and the vertiginous feeling caused by standing above it provoked dizzy staring rather than speculative exploration. The absolute nature of the concavity coupled with its lack of fixity did not (of course) produce the burning brilliance of which Irigaray speaks, but it did edge towards an effect of visual scintillation.

Kapoor exhibited a different work, *Untitled* (1995), in the group exhibition *Belladonna* at the ICA, London, 1996. This was made from metal, rather than powdered pigment. A rectangular shape of polished aluminium almost 1.5 x 1 metre was set onto the wall. In the centre of this rectangle the aluminium veered back into the wall space to create an oval recess or tunnel. The viewer was reflected in the highly polished surface, initially the right way up on the flat surround, then upside down as the concavity receded, then in a series of smudge-shapes in the interior of the cavity. The recess was just under a metre deep; despite the multiplicity of reflections, however, it did seem finite, with its dimensions fixed. The work had an immediate impression of being transgressive in a fashionable, 1990s, post-modern-chic manner: there were immediate sexual connotations in its oval shape and penetrative aspect. The reflections had a novelty value (a little like the distorting mirrors found in fairgrounds) rather than an effect of disrupting the viewers' space, place and perception. The size – much smaller than the average viewer – began to return it to object-status; and the size of the cavity, which appeared to be about head-and-shoulders size, appeared too illustrational an evocation of a birth canal. One could also have taken the piece initially as an illustration of Irigaray's concave mirror. Without wishing to suggest any direct or intentional correspondence on the part of the artist, anyone with even slight acquaintance with Irigaray's work might well have seen this too. Seen as such, it would fail

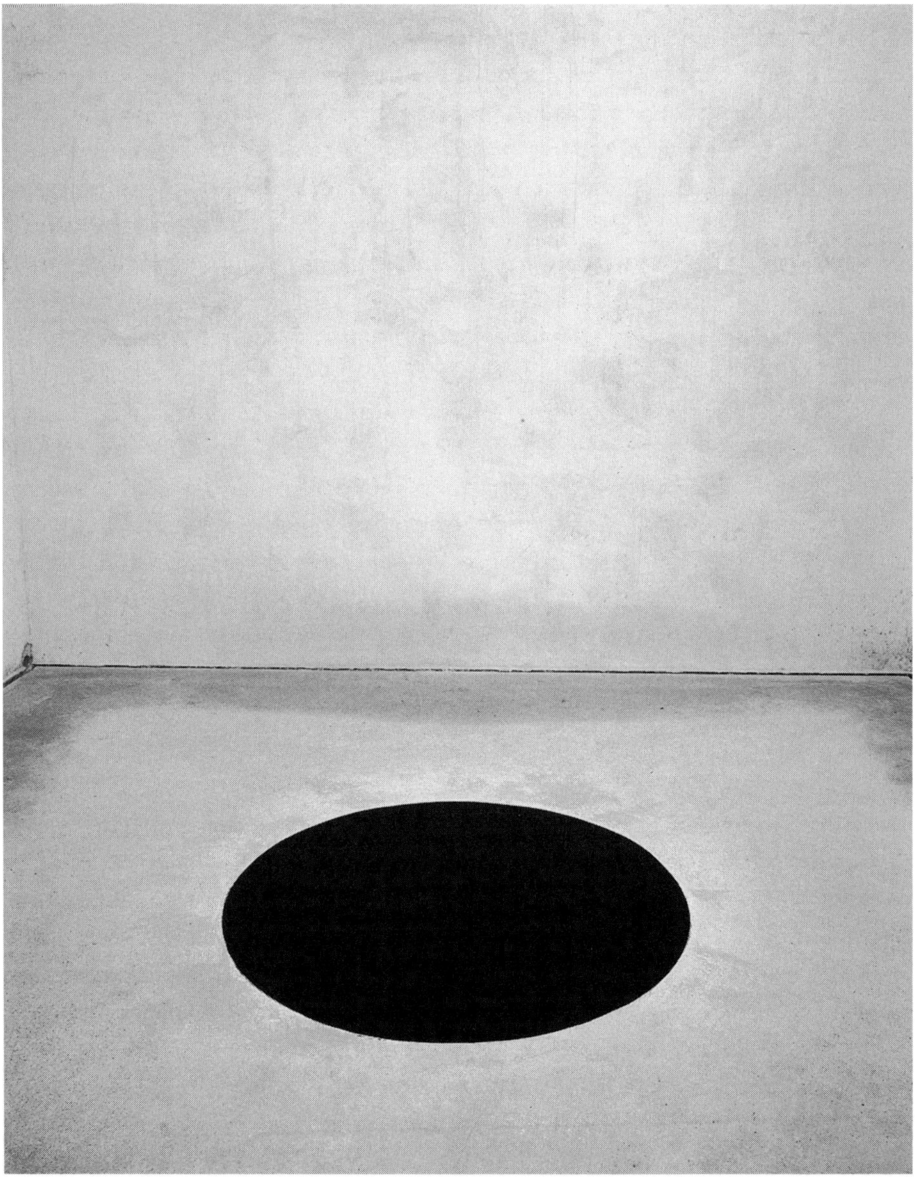

Anish Kapoor, *Descent into Limbo*: 1992. Concrete and Stucco 600 x 600 x 600 cm. Courtesy Anish Kapoor and Lisson Gallery London.

miserably: it was indeed a stand-in, a failed illusion of the scintillation and brilliance of which Irigaray speaks.

What is interesting also is the ways in which commentators have read the void in Kapoor's work as a threat, or as something fearful. For example, Germano Celant wrote of *Descent into Limbo*: 'The ordeal of the void, of limbo, is a necessary precondition to gaining mastery over nothingness and the self' – an evocation of a construction of male subjectivity through the deployment of the speculative gaze (Celant 1998). Kapoor himself has said of the voids in his work that 'this void is not something which is of no utterance. It is a potential space, not a non-space' (Kapoor 1990: 45).[6]

This begs the question: is my reading of *Untitled* a result of an intrinsic weakness the piece had as an artwork, or directed at its failure to illustrate Irigaray's work? Certainly, there is no indication that Kapoor is cognisant of Irigaray's work, nor would I wish to be so reductive as to suggest that this is the sole measure of the success or otherwise of his works. Getting pleasure from artworks one feels one 'ought not' to get pleasure from, and not getting pleasure from works one feels one 'ought' to get pleasure from are interesting and continuing problems for feminism; and works which illustrate pre-given (therefore fixed) theory, rather than being productive of their own discursive theory, inevitably have structural problems concerning how they create meaning. With *Untitled* the two were entwined: I could not see the work without immediately thinking of Irigaray. *Descent into Limbo* did not provoke thoughts of Irigaray's work until I made a comparison between it and *Untitled*. It was, however, more *productive* of Irigaray's analysis, in the way in which it provoked awareness of space, place and perception, vision and sensation, and provided a particular processing of experience. The paradox was that the possibility of such a scintillation as evoked by Irigaray was hinted at far more persuasively by the black spherical hole, with its production of vertigo and its disruption of the relation between its space, the viewer and the viewer's perception, than by the rather tacky aluminium false-mirror, which encouraged the speculative phallocentric gaze, tickling it rather than disrupting it. Kapoor's work of this period depends upon immaculate presentation in order to confound the speculative, penetrating gaze. Once the surface of the pigment had been disturbed in the Venice piece, the work failed. Whereas the success of *Descent into Limbo* hinged upon its ability to produce that shift in the viewer, rebus-like, from seeing a flat surface to seeing a substantial hole, and a subsequent oscillation of vision, the ICA work did not have the same effect upon viewers. Instead, the questions among viewers concerned not the form upon which we gazed, but rather the extent of its concavity – one, two or three feet – and playful dares to put one's hand inside to find out (the 'dentata' in this instance being in the shape of the watchful ICA guards). While one confounded the controlling gaze, the other attracted its speculations.

## SPECULUM

Irigaray is well aware of the associations of the convex mirror with gynaecological instruments and the knife-edge along which she travels – the attempt to develop an analogy in a syntax appropriate for women, while still speaking in a Symbolic that needs to undo its own phallologocentricity. Her aim risks a collapse back into phallocular structures:

> But, may come the objection, – defending again the objective and the object – the speculum is not necessarily a mirror. It may, quite simply, be an instrument to *dilate* [*écarte*] the lips, the orifices, the walls, so that the eye can penetrate the *interior*. So that the eye can enter, to see, notably with speculative intent. (Irigaray 1974: 180; 1985c: 144)

The group of words around 'speculum', including speculation, speculate and specularisation, are played with from the title of *Speculum* onwards, with their intellectual, financial and visual meanings being alluded to at different moments. Irigaray has said at least twice that she was unhappy with the translation of the title *Speculum, de l'autre femme* as *Speculum of the Other Woman*. The translation encouraged the understanding for an English language readership that Irigaray was suggesting both a straightforward mirror – in which, in a phallocentric structure, the subject sees the other of his same – and also the gynaecological instrument, the speculum, which Irigaray was then assumed to use as an analogy to speculate upon her 'other woman' – whom-soever, and in whatsoever relationship, she might have been. In both of these dissenting passages Irigaray states that the translation *Speculum On the Other: Woman* would have indicated more strongly a further meaning:

> In the title of *Speculum*, as throughout the whole book, I played on words, on meanings, to enable a different [*autre*] truth to appear. Thus, *speculum* denotes a gynecological instrument, though at an earlier period in our culture this term was used to denote the most faithful expression of reality possible. *Speculum mundi*, for example, was not an uncommon title and was what I had in mind. (Irigaray 1992b: 101–102; 1996: 59–60)

She expands upon this elsewhere:

> It's not simply a question of a mirror in which one sees oneself, but of the way in which it's possible to give an account of the world within a discourse: a mirror of the world. How I'm going to try to give an account of the world in my discourse. It's in this sense above all that I also played with the mirror, but not simply, because the mirror in a simple sense, in which I see myself, has served for the most part to constitute a masculine subject. (Irigaray in Hirsh and Olson 1995: 147)

So the speculum is not simply an instrument of phallocular hysteroscopy. Irigaray is using the analogy of the speculum not as maintenance mimesis (which Anish Kapoor falls back into, for instance) but as productive mimesis. This much should be evident from the overall text: the reflecting back of Plato and Freud upon themselves; the central section of the book named 'Speculum' pushing to either side the sections on Freud and on Plato; the titles of the three central chapters of that central section: 'Une mère de glace' ('The ice-glass-mirror mother'), '… And if, Taking the Eye of a Man Recently Dead, …' and 'La mystérique' ('the woman hysteric-mystic-mystery'); and so forth. This indicates a potential reserve in the structure of the speculum, and possibilities for a productive mimesis of it. The use of productive mimesis of the speculum shatters the ice-glass-mirror that is the two-dimensional representation, 'woman', exposing the device that it is and recognising the brilliance that is that mirror's backing, unseen and unknown in phallocular structures. Her speculum is not looking for an absolute or universal truth, but, as quoted above, for 'a different truth […] the most faithful expression of reality'. The word 'faithful', occurring here in *I Love to You*, is used through that book in close relation with the subject's recognition of the limits of his or her subjecthood in a relation of intersubjectivity. Its use in relation to the speculum denotes the nature of the subjecthood and its truth, its reality: a subjecthood that recognises the subjectivity of others, and, therefore, recognises also that it has limits, and that others cannot be reduced to its objects – or to itself.

The structure of the eye itself – or rather, the phalloculologocentric understanding of the eye and its vision – is also open for questioning. Irigaray summarised this as 'a given *plan/e*: a projection from a single source' (Irigaray 1974: 177; 1985c: 142), evoking the image of a slide projector, with the flat surface of the screen carrying the illusionary projected image, also a flat representation. One chapter of *Speculum*, 'Kore: Young Virgin, Pupil of the Eye', attends to Platonic thought, in particular 'reason – which will also be called natural light' (Irigaray 1974: 184; 1985c: 148) and the structures that support this analogy. The *kore* the pupil of the eye – is not a flat reflecting/projecting surface; it is the darkness marking the entrance from the external convexity to the internal concavity of the eye, a 'hole', a 'nothing to see'; a place where sight is underwritten by touch; a physically structural relationship between concavity and convexity, mediated through proximity and touch; the space and place through which the vision of the 'subject' really is turned upside down. Is this, a site of the interaction of sight and touch, and a site of patriarchal denial of touch, the causal site of the 'blind spot'? If so, why? The concave mirror, given the slightest entrance of light, will generate a scintillating brilliance so intense that it will burn anything within and anything that looks within. The gaze is more than dazzled; it is blinded; it will look, but see nothing. 'Then the gaze, aghast at such bareness, will have concluded that at any rate all brilliance was its own preserve, that it could continue to speculate without competition' (Irigaray 1974: 182; 1985c: 146). So, while its ability to create 'confusion' is noted, 'the concave mirror's potential for setting things afire is not mentioned' (Irigaray 1974: 186; 1985c: 149).

In Western patriarchy, the place from which women have been allowed to speak and act publicly is the site of *la mystérique* – the hysteric-mystic-mystery which is the name Irigaray gives to 'mystic language or discourse':

> This is the place where consciousness is no longer master, where, to its extreme confusion, it sinks into a 'dark night' that is also fire and flames. This is the place where 'she' – and in some cases he, if he follows 'her' lead – speaks about the dazzling glare which comes from the source of light that has been logically repressed [...]. Also about a 'burning glass' [*miroir ardent*]. (Irigaray 1974: 238; 1985c: 191)

What patriarchy understands in its representational economy is the ice-glass-mirror – *la glace* – when what could be understood is the brilliance of the soul-mirror – *la psyche*. It is this (sense of) vision which is at the centre of *Speculum*: the attempt, with words which evoke passion, to find ways of recognising the female, woman's, soul; the same attempt that is central to the enunciative position of *la mystérique*:

> And my eyes have proved sharp enough to look upon that glory without blinking. They would have been seared had they not been that simple eye of the 'soul' that sets fire to what it ad-mires out of its hollow socket. A burning glass [*miroir ardent*] is the soul who in her cave (re)joins with the source of light to set everything ablaze [*embraser*] that approached her hearth. Leaving only ashes there, only a hole: fathomless in her incendiary blaze. (Irigaray 1974: 246; 1985c: 197)

We could pause here to remember the painting by Berthe Morisot called *La Psyché* (1876), which images a young woman dressed in a chemise standing before a tall swing-mirror of the type called in France *une psyché*. It is ambiguous whether the title refers explicity to the mirror, or more eliptically evokes the Greek mythological figure of Psyché through the figure of the young woman. Psyché was a mortal woman who loved and gazed upon the god Eros. Carla Gottlieb says 'Living in a world of positivist values, the nineteenth-century artist does not play with the double meaning of the term' (Higonnet 1992: 279). I would, however, suggest that there is ambiguity in the painting, particularly in that we are aware that we do not see the whole of the image in the mirror that the woman in the pose sees. Not only do we see more of her, but we see her more clearly than we see her mirror image: its clarity is hers alone. Certainly, there is a tension between interior and exterior – the painting of the 'chemise' in the mirror is highly generalised, and could just pass as an image of the dress Morisot painted in *At the Ball* a year earlier. But there is also tension between the exteriorising of the image and the interiorising of thought suggested by the word 'reflection'. To project a content for the woman's thoughts is to limit the possibilities which Morisot herself may have been contemplating, as well as the nuances we can read into the representation of a woman and her reflection today.[7] The ambiguities can add to, rather than detract from, the present significance of *La Psyché*, and not *La Glace*, as a title.

## ATTENTIVENESS AND INTERSUBJECTIVITY

Women cannot represent themselves to themselves as subjects (let alone represent themselves to other subjects as subjects) while they are stuck in a representational economy of same and other, in which they are doomed to be forever other of the same. Women's relation to their self-image and to present images of women, womanliness and femininity is one that Rosalind Coward has identified as one not of narcissism, but of 'narcissistic damage' (Coward 1984: 80). But women can scarcely become subjects without representational economies that recognise their subjectivity, and which are, therefore, economies of intersubjectivity. What is crucial, to ensure the functioning of a syntax appropriate to women, is to build ways of attending to that syntax. It is not enough to develop a syntax in the Symbolic, then to assume that the methods of understanding it are unproblematic. If women collectively and painstakingly are developing visual languages which are appropriate, then we must not omit to attend to *how* we understand them. We must not continue developing such a syntax and our understandings of it (how we represent it to ourselves) without attending to the *methods by which* we come to those understandings. How do we look, listen, read? In this context, how do women experience artworks (by women)? And how is that experience then mediated, to oneself and to other subjects? What is an intersubjective relationship between the artist and the woman who looks at her work? How can it be developed?

In *I Love to You* Irigaray poses the initial questions: 'Yet isn't it time for us to become communicating subjects? Have we not exhausted our other possibilities, indeed our other desires? Isn't it time for us to become capable not only of speech [paroles] but also of speaking to *one another*? Which is not the same thing at all' (Irigaray 1992b: 81; 1996: 45).

If the subject and relations between subjects are not reconstituted, then things could get worse for women. Establishing 'a new economy of existence or being which is neither that of mastery nor that of slavery but rather of exchange with no preconstituted object – vital exchange, cultural exchange, of words [*paroles*], gestures, etc' (Irigaray 1992b 80; 1996: 45) is what is at stake here; indeed, one implication of *I Love to You*, when considered against the background of the earlier work, would be that a syntax appropriate for women would be impossible without this shift to a 'new economy' of exchange; another implication is that this change would inevitably begin to undo the languages of patriarchy (one does not move without the other), clearing the space for a syntax appropriate for women. The two must go hand in hand if women are to do something more than perform a maintenance mimesis upon patriarchy.

In a very pragmatic way, Irigaray indicates two structures of discourse that are already in use. These, she suggests, are models of, on the one hand, the form of discourse to be disrupted, and on the other, the form of discourse to be developed:

> ...there is a difference in subjective economy between the hierarchical transmission of an already established discourse [*un langage*] and language [*une langue*], order and law, and the exchange of meaning between us here and now. The first model of transmission or instruction is more parental, more genealogical, more hierarchical; the second more horizontal and intersubjective. The first model risks enslavement to the past, the second opens up a present in order to construct a future. (Irigaray 1992b: 81; 1996: 45–46)

These two models both help shape and are shaped by different structures of, and assumptions about, subjectivity, as can be deduced from their differing methods of giving and receiving: 'The first model operates by way of transmitted dependency, the second by way of reciprocal listening' (Irigaray 1992b: 81; 1996: 46). Thus is brought in a concern of Irigaray's that has increased since the late 1980s: that of working towards an anti-patriarchal culture (I mean by 'culture' the tenor of social, political and artistic interaction between subjects). This is a necessary development from her analysis of the non-subjecthood of women under patriarchy and her work towards possible subjectivity, Symbolic syntax and horizons for women. Women cannot become subjects in broader cultural and social structures that alienate them.

Referring back to the two models of transmission indicated above, Irigaray proposes a developed practice of *listening* as key to anti-patriarchal culture:

> Listening that does not exclude respect, especially for the other's experience, for the unique contribution *he* or *she* makes to culture beyond the transfer of information. The first model is not, strictly speaking, a model of communication. It is, at best, an information model, constituting knowledge as an aggregate of information and as the power [*le pouvoir*] it is likely to confer within institutions, in the opinion of colleagues or followers. The second model offers itself as an opening to a field of communication, as a world of the creation and exchange of thought and culture in which no man or woman can become master or slave for fear of destroying the given objective. (Irigaray 1992b: 81–82; 1996: 46)

This second model harkens back to comments that Irigaray makes about the structures of listening in the psychoanalytic scenario, both in *This Sex* and in essays such as 'The Limits of the Transference' (Irigaray 1985a, 1991a).

The phallocentric model of the relation between the analyst and the analysand retains power with the analyst, to whom belongs the gaze with its speculative, teleological structure and its need to discriminate form. Any practice of listening follows upon this structure and its configuring of the logos: distant, defining, controlling, turning what is said into information. But there is an alternative, where listening 'may let itself be *touched differently*':

> And this would mean that what is to be heard and accomplished is rather a different mode of the 'syntactic', in language and in the body. Let me add that as soon as your listening ceases to privilege meaning, the well formed, the visible, then the analyst's body, your own – in this connection we could take another look at what is called 'benevolent neutrality'... – is no longer protected by that sort of screen or referent. And so it comes into play 'differently' in transference. [...] We would thus escape from a dominant scopic economy, we would be to a greater extent in an economy of *flow*. (Irigaray 1977a: 144; 1985d: 147–148)

Here we have a description of a practice of listening which is (like that of sight) underwritten by touch; which is not predetermined by a certain economy of the logos which in turn rests upon a teleological scopic economy. It is a practice which works against the teleology of the classical analytic scenario, where the analyst works at '"narrating", dissecting, interpreting the transference of the (male or female) analysand alone', but one that recognises '*both* transferences. Here is one of the things at stake in analytic power. Analysts do indeed have transferences' (Irigaray 1977a: 144–145. Translation modified; 1985d: 148).

So overall in this advanced practice of listening we have a structure that recognises the subjectivity of the person who is speaking (does not reduce him or her to an object), and where the person listening does not deploy a 'benevolent neutrality' but instead recognises their listening, even their objectivity, as a subjective and bodily practice. It is a practice of engagement, not one of distance; a practice of communication between two subjects in which both are active participants; an active practice of intersubjectivity. It is a practice also which does not isolate the senses from each other, and which, as a practice, can be found in the intersubjective engagement of other senses. Indeed, Irigaray finds one of the most exemplary instances of this practice in the realm of sight and the gaze (as will be discussed below). Irigaray's discussions of this practice and this quality can advance possibilities for engaging with artworks.

It is useful at this point to shift the terminology for the woman who experiences or encounters the artwork away from 'the viewer' with its naming of sight as the only sense which is involved, and also away from 'the female gaze', which, for all its theorising, still appears to imply a simple inversion of the theory from which it developed, of the phallocentric male gaze. The word 'audience' has overtones of sociological surveys and of the theatrical, but does have the benefit of retaining a trace of Irigaray's interest in the practice of listening. I will call it a practice of attentiveness, as I think this suggests a combination of chosen activity, non-imposition and being-a-subject; and use the phrases 'the attentive woman' or 'the attentive audience', on the understanding that attentiveness involves more than one sense, and presupposes a move towards intersubjectivity.

Essential to a practice of intersubjectivity is a recognition of the limits of the subject. If the other subject cannot be reduced to an object and so cannot be reduced to being the other of the same, then the subject has to recognise his or her limits. For Irigaray, recognition of gender identity and gender difference is key for the subject's recognition that he or she is not everything:

> In this way, to recognize an identity in oneself is itself to overcome instinctual and egological immediacy by recognizing the negative in the self. 'I am sexed' implies, 'I am not everything'. Identifying with my gender amounts to entering the world of mediation provided I recognize the existence of the other gender. There will thus no longer be the simple identity of my will with itself since respecting my nature as generic identity constrains the immediacy of my will.

> But this constraint does not emanate from an abstract or impersonal law. It is established on the basis of the objectivity of who I actually am. Before being limited by others, I am limited by myself owing to the objectivity of my sexed body and to the particularity that ensues from my inscription in a genealogy. In this sense, there is no immediate subjectivity. This is an incorrect concept, notion or expression. (Irigaray 1992b: 91–92; 1996: 51–52)

This is a subtle structure of accounting for a relation to mediation. If the subject recognises an identity, then the will is constrained: the will has to recognise that the subject is not everything, that there are other identities. The sexed body, productive of particular structures of subjectivity, is also productive of the limits of that subjectivity – the negative of subjectivity being the recognition of other subjectivities. With the recognition of those limits comes the necessity for mediation. The subject, in a situation of intersubjectivity, cannot rest in a state of immediacy to itself or to other subjects.

Irigaray does state explicitly her privileging of gender difference over other differences – for example: 'But I think that it's because I'm able to situate *there* [i.e.: between woman and man] the difference and the negative which I will never surmount [...] that I'm able to respect the differences everywhere: differences between the other races, differences between the generations, and so on. Because I've placed a limit on my horizon, on my power' (Hirsh and Olson 1995: 161). This is, of course, a contentious position. One of the most considered and interesting critiques of it is from Henry Louis Gates (Gates 1988). He criticises Irigaray's lack of concern for daily struggle and opens up consideration of white men's specularisation of black men, and gay male specularisation. Unfortunately, his analysis is based on a reading only of *Speculum* and *This Sex*, and was written before Irigaray's work on intersubjectivity was published in English. I think Irigaray would agree with Gates when he says: 'We must also interrogate [white, patriarchal representation]'s material conditions of emergence – and thus take a very practical interest in patriarchy as an everyday practice with specific conditions of reproduction' (Gates 1988: 622–623). Irigaray has insisted within *This Sex* that 'in order for a woman to reach the place where she takes pleasure as a woman, a long detour by way of the analysis of the various systems of oppression brought to bear upon her is assuredly necessary' (Irigaray 1977a: 30; 1985d: 31), and in books published in the 1980s and 1990s (such as *I Love to You*, *Je, Tu, Nous*, and *Democracy Begins Between Two*) this early acknowledgement of the need for action on civil rights and structures is developed.

As might be imagined, achieving intersubjectivity is far from being the same process for each gender, not least because men and women have a different relation to the Symbolic in our present culture. Thus what is necessary is not only a sense of the limits of identity, but a sense of identity that is more active: what Irigaray calls a *relational identity*, a subjective identity that recognises that each gender has its own particular problems to overcome in order to achieve intersubjectivity and thus attentiveness, with other subjects both of its own gender and of the other gender: 'Such a relation [of attentiveness] can only come about if man renounces the domination of nature and of the economy of subjectivity, and if woman has the ability to govern her nature so that she becomes subjectivity' (Irigaray 1992b: 82; 1996: 46). Men must recognise that their subjectivity has limits; while women must realise their identity as subjects and, therefore, their need for subjective mediation:

> Men and women must modify their relational identity. Certainly, women 'spontaneously' privilege the relation between subjects and men the relation to objects. The feminine subject constructs itself through a relation to the other, the masculine subject through the manufacture of objects and worlds starting from which it is possible for him to exchange with the other. Let us say the woman must learn to put some objectivity susceptible to being shared between *I* and *you*: this relation must not remain, for her, at the level of need and of subjective immediacy, otherwise the you risks disappearing as *you*. The man, on the other hand, needs to rediscover the other as subject beyond his universe of objects. What the one and the other lack in order to realize their relation is a dialectic between subjectivity and objectivity, at the same time proper to each and common. (Pluhácek et al. 1996: 355)

In this passage, Irigaray returns us to the highly pragmatic nature of this relationship: indeed (to treat it pragmatically), it could serve as an analysis of the crisis of representation in the art world. Historically, women artists have had to make work which can be seen to be a maintenance mimesis of the patriarchal languages of men; while at the same time that work has been written about as if it were a symptom of their *immediacy as women* (a phenomenon well charted within feminist art history). More recently, the apparent breakdown of the visual languages of art has served only to present the father–son power struggles of the maintenance mimeses in a slightly altered guise. The space that seems to have opened up for developing subjectivities is still generally for men, about the production of the object (often as spectacle) and not about developing an awareness of the other subject and the possibilities of intersubjectivity. The market keeps excelling itself, not only (and most clearly) with palpable objects (paintings, sculptures, etc) but with the selling of objects of little or no monetary value (Richard Long's stone circles, David Mach's sculptures made from wire coat hangers, matches, etc) and the marketing of body art (from Pietro Manzoni's canning of his breath and shit to photographic documentation of performance work being promoted to the level of artwork itself). Aspects of conceptual work could be considered as avoiding this; but some which clearly rely upon a degree of intersubjectivity, such as Sol LeWitt's wall drawings and Lawrence Weiner's descriptive statements, nonetheless compromise this by only being available as *objects* on the market. They can only be accessed once they have negotiated the market (been sold) and have been reproduced by the owner. All of these correspond to Irigaray's identification of men's patterns of 'communication': 'For men's teleology implies rather an abandonment of immediate communication – of intersubjectivity and dialogue – in order to set off in quest of an *oeuvre* (in which they usually alienate themselves) and, among other things, a spiritual journey compelled by a transcendence appropriate to their ego' (Irigaray 1992b: 157; 1996: 100).

For women, the situation is slightly different. Of course, some are still permitted a place through their maintenance mimesis of patriarchal languages; and in some cases their work is still written about as a symptom of their immediacy. In addition, particularly for those who acknowledge their gender, the expression of a subjectivity through an appropriate syntax has become an issue.

Janine Antoni's performance *Loving Care* (1992) is one example of this. Having dipped her long hair in Loving Care hair dye – rumoured at the time to be the brand used by her mother – Antoni then proceeded to 'mop' the floor of the gallery with it. *Loving Care* was first presented as an installation at the Hunter College Vorhes Gallery, New York, with the audience seeing only the results of the 'mopping'; but later that year was presented as a performance at the Anthony D'Offay Gallery, London. It has since been repeated elsewhere. Interestingly it is through the photographs of the performance that it is best known. The photographs show Antoni, dressed in black polo-neck tee shirt and leggings (and plastic gloves). She dips her hair in the bucket of dye and then, half on all-fours, half lying, she wipes the floor with her wet hair. One understanding of this work could be that Janine Antoni was performing a mimesis of the 1950s works of Yves Klein which involved painting the naked bodies of women models then using their bodies to make marks: indeed Dan Cameron has made the link between *Loving Care* and the Yves Klein works (White and McParland 1995: 45). It could be argued that it is a productive mimesis: she reasserted a female genealogy (the link with her mother, and earlier works by feminists such as Mierle Laderman Ukeles' *Hartford Wash* [1973] or Shigeko Kubota's *Vagina Painting* [1965])[8] while bringing to mind the irony of the product name, 'Loving Care' – it is, after all, a product to aid women in performing the masquerade, femininity, and not about loving the subject, woman. It is also a highly ironic reference to 'women's work' – the 'loving care' of usually unseen tasks of cleaning subverted through making the clean floor dirty. There are also clear echoes of Jackson Pollock's action painting, although as Amelia Jones has pointed out, in Namuth's photographs of Pollock, the painter remains on his two feet, while Antoni is on the floor (Jones 1998: 281). He ranges and hovers over the surface, controlling it; she is sprawled upon it, in touch with it.

But another understanding can be gleaned from the photographic documentation. We see Antoni dipping her hair in the bucket and methodically working her way from one end of the gallery to the other, leaving great sweeping marks on the floor. The audience are in the background, moving back, and out of the gallery door, where they peer through the windows. The final photograph shows the floor covered with the marks of the dyed hair, the bucket left near the door, opening-night detritus (or empty packets of hair dye?) left on a window sill. The gallery is otherwise empty, the audience outside. What is happening here? Is this woman articulating subjectivity, or turning herself into an object – or indeed abjecting herself before the speculative gaze of the viewers? The relation between the subjectivity of the photographer as mediated through the photographic image, and the subjectivity of the performer, as mediated through the performance, is often at odds, and sometimes fraught. Things can be suggested through the photograph that may not have been prominent in the performance, and once caught in the image they can become iconic, misleading metonyms for the artwork. Some of the photographs of *Loving Care* appear to be taken too close, in an intrusive manner where the photographer may well be interfering with the activity of the artist, as if the photographer was confusing the artist with the artwork. In other photographs there is a relation suggested between the audience and the artist. The audience consists of people standing, talking, laughing, cameras in hand, looking down at the artist on the floor at their feet: they are images that suggest that rather than articulating subjectivity the artist is in the process of becoming object, or that she is abjecting herself. If this is what happened (I was not present at the performance) then either way – object or abject – she denies any possibility of articulating her subjectivity and of an attentive, inter-subjective, presence from (and relationship with) the audience. The final photograph of the empty gallery, post-performance, appears to be more eloquent of a mediation of subjectivity.[9]

## INTERSUBJECTIVE OBJECTS

In order to achieve intersubjectivity, the subject has to recognise that the other subject is irreducible to themselves. A model for this can be found, argues Irigaray, in the irreducible difference of gender (Hirsh and Olson 1995: 160). Gender difference and gendered subjectivity works across other forms of difference, and the subject's recognition of difference and of the other subject is rooted in the experience of sexual difference and its irreducibility. For a subject, woman, to recognise the difference that is another subject, woman, she has first to be a woman – to have her subjecthood – and secondly to have a relational identity – to have an awareness of her limits, and that the other subject is irreducible to herself. The subject, woman, is still more likely to reduce the other subject, woman, to herself, than she is to reduce the other subject, man. This is more to do with identity than with identification; by which I mean that it is a matter of ontology, of the relation to origin and the subsequent relationship with the mother, which is still in a state of immediacy:

> Woman must be able to express herself in words, images and symbols in this intersubjective relationship with her mother, then with other women, if she is to enter into a non-destructive relationship with men. This very special economy of woman's identity must be permitted, known and defined. It is essential to a real culture. It means supporting, not destroying, the mother-daughter relationship. (Irigaray 1989: 37; 1994c: 19–20)

It is not so much that what is needed here (between mothers and daughters, and then between women) is a reassertion of limits; what is necessary is an insertion – a bringing into play – of objects. Becoming the subjects, women, cries out for mediation between women: 'Unable to create their own words, women remain and move in an immediacy without any transitional, transactional object. They take-give without mediation, commune without knowing it with and in a flesh they do not recognize' (Irigaray 1985a: 293; 1991a: 105). So there is a fundamental need for women to create objects in an appropriate syntax; objects that function transactionally between them in order to achieve a form of intersubjective mediation. Indeed, in her list of highly pragmatic recommendations to aid the creation of space between mothers and daughters, Irigaray suggests 'Between mother and daughter, interpose small handmade objects to make up for losses of spatial identity, for intrusions into personal space' (Irigaray 1990a: 55–56; 1993i: 49). Evidently not tokens to assuage guilt after traumatic rows, these objects are the development of a syntax in the mother–daughter relationship; one that will create the third space of mediation, and avoid women collapsing back into immediacy: what we might call a gift-space/object.

To extrapolate from this, therefore, the art object *between* women can then be understood as a means of attending to an intersubjective relation *if* we recognise it as a gift of a means of mediation between subjects, rather than as a stand-in for the objectness of the other, as phallocentric man does with his production of objects. There is a risk however. A woman may make an object – an artwork – as a means of mediation and offer it in all good faith as a space through which mediation can occur. But this does not guarantee that the woman to whom it is offered will be a subject able to accept and produce intersubjective relationships between women, or able to be attentive. This risks a hurt to the subjectivity of the woman who gives the space / object (Irigaray 1985a: 298; 1991a: 110). In part, this risk may be ameliorated by the nature of the enunciation, the presenting of the gift-space / object. We can look here at the offer of love. Irigaray explains her use of the phrase 'I love to you':

> *I love to you* thus means: I do not take you for a direct object, nor for an indirect object by revolving around you. It is, rather, around myself that I have to revolve in order to maintain the *to you* thanks to the return to me. Not with my prey – you become mine – but with the intention of respecting my nature, my history, my intentionality, while also respecting yours. Hence, I do not return to me by way of: I wonder if I am loved. That would result from an introverted intentionality, going toward the other so as to return ruminating, sadly and endlessly, over solipsistic questions in a sort of cultural cannibalism. (Irigaray 1992b: 172–173; 1996: 110)

Irigaray is here suggesting an approach to an intersubjective mediation through the phrase 'I love to you'. If we take this as a model for extended forms of intersubjective communication, then it suggests practices of enunciation – of creating intersubjective objects – that neither reduce the other subject to an object, nor uses them to reflect back one's subjectivity. If we then further extrapolate from this to the making of art, it suggests a practice that is respectful of the subjectivity of the artist (i.e. which is not a maintenance mimesis but instead aids the woman artist in becoming the subject, woman) and that is offered as a mediation between attentive subjects, not as a spectacle whereby to win approval. 'Attentiveness' here is thus actively two-way, not only about the audience, woman. For the artist, it is not only about the private, studio practice of making her work, but also about the broader aspects of enunciation through the making of art: the practices of the market, exhibiting, documentation, criticism, teaching or lecturing and so forth. This suggests that women artists continue to get more attentive to these practices *as* practices (that they get more 'difficult'?) and make the shift from treating their artworks as objects of distance (as galleries tend to), instead treating them as objects of mediation, or, rather, objects through which mediation can happen. It means taking further responsibility for the work, whatever its material nature: in particular, painstaking exactitude over the installation of work, but also, for example, in the heart of the gallery system, insisting upon a veto – and making positive suggestions about – other aspects of the gallery's activity.

Without wishing to point the finger at individuals, personal experience of working as a critic and art administrator suggests that the epithet 'difficult' is more readily applied by curators to artists who are women than to artists who are men; indeed, the man who is exacting about the context in which his work is presented may be described as 'committed' or 'professional'. I would read this as symptomatic of two things: firstly, the problematic of phallogocentric representations of 'woman', and secondly, the strategies some women already employ to disrupt or open up the structures of various gallery situations. This may of course involve a fundamental questioning of the methods and practices of the art market, which in turn involves risk. The livelihoods of artists are precarious, particularly those who are young and for whom a 'name' and therefore a market has not yet been established. Vast sections of the art market are not geared towards avant-garde practices and would regard any challenge to their own practices as destabilising of their business premise. On the other hand, those sections of the art market that do deal with avant-garde challenges are of course well versed in the incorporation of such challenges in the name of novelty and thus of market expansion. We can think here of early video and performance artists, who used such formats as a means of disrupting the cultural real-estate market, and for whom video was either a simple means of documentation of the actual work – the performance – or an accessible and democratic art form, and distributed and priced their videos accordingly (artists such as Martha Rosler still pursue this strategy, and her video works can be purchased from museum shops, priced in the region of $25). Often now, however, many video works come in strictly limited editions through the dealers and command prices on a par with less replicable art forms. The art market proves itself adeptly resilient to such challenges.

Irigaray discusses the reciprocal activity of listening in one chapter of *I Love to You*. She outlines it as a highly exacting practice of concentration, attentiveness and silence: an emptying of the ego in order to offer the other subject 'the possibility of existing, of expressing your intention, your intentionality, without your calling out for it and even without asking, without overcoming, without annulling, without killing'. The situation she is assuming here is one of discussion between two subjects: 'one *with* the other in the serenity and the occasion of *being with*, respecting difference' (Irigaray 1992b:

184; 1996: 118). Is it then possible to move the model of practice she offers here and apply it to an attentive audience of an artwork? Is it possible to apply practices from face-to-face communication, with the mediation of the spoken word and of bodily gesture, to the situation of encountering the mediating object of the artwork? I think so, precisely because it is a *set of practices* that are given – emotional, intellectual, spiritual practices carried out in and through the body. The risk here would be that the artist would still be treating her work as a object of distance, rather than an object through which mediation will take place; in which case the gift of attentiveness from an audience, if it is acknowledged by the artist, will be either ignored, or (mis)taken as a response to the question 'am I loved?'. Irigaray does not mention this risk and its effects on the attentive subject. But what is offered by this attentive audience is not the gift-space/object mentioned above: instead, her practice of attentiveness is part and parcel of being-a-subject. Part of becoming the subject, woman, is an acknowledgment that the other subject is not reducible to the self, and that an active practice of intersubjectivity is necessary. Thus the gift of attentiveness, insofar as it is a gift, is a gift of flow from *one* subject to *both* subjects, as the following passages indicate:

> I am listening to you, as to another who transcends me, requires a transition to a new dimension. I am listening to you: I perceive what you are saying, I am attentive to it, I am attempting to understand and hear your intention. Which does not mean: I comprehend you, I know you, so I do not need to listen to you and I can even plan a future for you. [...]
>
> I am listening to you not on the basis of what I know, I feel, I already am, nor in terms of what the world and language already are, thus in a formalistic manner, so to speak. I am listening to you rather as the revelation of a truth that has yet to manifest itself – yours and that of the world revealed through and by you. I give you a silence in which your future – and perhaps my own, but *with* you and not as you and *without* you – may emerge and lay its foundation. [...]
>
> This silence is the condition for a possible respect for myself and for the other within our respective limits. (Irigaray 1992b: 180–182; 1996: 116–117)

These are practices that can be adopted by attentive audiences. Irigaray describes this silence as 'a space-time'(Irigaray 1992b: 182; 1996: 117) made possible by recognising the irreducibility of the other subject. Maybe then our encounters with the gift-space/object, the artwork of the other subject, are wholly appropriately regarded as chances for intersubjectivity, times to avoid 'subjective affect [...]. Sentiment [that] will bind one to the other, often in one direction and not reciprocally' (Irigaray 1992b: 179–180; 1996: 116–117).

In an earlier evocation of this attentiveness, Irigaray frames the discussion in terms of art. First she uses the term in its meaning of 'skill'; then quickly shifts to use its meaning as creative practice, and discusses art and aesthetics as social practice:

> For a dialectic of the couple to occur, we need an art of perception that cannot be reduced either to a pure innerness or a pure outerness but passes ceaselessly from one to the other. This art requires that concrete perception be detailed and attentive, a perception that as autoaffection is individual, is copulative as the privileged space of hetero-affection, and finally is collective. (Irigaray 1987h: 159. Translation modified; 1993k: 144)

She suggests that such an art can be found in some cultures of the East, particularly India. This passage alerts the reader to the aesthetic and visual possibilities of mediation, though she is adamant that 'there is a danger that ethics should become a part of aesthetics and seen as secondary to the life of the people, pleasant but not essential to spiritual development' (Irigaray 1987h: 159; 1993k: 145). Does this mean that Irigaray considers aesthetics beneath ethics? I think it is an analysis of the present relation between the two in our culture. In *I Love to You* she indicates that in some other cultures an ethical dialectic of the (sexual) couple is expressed aesthetically:

> In cultures where sexual attraction is cultivated, certain gestures express the desire for coming together, for union.
>
> A greeting is made by the whole body.
> A request for carnal union may be expressed by the hands.
> Hands are placed in different positions depending on the degree of union desired.
> These modalities of speech and gesture can be brought into relation with:
> forms
> colors
> sounds
> fragrances
> breath
>
> appropriate to man and to woman and to each of their *chakras*.
>
> Love, even carnal love, is therefore cultivated and made divine. The act of love becomes the transubstantiation of the self and his or her lover into a spiritual body. It is a feast, celebration, and a renaissance, not a decline, a fall to be redeemed by procreation. Love is redemption of the flesh through the transfiguration of desire for the other (as an object?) into desire with the other. (Irigaray 1992b: 218–219; 1996: 139)

What is significant through this passage is that the ethical relation of the couple has an aesthetic mediation; it is mediated *through* the aesthetic relation and perceptible through different senses. It is not a question of establishing an ethical relation, and adding the aesthetics, nor of seeing an aesthetic representation distanced in time and space from the ethical relation. It may be a question of reconsidering the Western term – and processes of – 'aesthetics'. Certainly, it assumes that at its most developed and intimate level, inter-subjectivity is a practice both of ethics and aesthetics: of beauty. This is emphasised in the discussion of certain Eastern cultures:

> What is remarkable in these traditions is the fact that thought is ready to listen to nature, to the sensible. The famous example of this is Buddha contemplating a flower. For him, this gesture probably represents the perfect act, since it respects nature while becoming spiritual. The overcoming of matter by spirit or the privileging of the speculative over the sensible is, therefore, no more. Buddha becomes spirit while remaining sensible, awakened flesh. Surely this is a fine [*une belle*] lesson in love? (Irigaray 1992b: 219; 1996: 139–140)

Here we have again the evocation of listening in relation to a visual contemplation, and a working of spirit and flesh together: a 'lesson in love' for both men and women.

## FLOWERING OF SELF

Irigaray's references to yogic practices and to Buddha can be challenging to a Eurocentric audience, both to our sense of positioning in relation to cultural difference, and to a wariness of a New Age supermarket-trolley approach to spirituality. However, such references have been for a number of years, and are increasingly, a significant element within the overall parameters of her work. Gayatri Chakravorty Spivak has noted how 'French theorists such as Derrida, Lyotard, Deleuze and the like, have at one time or another been interested in reaching out to all that is not the West, because they have, in one way or another, questioned the millennially cherished excellences of Western metaphysics' (Spivak 1988a: 136). The problem of the interest this strand of Western philosophy has in the non-Western lies in the shape of what she calls its 'turn', analysed as 'a desire marking the place of the management of a crisis'. The reversal of the binary opposition, 'the so-called non-West's turn toward the West', works to deconstruct the Western intellectual desire. As a result, her work of the moment was 'to show how in fact the limits of the [Western] theories of interpretation that I am working with are revealed through the encounter of what can be defined as "non-Western material"' (Spivak 1990: 8). This analysis outlines what is a continuing complexity of interrelationship between Western and non-Western intellectuals and thinking, where an asymmetric relation is still caught in an imbalance of power.

Irigaray's project is also (though differently) one of working at 'the limits of the theories of interpretation'. She has in recent years published essays and a book drawing upon Eastern traditions and theories of breath, particularly as found in Indian yogic practices (for example Irigaray 1999a); (Irigaray 1997, 1999b, 2002). I find it interesting that beyond these publications her references to Buddha and contemplative practices occur mainly in texts which are neither aimed at a readership which is academic or with a specialist theoretical interest, nor are they polemic. This removes the references from a mimesis of a Western discipline and from a potential interpretation of advocacy. While I do not wish to remove Irigaray from the problematic structure of intellectual desire mapped by Spivak, it is important to note that such references are highly particular and focused. So too is their context – discussions of practices of intersubjectivity and attentiveness. This places her turn to the non-Western at one remove from the desire which reduces a heterogeneity of peoples to an assumed unified class.

It is important to recognise that Irigaray is discussing practices, and not ritual, religion or cultures. She has recently stated this explicitly:

> Like some recent philosophers of the West, I needed to turn myself toward the East in order to find guides and basic principles of method. I did this differently than the Western masters. I did not claim to incorporate the knowledge of Eastern masters in my knowledge, nor even to pass from their words to my words. This type of transmission appeared to me to have become obsolete. I followed the teaching of masters for whom a daily practice – in fact, yoga – was what could help awaken or reawaken and discover words and gestures carrying another meaning, another light, another rationality. (Irigaray 2002: 6)

The yogic and meditative practices to which Irigaray refers can be found in the differing cultures of India, Japan, Tibet, Korea, China, Burma and many other countries, and their relation to the daily ways of life and religions of these places is complex. This is not least because these practices are independent from formal religious structures, and instead actively return the responsibility for morality and ethics to the individual practitioner. For example, although it is often classed in the West as a religion, Buddhism is a philosophy; most manifestations of it do not centre upon a belief system, god or gods. In *Between East and West*, Irigaray makes frequent mention of structures of 'philosophy or religion'.

Irigaray's focus, as I say, is upon yogic practices from India and found within Hinduism, and in particular, upon practices of breathing. She has also, however, made mention of Buddha's gaze upon the flower – a story of particular interest for discussions of visuality and subjectivity. Irigaray has said that 'to meditate on physical gestures, in particular the cosmic respiration of the Buddha, rather than on the logical subtleties of a Buddhist discourse [...] is, as far as I am concerned, a deliberate choice which is careful to respect aboriginal cultures.' I will turn to Zen thinking and interpretation at this point as it is the most clearly philosophical Buddhist discourse of meditation and attentiveness. Within its literature, as one of its central problems or anecdotes, is discussion of the moment of Buddha's gaze at the flower, to which Irigaray refers as a model for intersubjectivity. This, and other problems, are presented within Zen as practices of analysis through which, over time, the individual can come to terms with his or her interaction with others.

The *Mumonkan*, one of the classic Zen texts by the thirteenth-century Mumon, is a collection of 48 problems. One recounts the case (or anecdote) of Buddha and the flower, with Mumon's commentary upon it. The case is this:

> Once when the World-Honoured One, in ancient times, was upon Mount Grdhrakuta, he held up a flower before the congregation of monks. At this time all were silent, but the Venerable Kasyapa only smiled. The World-Honoured One said, 'I have the Eye of the True Law, The Secret Essence of Nirvana, the Formless form, the Mysterious Law-Gate. Without relying upon words and letters, beyond all teaching as special transmission, I pass this all on to Mahakasyapa'. (Blyth 1996: 76)[10]

R.H. Blyth, in his extended commentary upon the original text and his translation, gives us some insights which can aid our understanding of Irigaray's interest in this moment of the Sakyamuni Buddha. The title Buddha itself 'comes from buddh, to be completely aware, and was translated into Chinese by [the symbol meaning] to perceive, be awake, and [the symbol meaning] gnosis. The original meaning of [the symbol meaning Buddha] is to flourish. It was used for its sound' (Blyth 1996: 74). So here we have the person who 'performed' this action referred to initially as completely aware, and as mystic knowledge in perception (gnosticism itself was of the second century AD). In an attractive move, it is the *sound* of the symbol meaning 'to flourish' that determines this later visual/written representation. Blyth says 'the important thing is not the life and death of Sakyamuni, nor his teachings, but his enlightenment. Not his words but his silence, not his acts but his un-acts are what we would grasp' (Blyth 1996: 75). This practice of enlightened silence begins to resonate through a re-reading of Irigaray's understanding of listening or attentiveness. The moment of the gift of space-time within a relation of intersubjectivity can be found in this teaching.

Blyth says of the moment between Buddha and Kasyapa 'We might call this a love scene' (Blyth 1996: 76–77). It could also be read as a moment of mediation of a reversible and open transferential relationship. Buddha's state of enlightenment was his 'gift' to Kasyapa: 'It would be a great mistake to think that Kasyapa smiled as a sign that he understood something or other. His "breaking his face" was the opening of the flower' (Blyth 1996: 80). The flower and Buddha's gesture are not reduced to being Kasyapa's objects, his 'others', just as the flower is not reduced by the Buddha. As Irigaray indicates 'We also misinterpret him [Buddha] if we reduce him to discourse […] while forgetting his gestures. The Buddha makes himself gestures. He even gives up speaking […]. Speaking generally supposes an object of speech. Now the Buddha renounces every object, the object always being partial, nonabsolute, a cause of conflicts, sorrows'(Irigaray 2002: 36). This is what is mediated – the moment of intersubjectivity, of enlightenment, *not* a truth *about* the flower: 'what Zen wishes us to avoid [is] the dividing of the flower and its meaning […] When "the bright consummate flower" is really seen, the flower sees itself. The self flowers' (Blyth 1996: 80).

It becomes difficult to differentiate between the dissolving of the ego in the practices indicated in such texts, and the dissolving of the ego indicated in Irigaray's texts on intersubjectivity, informed as they are by her practices of psychoanalysis. Their impulses differ radically: 'This "otherwise" has nothing in common with the discovery of some unconscious […] The practices of diverse kinds of breathing certainly reduces the darkness of the shadows of Western consciousness. But above all it constitutes the mental in a different way' (Irigaray 2002: 6–7). However, some of their practices and effects resonate clearly; indeed, Irigaray has made this resonance implicit at particular moments. Ten years before explicitly indicating Buddha's contemplation of the flower, she wrote in *Je, Tu, Nous* a meditation upon the extreme difficulty of not reducing the other subject to an object, in which the subject-not-to-be-so-reduced was written as a flower:

> Do you want the flower to open only once? The unveiling of the opening would then belong to you. The beauty or truth of the opening would be your discovery. Proposed and exposed in one definitive blossoming. The nightly closing of the flower, its folding back into itself would not take place. […] Fixed display, rapt – an immortal show. Unattainable, thus transported outside itself. (Irigaray 1982, 1992a)[11]

This would sit comfortably with some Buddhist teachings. For example, Joshu Sasaki Roshi has written: 'We all have a personal consciousness which looks at things as objects. [...] When that personal consciousness becomes free of the need to look at the pine tree as object, then your personal nature becomes perfect' (Sasaki Roshi 1974: 88). To refigure this in Irigaray's terminology: the other subject retains its subjecthood as you recognise its irreducibility to yourself and its irreducibility to being your other: 'one *with* the other in the serenity and the occasion of *being with*, respecting difference' (Irigaray 1992b: 184; 1996: 118).

One of Irigaray's most far-reaching passages on Buddha concerns the realm of the visual and his 'gaze' at the flower:

> There is no question, then, of renouncing the sensible, of sacrificing it to the universal, but rather it is cultivated to the point where it becomes spiritual energy. And so the Buddha's gazing at the flower is not an inattentive or predatory gaze, nor the decline of the speculative into flesh. It is both material and spiritual contemplation, furnishing thought with an already sublimated energy.
>
> This contemplation is also a training in finding pleasure while respecting what does not belong to me. Indeed, Buddha contemplates the flower without picking it. He gazes at what is other to him without uprooting it. Moreover, what he is gazing at is not just anything – it is a flower, which perhaps offers us the best object for meditation upon the appropriateness of form to matter.
>
> Buddha's gazing at the flower might provide us with a model. So might the flower. Between us, we can train ourselves to be both contemplative regard and the beauty appropriate to our matter, the spiritual and carnal fulfilment of the forms of our body. (Irigaray 1992b: 48–49; 1996: 25)

Here, in this non-patriarchal gaze, we find one of Irigaray's most developed accounts of becoming a subject and intersubjective communication. The nature of the particular body is respected (not sacrificed to a spurious 'universal') while at the same time fragmentation is remedied. Flesh and spirit are one in the subject; the subject becomes in its recognition of the other subject. Communally, in intersubjectivity, in love to each other, we achieve our beauty: 'Thus, neither the one nor the other will take the initiative of plucking [*cueiller*] the bloom in order to contemplate it. Both contemplate [*recueillis*] and bloom. Opening and closing themselves in order to keep giving each other that which they could never have brought to life' (Irigaray 1984: 180; 1993d: 194).

The self flowers in an intersubjective relation. The removal of objects – even of objects of speech – does not mean the end of mediation: on the contrary, it enables a profound intersubjective mediation. The role of artworks for women here is complex. Women in our culture have no easy access to a syntax through which they can mediate their subjectivity. This syntax – still a cultural reserve yet to come – needs to be worked upon, developed: its gestures and practices need to be tested and explored: 'Don't restrict yourself to describing, reproducing, and repeating what exists, but know how to invent or imagine what hasn't yet taken place' (Irigaray 1990a; 1993i: 49). While women are in a state of immediacy and without the syntax to mediate their subjectivity, 'objects', (non)objects and gift-space/objects – need to be interposed to compensate for the lack of space of mediation. Artworks have a role here. In order that these do not perform a maintenance mimesis upon the subject–object practices prevalent in the art world, attention will need to be paid to the appropriate syntactical morphology and gestures. Irigaray's thinking can help make legible some of these practices which are presently very much the 'reserve' of art discourses – that which is not seen, not reflected upon within them. This will be the subject of the next chapter.

# PART 2

# Body and Legibility

# 3

# Morphology

In this chapter I want to examine the potential of the term 'morphology' as Irigaray uses it for reading certain material practices in art. The aim is to allow for the play of a *morpho-logic* as prior to, while also allowing for, the production of an appropriate syntax for women in the Symbolic. While the term 'morphology' is from the Greek *morphé*, meaning 'form', and is used in the field of biology, it does not automatically imply an anatomical reading. In biology it does not refer to deterministic analysis of forms in themselves, but to a method of discerning patterns of *relationships between* forms (as is known to plants-women and plants-men, and thus explaining why flowers as superficially dissimilar as buttercups and delphiniums are in the same family: they share a morphology). 'Morphology' is also used as a term within linguistics (the subject in which Irigaray presented her first doctorate (Irigaray 1973)), where it names a method of studying the component parts of words and of language. So while there is a biological implication in the use of the term 'morphology', to reduce it to the anatomical, as some critics have (for example, Moi 1985: 143), is to restrict its possibilities. Furthermore, when Irigaray uses the term we are always also in the realm of linguistic structures. It is a concept that opens up the possibilities of different legibilities.

### MORPHOLOGY AS *DIFFÉRANCE*

Irigaray insisted on the distinction between anatomy and morphology from an early point: 'I think we must go back to the question not of the anatomy but of the morphology of female sex' (Irigaray 1977b: 64). More recently she has reiterated her distance from Freud's thesis that anatomy is determinant, a position which is 'authoritarian, final and devalorizing for women' (Irigaray and Lotringer 2000: 150). She uses the term 'morphology' precisely to name the site of a discursive and dynamic relationship between a subject's empirical living in the body and in the Symbolic; a relationship which does not go in one direction, but where the way the subject understands the body is significant in determining an appropriate syntax in the Symbolic; and where in turn the subject understands – or reads – the body through that syntax. The subject then 'sees' anatomy according to the signifiers of that syntax. The 'objectivity' granted this understanding is thus determined in a dynamic relationship with the subject's language-inflected subjectivity. As Irigaray says, 'of course no woman has the morphology of another' (Irigaray 1985a: 300; 1991a: 112).

This, of course, can be applied to both men and women. As Jane Gallop points out:

> When she speaks of 'the sex which is one', she is not speaking of male genital anatomy but rather of an already phallomorphic conception of male genitals, that actually has only a selective relation to male anatomy. Irigaray, for example, nowhere mentions the testicles. Male genital anatomy does not determine phallomorphic logic, but rather phallomorphic logic determines a certain unitary perception of male genitalia. (Gallop 1988: 94)

Indeed, an initial, resistant, reaction to reading Irigaray's enunciation of the multiplicity of women's sexual pleasure and sexual organs (Irigaray 1977a: 28; 1985d: 28) can be to reflect that men's sexual pleasure and sexual organs are also multiple: not only the testicles, but the scrotum, the glans, the foreskin (if not removed) – to say nothing of the touching of the foreskin and the glans, the flow of blood and the stretching of skin, the passage from detumescence to tumescence and back…

But this is surely Irigaray's point, that erecting the phallus as a unitary determinant then produces '*the* penis [as] being the only sexual organ of recognized value' and women's sex organs as 'never amount[ing] to anything but a clitoris-sex that is not comparable to the noble phallic organ, or a hole-envelope that serves to sheathe and massage the penis in intercourse' (Irigaray 1977a: 23; 1985d: 23). Men's sex organs are seen as singular through phallocentrism – 'the penis'; and women's are seen only as an other which reflects this unit – the nothing-to-see, determined in a negative relationship to the one. As Elizabeth Grosz points out: 'bodies are not conceived by Irigaray as biologically or anatomically given, inert, brute objects fixed by nature once and for all. […] Her emphasis on morphology in place of anatomy indicates that she has stepped from the register of nature into that of social signification' (Grosz

1989: 112). This social, discursive, understanding of the term 'morphology' is developed by Maggie Berg. She removes a determinant, indexical link from the relationship between language and the body in favour of the morphological relationship:

> An indexical sign, as Silverman explains, is understood to be existentially connected to its referent, whereas a morphological or iconic sign merely draws attention to formal resemblances. If Irigaray criticizes the phallomorphism of discourse, she does not make any claims about which comes first, the penis or the phallus; in fact, she suggests that the focus on the penis in the construction of male sexuality is a consequence of values inscribed in discourse. (Berg 1991: 54)

In this we can begin to see how a different morpho-logic might represent both sexes differently. A single morpho-logic is in play at present, imposing its formations of language: a morphology of singularity, sameness (Irigaray 1985b: 271–317; 1991c: 96–97). Questioning this morphology does not mean retreating to anatomy, but breaking the tautology where only men's sex is spoken – a repetitive, mirroring, maintenance mimesis.

Thinking differently about the relationship between the body and language is clearly complex: thinking through a morphological relationship disrupts the clear-cut binary relationships found so frequently within phallomorphic thinking, even as one understands how they are produced. One example of the difficulty is found in an early article by Margaret Whitford. Here, she distinguished between the empirical (defined as 'biological and social') and the textual – 'the "female", "feminine" or "other", where "female" stands metaphorically for the genuinely other in a relation of difference' (Whitford 1986: 7). Leaving aside 'the genuinely other' as suggesting an authenticity which does not figure in Irigaray's writing, there is another problem with this absolute distinction between the two realms, outlined by Maggie Berg in her refusal of it:

> Far from being a trap, however, some sort of identification between 'woman' as a discursive construct and woman as a 'biological and social' entity is absolutely necessary and is central to Irigaray's work. Had Whitford recognized that masculine and feminine are in a relation of '*différance*' rather than 'difference' in Irigaray's work, she would not, I maintain, also have made the misleading split between empirical and textual women. (Berg 1991: 55)

'*Différance*' – a neologism combining 'to differ' and 'to defer' – is a concept developed by Jacques Derrida 'to remind us that difference is not a consequence of identity but, rather, makes identity possible' (Berg 1991: 55). He defines the term as: 'the systematic play of differences, of the traces of differences, of the *spacing* by means of which elements are related to each other. This spacing is the simultaneously active and passive [...] production of the intervals without which the "full" terms would not signify, would not function' (Derrida 1981: 27).

This spacing is both active and passive as it is the combination and confusion of differing and deferring. It is in this play that identity becomes possible, rather than identity leading to a recognition of difference. '*Différance*' is 'a structure and a movement no longer conceivable on the basis of the opposition presence/absence [...] Differences are the effects of transformations, and from this vantage the theme of différance is incompatible with the static, synchronic, taxonomic, ahistoric motifs in the concept of *structure*' (Derrida 1981: 27–28).

A fixed structure opposing presence/absence would produce a master-discourse of difference, while the play of *différance* produces transformation and structure together, and thus concepts of difference that are contingent. *Différance* is not produced by something beyond itself; it is necessary before any distinctions in seemingly circular relationships (for example, speech-language-speech) can be made (Derrida 1981: 28). For example, when speaking of gender, as Griselda Pollock has pointed out, the sociological understanding of gender difference or the psychoanalytic understanding of sexual difference in language may produce Man and Woman as distinct – different – categories that appear to be 'the fixed poles of a natural opposition'. However, these 'are but two relative signifiers in a chain down which meaning is constantly deferred'. *Différance* enables us to see a structure 'whose effect is *binary division* while it is in fact a *signifying system* that arbitrarily creates distinctions which are always co-dependent, co-extensive and shifting' (Pollock 1999: 30). In other words, difference is impossible without *différance*. Clearly, this supports Irigaray's notion of non-oppositionally gendered identity – intersubjectivity, the play of couples, sexuate subjectivity.

We can see here how morphology, in the site where it is, a spacing between body and signification, is an instance of *différance* at work (play). It is both a producer of gendered subjectivity, and also (in that very space between body and language, between empiricism and text, coming before any distinction between the two) it is productive of structure and transformation in that relationship. This is not disproved by the earlier discussion of man's morpho-logic as singular; a phallocentric morphology will produce structures of sameness while remaining what is only one morpho-logic. There are others.

In a phallocentric morpho-logic, and defined as other of the same, women have been denied the play of *différance* that will give them access to becoming sexuate subjects; denied the play of *différance* that will be productive of an appropriate Symbolic syntax; denied this, because the *différance* made possible by women's morphology can not be recognised by a phallic economy (Irigaray 1987g: 194; 1993j: 180). Through bringing women's morphology into play, phallic morpho-logic will have to shift (Irigaray 1990a: 68; 1993i: 59). Women's bodies will no longer be available as objects for men; no longer will women be other of men's Same. Once their subjectivity in and as *différance* with and from men's subjectivity is recognised, so too the necessity of intersubject relationships will be recognised. This will be aided by the deployment of a morpho-logic appropriate to women: the morphology in play between women's bodies and their syntax in the Symbolic, productive of that appropriate syntax and of appropriate symbolic (cultural) representations of women's bodies.

## THE LIPS AND THE MUCUS

The terms that Irigaray uses most often in order to mediate the play of women's morphology are those of 'the lips' and, increasingly through the writings of the 1980s, 'mucus'. 'The lips' as a term is inclusive of ambiguity, particularly in the French, where *lèvres* refers both to the lips of the mouth and the labia of the vulva (Gallop 1988: 98). Women's morphology produces a site for itself in this term: *not* the lips of the mouth, not the lips of the genitals, but at the same time *both* the lips of the mouth *and* the lips of the genitals: 'the lips', as a term, is the site of a play between them. The lips are at least two in at least two ways: both in the play between the (not)mouth and (not)vulva, and also in the internal morpho-logic of such (non)references. This morphological always-plural (i.e., which is not a one + one + one + . . .) is a point of distinction from phallomorphism, which counts in ones:

> We are luminous. Neither one nor two. I've never known how to count. Up to you. In their calculations we make two. Really, two? Doesn't that make you laugh? An odd sort of two. And yet not one. Especially not one. Let's leave one to them: their oneness, with its prerogatives, its domination, its solipsism: like the sun's. And the strange way they divide up their couples, with the other as the image of the one. (Irigaray 1977a: 206–207; 1985d: 207)

It is noticeable that Irigaray does not produce a name for this morphologic of women. Instead, she works with it in her writing. The lips' lack of oneness means that they do not have a graspable, unitary form; to give this morphology a name would be to revert to phallomorphic practice, to place it in patriarchal limits.

As well as being nameless, this lack of form is referred to frequently by Irigaray. In an often-quoted passage, as part of her accounting for phallocentric vision and phallomorphic syntax being unable to see woman's sexuality, she describes the female genitals as lacking a form of their own:

> This organ which has nothing to show for itself also lacks a form of its own. And if woman takes pleasure [*jouit*] precisely from this incompleteness of form which allows her organ to touch itself over and over again, indefinitely, by itself, that pleasure [*jouissance*] is denied by a civilization that privileges phallomorphism. The value granted to the only definable form excludes the one that is in play in female autoeroticism. The one of form, of the individual, of the (male) sexual organ, of the proper name, of the proper meaning... supplants, while separating and dividing, that contact of *at least two* (lips) which keeps woman in touch with herself, but without any possibility of distinguishing what is touching from what is touched. (Irigaray 1977a: 26; 1985d: 26)

This passage shows a constant slipping between the lips of the bodily vulva and the (not)vulva of women's morpho-logic – in fact, this gives us an understanding (reading) of the vulva *through the means* of such a morphologic. The words '*jouissance*', 'phallomorphism', 'definable', 'meaning' and 'at least two', remove it from the realm of the simply anatomical (while also providing plenty of confusion for those who understand 'morphology' as a synonym for anatomy). The non-form qualities of the genitals are in play with the non-form qualities of women's morpho-logic – a process which is not completable:

> from this movement is born, self-perpetuates, self-develops, a formation of desire, an imaginary of the sexuate body which never detaches itself as form(s) from the matter which generates it. Form and matter – and even the distinction between the terms is foiled – beget one another endlessly, and no form can be extrapolated from the body-support that gives birth to it. (Irigaray 1985b: 273. Translation modified; 1991c: 97–98)

So women's morpho-logic, in play between women's body and language, in a play of *différance*, is the place of the birth of the imaginary: *women's morpho-logic, which has its own material practices, is the necessary precursor to the distinction of a Symbolic syntax appropriate to women* (this point is crucial). And without this syntax, as we have seen, women remain in a state of immediacy, without access to their subjectivity, since subjectivity is entwined with signification.

Irigaray expresses this threading very clearly in 'When Our Lips Speak Together', in language which is not a 'poetics of the body', not '*écriture feminine*', but an attempt to write of and through the morpho-logic of women: the *parler-femme*, the witnessing woman:

> If we don't invent a language, if we don't find our body's language, it will have too few gestures to accompany our story. We shall tire of the same ones, and leave our desires in latency, unrealized. Sleep again, unsatisfied. And fall back upon the words of men – who for their part, have 'known' for a long time. But not our body. Seduced, attracted, fascinated, ecstatic with our becoming, we shall remain paralyzed. Deprived of our movements. Rigid, whereas we are made for endless change. Without jumps or falls necessary. And – without repetition. (Irigaray 1977a: 213. Translation modified; 1985d: 214)

The 'we', 'you', and 'I' through 'When Our Lips Speak Together' should not be reduced to anatomy in either the generalised sense (reduction to the genitals and the mouth); but neither should they be anthropomorphicised (reduced to a quasi-narrative between two women). Instead, they can be seen as the play of the *différance* of a woman's morpho-logic: (not)lips, (not)vulva, form and matter endlessly begetting each other. The only way in which such a contemplation can come about – the only way to mediate what would otherwise be an immediate, distanceless proximity, the morpho-logic of two lips touching – is through the morpho-logic of mucus: 'Your skin and mine, yes. But mine goes on touching itself indefinitely, from the inside. Secreting a flow which brings the sides together. [...] It flows between. Not held or held back by a source. The source already rises from the two caressing' (Irigaray 1982: 18; 1992a: 15).

Irigaray discusses the facets of the morphology of mucus and mucous membranes most fully in 'The Limits of the Transference' and in *An Ethics of Sexual Difference*, where she indicates that a distanceless proximity can be dangerous for both subjects when it results in a maintenance mimesis of the representation, 'woman':

> Mimetic appropriation by women is still the most terrible thing of all because it is practised without any feminine ideality or model. The absence of an ideal maternal and female figure [*figure idéale*] for women results in the fact that mime between women becomes the flaying of one woman by the other, the reduction of the skin and of the most mucous to forms [*figures*] into which they flow in order to exist, often quite unconsciously. They take the appearance of the other before there is any image, and may leave her their own, which they no longer want, for lack of a self-representation to venerate, contemplate, admire or even adore. (Irigaray 1985a: 299. Translation modified; 1991a: 110–111)

In 'this distanceless proximity between women [...], distanceless because no symbolic process allows us to account for it' (Irigaray 1985a: 295–296; 1991a: 107), occurs a form of maintenance mimesis – but a maintenance of an identity which has no subjectivity, no ideal, no Symbolic syntax of its own. Instead, that mimesis strips away the possibilities of mediation and a syntax through maintaining a disregard of women's morphology. There is, I think, a deliberate ambiguity in Irigaray's use of the word '*figure*' here: an ideal female model for women would require some form of configuration within a syntax appropriate to women; the manner of gestural mimesis which is described here is the result of a proximity so unmediated that it does not recognise that the other is not that female ideal model and that it has no mediation, and instead displaces the site of the ideal through a mimesis of the representation, 'woman'. In doing so the woman displaces the morphology of the mucous (flays it back, even) with a reduction to a form – a reassertion of phallomorphologic, 'a gesture which involves a sort of capitalization of the mucous membrane, an exteriorization of what is most inner' (Irigaray 1985a: 298; 1991a: 110). The possibility of (and possibilities ensuing from) a woman's morpho-logic are eclipsed by the fatal misrecognition of the phallomorphic form that is the representation, 'woman'.

## MUCUS AS MEDIATION

To recognise the morphology of the mucus and realise its morpho-logic is thus a priority. Its realisation is crucial for woman–woman relationships; it is also crucial for woman–man relationships and for a woman's relationship with herself – her self-mediation through an appropriate symbolisation:

> However, it is possible that the mucus corresponds to something that needs to be thought through today. For different reasons and imperatives:
>
> – any thinking about the female has to think (through) the mucus.
>
> – No thinking about sexual difference that would not be traditionally hierarchical is possible without thinking (of) the mucus. (Irigaray 1984: 107. Translation modified; 1993d: 110)

The morphology of the mucus is that which mediates a woman to herself, and also mediates her, in her difference and specificity, to her lover. It will inform an appropriate syntax and provide for its legibility. It is the mark of her sex, and it is the mark of mediation. The lips are, morphologically, a threshold; ajar, but touching;[1] not closed; not skin (surface closure), not flayed (internal made external), not a unitary form of flesh (non-mediating); but rather, mucus: the site of mediation.

What I discern here in my reading of the morphology of the mucus is a morphology that allows for both the relinquishing of control and the presence of the subject demanded by the intersubjectivity and attentiveness discussed in the last chapter. Recalling the flowering of the subject that was the Buddha's gaze upon the flower (one of many references to flowers which should not, I think, be misread as a patriarchal representation of femininity), Irigaray evokes the potential of the mucus: 'The flesh of the rose petal – sensation of the mucus regenerated. Somewhere between blood, sap, and the not yet of efflorescence. Joyous mourning for the winter past. New baptism of springtime. Return to the possible of intimacy, its fecundity, and fecundation' (Irigaray 1984: 185; 1993d: 200). And this 'return to the possible of intimacy' can be found in the way the mucus marks the limits of the subject as it performs a mediation between subjects. Articulating the limits between women is problematic: 'the very openness [*l'entreouverture*] of their bodies, of their flesh, of their genitals [*sexe*] makes the question of boundaries difficult' (Irigaray 1985a: 300; 1991a: 112). What is necessary, then, is a site of a 'third term' – a site that is neither one subject nor the other (and that will thus prevent each woman reducing the other to herself), but is also not abstract.

Throughout the discussion of how this may be achieved in the psychoanalytic transference between a woman analyst and a woman analysand, Irigaray uses the morpho-logic of the mucus to provide an understanding of the processes. Once again, it is the lack of an appropriate syntax that can prove fatal for the two women attempting to achieve subjecthood and intersubjectivity through the psychoanalytic transference. In order to allay this danger, the two subjects have to produce a (non)object – the third term – between them:

> How are they constantly to make greatest and smallest meet? And above all, move from one qualitative to another? A difficult energetistic question, especially when there is no object, no comparison between the two poles. They must become creations. Art *objects*? In that way two subjects can advene one to the other, and an alliance between the two becomes possible.
>
> This is not so much a problem of mastery as the question of a creation allowing participation in the *jouissance* of the object or its cocreation: a useful work because it marks, without destruction, the limits of energy, of the flesh and of the body, of desire and its possibilities. The creation or elaboration of the object becomes an architectonic of the body, of a life and a death that does not kill the other. This creation might be the only thing that could allow the resolution of the transference. (Irigaray 1985a: 301; 1991a: 112–113)

Without the morpho-logic of the mucous in play in the analytical process, this resolution would be impossible. The object would otherwise remain the over-valued object of phallocentrism identified in the last chapter; possibly, if the fatal mimesis by one woman of the other has taken place, a symbolising of mucus in a phallocentric syntax. The 'object' that is created, however, is something more like a fluidity of creation itself: the work of creating a subject is a co-creation in the analysis. This must start not from the premise that one woman is the subject and the other is her object (nor that the other is the object of the analysis); but that both are potentially subjects in a relationship of intersubjectivity: 'a communication or communion which respects the life of the other whilst still tasting the strangeness of his/her desire. [...] Access to this is essential if there is to be an other' (Irigaray 1985a: 303. Translation modified; 1991a: 114–115).

In this way the transference takes place not as a pouring of one subject into the other, with the resultant annihilation of both, but as two subjects, women, retaining their boundaries, relating through the play of the morphologic of the mucus. The morphology of mucus – its (non)form, its other-translucency, its resistance to being mastered by either subject, its specificity to each woman, and its mediation of the woman to herself – provides a pattern for the morphology of the mediation between the women. The 'object' to be created is this work.

Once the patterns of the morpho-logic of the mucus are recognised, they can be worked for elsewhere. I should like now to look for its patterns in practices of art-making: how it might be discerned in the use of certain media. Further, I will explore how, as a result, those media may function as material through which mediation between subjects may take place.

## MORPHOLOGIES IN MATERIALS

Various commentators have attempted to describe Irigaray's use of the morphology of lips and the mucus within extant grammatical formations. Most of them fall short of the way in which she herself uses such a morphologic – 'already-constructed theoretical language does not speak the mucus' (Irigaray 1985a: 302; 1991a: 113) – and thus also fall short of being ways in which we might think anew about practices of making art, and the languages we use through which we can develop an appropriate syntax. For example, Margaret Whitford points out that 'readers do not hesitate to use the term "metaphor" when they discuss Irigaray's work; some, but not all, realize that there is a problem here' (Whitford 1991b: 71). Whitford herself falls foul of these problems when she refers to the mucus as bodily – betraying a slippage between the adjective 'the mucous' [*le muqueux*] and the noun 'mucus' [*mucus*] – and suggests that what is needed is 'to symbolize the mucous' (Whitford 1991b: 106). Here she appears to slide from using the term 'symbolic' in its psychoanalytic meaning ('the Symbolic'), to using it as one might refer to symbols within symbolism. Thus she is able to refer to Irigaray's 'images of the body' such as the two lips and mucus, and say 'that what Irigaray has succeeded in doing [...] is to provide *images of women's bodies* which have become material for symbolic exchange between women, and which therefore have already in a limited domain and to a limited extent exceeded the parameters of patriarchal representations of women' (Whitford 1991a: 98). To me, this is a rather literary way of reading Irigaray's writing, and one which comes perilously close to encouraging a reading that falls back into the capitalising[2] of the verbal or visual metaphor. It also undermines her discussion of 'the lips' and the mucus as an example of metonymy, rather than metaphor (Whitford 1991c: 177–185).

Jane Gallop has a similar problem: 'Vulvomorphic logic, by newly metaphorizing the body, sets it free, if only momentarily. For as soon as the metaphor becomes a proper noun, we no longer have creation, we have paternity' (Gallop 1988: 96). This appears not to realise the trap of producing the (highly reductive) term 'vulvomorphic logic' as a noun after a rather elegant disquisition on the problem. Maggie Berg notes this. However, after quoting Irigaray on the need to ascertain whether 'the motifs of "self-touching" [...] might not imply a mode of exchange irreducible to any centering, any centrism' (Irigaray 1977a: 76; 1985d: 79) and saying 'she does not wish to displace Lacan's phallus with the lips, which would be a phallocentric strategy', Berg supplies her own term of 'lipeccentrism' (Berg 1991: 68–69). This runs the danger of being defined by its otherness to the (phallic) centre. (These problems highlight why I persist in using the cumbersome indication of 'a morphology appropriate to women'.)

Instead of symbolising mucus as such, we need to recognise in it the play of '*différance*', and its morphological patterns, and develop from that site morphologies of mediation and, contiguously, of other syntaxes in the Symbolic. There is no doubt that this problem in critiques of Irigaray can be seen as the crux of an interesting problem with Irigaray's writing itself: how, at present, can we work simultaneously with and against the structures and tropes of the Symbolic currently provided by our culture? How does one produce the element of mediation – the third term, the gift-space/object, the appropriate syntax in the Symbolic – and its representations, without capitalising? How do we self-represent without reproducing (to ourselves or to others) the phallomorphic representation, 'woman'? How do we resist incorporation while retaining legibility, developing appropriate syntaxes for legibility? In different ways, these questions have resonated throughout this present text.

As Whitford does, Diana Fuss also distinguishes between metonymy and metaphor in Irigaray, suggesting that 'the "two lips" operate as a metaphor for metonymy' (Fuss 1990: 66). This seems to me to be closer in *structure* to an understanding of what Irigaray's writing is doing – what work her work is doing – but still with the risk of retaining phallogocentric understandings and functions of the terms 'metaphor' and 'metonymy'. Metaphor has been hugely dominant in the way we talk about art and art-making, even of radical practices. Mary Kelly, for example, has spoken of the roles of metaphor and metonymy in making work:

> I'm sorry I have to resort to some kind of essentialism here, but how do you describe a feeling for certain materials, how do you make that translation? It's interesting to see how much the whole idea of metaphor is central to what causes visual pleasure. [...]
>
> Another feeling that's very common is that you're never satisfied. That places you within the axis of metonymy of desire, which is also very productive to examine in terms of who you really are desiring to speak to in the work. (Kelly and Pollock 1992: 193–197)

This is why I think that in considering art we need to return to an understanding of the functioning of morphology, and of the morpho-logic of 'the lips' and of the mucus: to attempt to locate a morphology that can enable a mediation through materials – an enunciation which is legible and productive of discourse – in an appropriate syntax; what Kelly calls 'a visualisation and a theorisation simultaneously [...] a construction of meaning that's tying together with form and content' (Kelly and Pollock 1992: 193), where maybe structures of metaphor can function in relations of *différance*.

What we can see Irigaray doing – practising – in her work and the concept of '*parler-femme*' is not so much in a reductive sense 'speaking as a woman'[3] but rather speaking *in* the morpho-logic of 'the lips' and the mucus. Thus, the task for us reading her work is not to distinguish between metaphor and metonymy, but to realise the play of *différance* between the language which is spoken or written and that which is said within that language (they may well be contiguous): its morphology. This would then allow us to approach, develop and be attentive to the motifs within that speech without capitalising them as a *result of our use of ('speaking' and 'reading') the language*, without returning them to metaphor or phallomorphic object. Irigaray hints at this early in her work, commenting upon motifs such as 'self-touching' within the work:

> But of course if these were only 'motifs' without any work on and/or with language, the discursive economy could remain intact. How, then, are we to try to redefine this language work that would leave space for the feminine? Let us

> say that every dichotomizing – and at the same time redoubling – break, including the one between enunciation and utterance, has to be disrupted. Nothing is ever to be posited that is not also reversed and caught up again in the *supplementarity of this reversal*. To put it another way: there would no longer be either a right side or a wrong side of discourse, or even of texts, but each passing from one to the other would make audible and comprehensible even what resists the recto-verso structure that shores up common sense. If this is to be practised for every meaning posited – for every word, utterance, sentence, but also of course for every phoneme, every letter – we need to proceed in such a way that linear reading is no longer possible: that is, the retroactive impact of the end of every word, utterance, or sentence upon its beginning must be taken into consideration in order to undo the power of its teleological effect, including its deferred action. (Irigaray 1977a: 76–77; 1985d: 79–80)

The play of the morpho-logic (including its play through the media of the artwork) precedes the distinction of the Symbolic syntax appropriate to women: the motifs and representations occurring within it – that which we wish to say in it – cannot be anticipated in advance; nor can the degree of contiguity between the two. Continuous vigilance regarding the play of the morpho-logic in the structure of the Symbolic is required: in a constant multiple movement we have to work with and through the language to hand (both in its substance and its representations), back to its informative morpho-logic, and return again to language.

This prompts me to remember the partial nature of this present text: it is a practice of writing, not a practice of making art. As such, it should not presume to tell artists what to do, but rather should be at that moment of re-engaging with, in order to make legible, the morphological structures informing artworks and the practices of making them and reading them. What is at stake here is the morpho-logic informing both our making of artworks, and how we represent the representational practices of art to ourselves. Lynda Nead has noted how, within writing on art:

> ...the artistic subjectivity that is registered by the brushwork and surface is sexualized. Art criticism writes sex into descriptions of paint, surface and forms. The category of art does not permit a sexuality that is an obvious and provocative element, but a certain kind of phallocentric textuality can be articulated in the discussion of a painting's handling and style. The sexual, then, is distanced from the subject represented on the canvas and is reinscribed through the metaphorical language of connoisseurship. (Nead 1992: 58)

In recognising the morpho-logic of the mucus and the lips, the whole approach of thinking through metaphor would need to be undone; the recognition and privileging of metaphoric elements before other elements would be opened for question. As with Irigaray's work on vision, this does not mean that metaphor would be expunged: rather, that its role in producing phallocentric representations should be recognised, and the prior workings of a phallomorphologic be disrupted by the need to recognise a morphology of the mucus. This returns us to the materiality of art-making, and to the problem of approaching a medium and working with it as that element of mediation – the third term, the gift-space/object of co-creation – in which enunciation in an appropriate syntax in the Symbolic is possible. Thus, 'representational practices' in artworks are in an interdependent and discursive relationship with the practices and processes engaged with by the artist in her use of media. The medium, therefore, must be recognised by the artist and the attentive audience as an element in a discourse productive of representations which remain without capitalising – if you like, one set of signifiers among others in artworks as non-capitalised objects.

The medium recognised historically as the one privileged among art practices is paint. Griselda Pollock argues, moreover, that:

> Since the late eighteenth century, and certainly since the beginning of [the twentieth], the term ['painting'] has referred to the hegemonic cultural form which is constituted by the combination of a subject (the artist), an activity (the practice in the studio) and a web of symbolic meaning woven through that figure in that space by means of the economic investment in the commodity it produced (Pollock 1992: 159).

In analysing the critical structures of modernism which capitalise the medium, Paint, and the practice, Painting, as product of the Artist, Pollock writes of the signification of paint and the act of painting within Greenbergian modernism:

> The purity of the visual signifier, seemingly emptied of all reference to a social or natural world, is still loaded with significance through its function as affirmation of its artistic subject. Abstract Expressionism is a celebration of the 'expressivity' of a self which is not to be constrained by expressing anything in particular except the engagement of the artistic self with the processes and procedures of painting. Thus 'painting' is privileged in modernist discourse as the most ambitious and significant art form because of its combination of gesture and trace, which secure by metonymy the presence of the artist. These inscribe a subjectivity whose value is, by visual inference and cultural naming, masculinity. (Pollock 1992: 142)

As Pollock's essay indicates, the moment of modernism and its structuring of 'the Artist' has been massively disrupted by post-modernist and feminist critiques and practice. She names artists such as Barbara Kruger, Lubaina

Himid, Martha Rosler, Jo Spence and Mona Hatoum whose 'strategic practices [ensure that] their work is a site for a sustained analysis of the meanings of sexual difference authored by culture, across which "cultural body" they inscribe feminist readings' (Pollock 1992: 154) – practices which include disrupting the privilege accorded paint.

It is interesting to note, however, that when it comes to painting, some feminist critiques have simply enacted a reversal upon the Greenbergian emptying of all meaning other than 'the engagement of the artistic self with the processes and procedures of painting', and have instead emptied paintings by women of all meaning other than that discerned in their images. One example of this occurs in Peggy Phelan's *Unmarked: The Politics of Performance*, where a discussion of paintings by Mira Schor omits any engagement with the materiality of the work (other than to give their dimensions, configuration when hung and the fact that some utilise rice paper) in favour of a discussion of the overt representations of the imagery (Phelan 1993: 51–60). This is surprising, given both the subtitle of the book, and other discussions within it – for example, of representations in films by Yvonne Rainer as products of material and image in a dynamic relation – but symptomatic of the sway held by Painting and the long reach of the discourses around it. If Painting (as capitalised act) is left undisrupted by feminist theorising in the culture, then not only will feminists who are painting remain marginal, their strategies reduced to ones of choice of medium, but also, crucially, any feminist interventions into the practices of painting may well remain broadly illegible, even to other feminists. In some respects – both because of its historical signification, and because of some of its material potentialities – the practice of painting could prove a major testing ground for the possibilities of non-phallomorphic developments of an appropriate syntax. It should be clear that I am not arguing for a return to formalism:[4] it would be easy to capitalise mucus by capitalising paint, understand 'Paint' as a phallomorphic metaphor for mucus. Instead, I want to try to arrive at an understanding of painting as one site of mediation within the morpho-logic of the mucus. First, I would like to indicate one example of how the work of one woman has been brought into a state of semi-legibility, but no further, by the terminology of present feminist criticism.

## LEGIBILITY: LAURA GODFREY-ISAACS

Laura Godfrey-Isaacs first came to prominence in 1990 when she received a Momart Fellowship at the Tate Gallery, Liverpool. At that time, and until 1992, she was working with oil paint, but subsequently she has worked with a variety of media including resin, plasticine and expanded polyurethane. The properties of oil paint were pushed to the limit in her paintings, which ranged from one foot to over ten foot wide. Usually single colour – for example the *Red Series* (1991–1992) – her technical interest was in working with the contrasting liquidity and solidity of the paint, its qualities when skinning and drying, and when mixed with different oils and varnishes. This was developed in the series of small *Padded Paintings* (1993–1994) to the extent that the paintings would be built up with scrapings of dried paint and varnishes, layer upon layer, until they were inches thick. The related *Alien Blobs* (1994) were moved off canvas, and worked with resin, until the largest was 25" x 15"x 10". In the *Monstrous* series (1995), Godfrey-Isaacs started making free-standing sculptural pieces, using similar techniques of pouring and layering, but on a large scale with polyurethane. The malleability of plasticine, clay and dough has been explored in series of small sculptures (1995), and in the wall pieces called *Plasticine Paintings* (1995).

Whatever the media in these paintings and related works, critics have located the signifiers of Godfrey-Isaacs' work somewhere between its imagery and its material, and its significations in the realm of the body, its wet interior and its skin. The works have been read as exploring qualities of their media in order to express interest in and metaphors for viscera and bodily fluids. Simon Watney writes:

> Laura Godfrey-Isaacs is well known for the emphasis in her work on the liquidity of paint, its viscous, tick-tacky, messy gooey qualities. [...] Obliged to think of the painted surface through metaphors of skin and flesh, Godfrey-Isaacs' work takes us to the other side of skin, to the clinically exposed insides of the organism – gleaming, wet, animal, and to most of us largely unrecognisable and incomprehensible (Watney 1995).

Godfrey-Isaacs' work has been written about predominantly in two styles, even in gallery-generated texts intended to support and elucidate: either in a mock-transgressive voice, reminiscent of the advertising of cream-cakes to women ('naughty but nice'), or assuming that their engagement with feminist theory is transparent. Leah Karibian, in a conversation with the artist about the *Padded Paintings*, assumes the latter position, and tries to retrieve the works for formalist analysis:

> You seem to have taken a step out of the critical fold in which your practice was previously protected, or let's say supported. You've stepped away from certain well-established feminist narratives on the body into areas where those arguments are less applicable. In particular, I'm thinking about the way your new work openly flirts with the language of modernist formalism [...]. The thrill

> for me is seeing a feminist artist play around with formal concerns – to enjoy them. It's been such a male preserve in the past, and a language that feminist practitioners have denied themselves – almost on moral grounds. Audiences have had to go without. But now you're in there, having a great time, altering formalism through informed practice. (Karibian et al. 1994)

This is worrying for a number of reasons, most pertinently here, because of the opening it provides for a return to formalism. Godfrey-Isaacs responds to Karibian: 'I definitely stepped out of that practice which directly references the gendered body, and the culturally defined body'. This opens a space for discussion of 'indirect' references of such a body; but the opening is

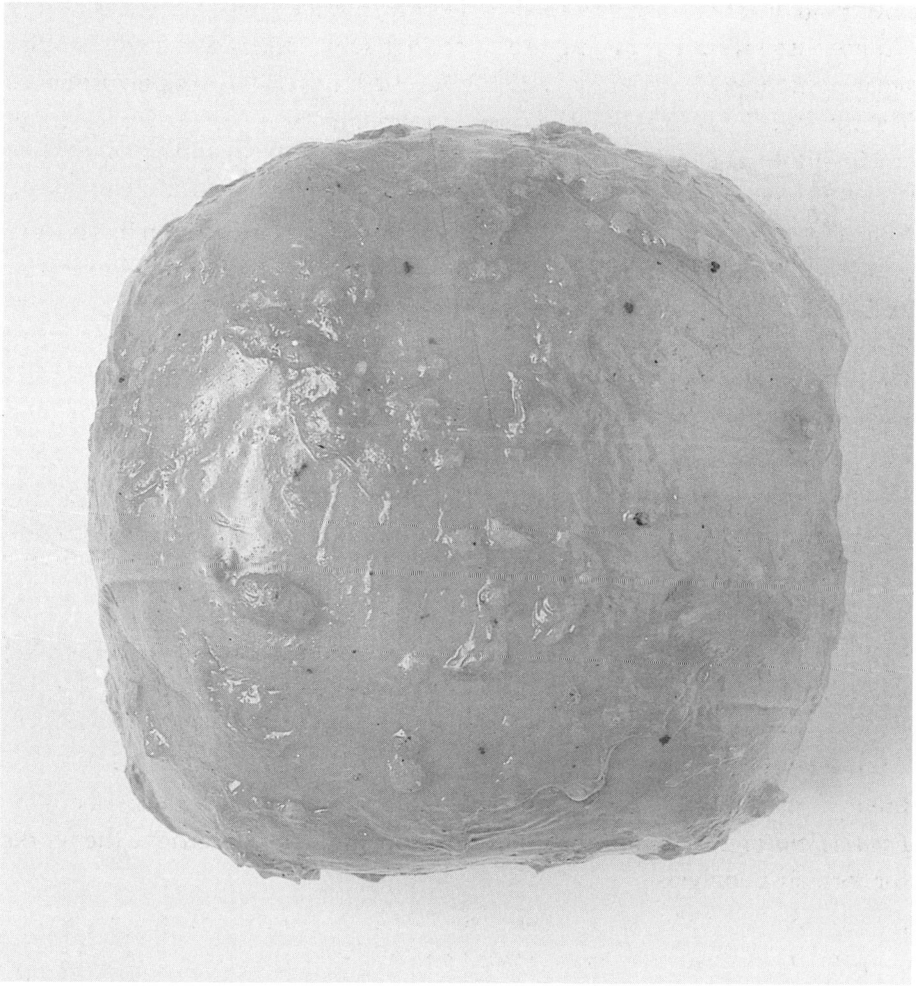

Laura Godfrey-Isaacs, *Padded Paintings*: (detail), 1993–1994. Oil and gel on canvas, 6″ x 4″. Courtesy of the Artist.

immediately closed by another participant in the discussion who, prompted by Karibian's comments, validates the work by comparing it with 'masters' of Abstract Expressionism: 'it's a Frank Auerbach or a Karel Appel painted with mashed up Baked Beans [...] I had this rather charming image of Auerbach larding on the beans in heroic fashion but which in fact was an image of a child playing with its food' (Karibian et al. 1994). The dangers of positioning the work in such a discourse become clear: no matter how wittily it is phrased, we are left with a reading of the works of the woman artist (Godfrey-Isaacs) as, 'in fact', infantile, unintentional, simulations of work by the grand male figures of Abstract Expressionism.

From the outset, Rosemary Betterton's *An Intimate Distance: Women, Artists and the Body* directs the reader to consider Godfrey-Isaacs' work as significant (Betterton 1996). A detail of the painting *Pink Skin* (1992) wraps around the whole cover of the paperback. Betterton dedicates one passage of the book to the paintings of the early 1990s, and another to the resin and polyurethane works of the exhibitions *The Alien and the Domestic* (1993) and *Monstrous* (1994). While these passages do go some way towards providing a theoretical discourse for the works, they are caught by attempting to fit the them into a pre-existing theoretical structure which is not, ultimately, sufficient, but tangential to other structures suggested by the works. Having referred to the *Alien Blobs* series as 'such fetish objects' as those found in a 'bulim[ic] [...] fetish structure' (Betterton 1996: 151–152), Betterton then gives the *Padded Paintings* a related context: 'If the problem for daughters in separating from their mothers is represented in terms of a process of disavowal (I am not like her, but all the same), then this work functions in a similar way as a fetish which both alludes to and denies that loss' (Betterton 1996: 153).

Betterton's analysis takes us some way towards an active feminist reading of the paintings; but the problem is indicated in that 'if' and 'then'. I will take her arguments as a starting point, and then try to move it a step forward. Further legibility can be gained through recognising a morphology of the mucus in that structure. *If* the problem for daughters in separating from their mothers is *not* seen as caught in a phallocentric bind, requiring disavowal in a phallomorphic syntax *but instead* seen through a morphologic of the mucus, then these works can be read as attempts at mediation in an appropriate syntax. Form and matter can be read as begetting each other in a play of *différance* productive of syntax, rather than form being read through a phallomorphic syntax as metaphor or fetish. The project they speak of is then read not as one of providing a fetish to stand in for the relationship with the mother, but of providing the gift-space/object which ensures its continuation through constructing the means of its mediation. The works can then be read also as more productive of the 'intimate distance' of Betterton's title.

It is perhaps indicative of the complexity of the problems facing critics and theorists that when Betterton touches upon paintings such as *Pink Skin* she does so in the context of opposing 'painting "femininity"' to 'painting women'. She describes them as 'explor[ing] the metaphorical and literal equivalencies between the feminine body and the surface and textures of oil paint' (Betterton 1996: 96).[5] When critiques (like those of all the writers cited on Godfrey-Isaacs' work) are built upon structures of metaphoric narrative between media and signification, then they will not survive the artist's radical shift of media. In the late 1990s Godfrey-Isaacs started making work from knitting. Much of the material used in them – knitted sheets, squares and pillows – was made collaboratively by the artist, her mother and other earlier generations of women in her family, during her pregnancy and the early life of her first child.[6] No longer possible to read as narratives of sexual metaphor, they would add to my argument to read her work as the site of a mediation of, rather than a fetish for, an intersubjective relationship between women.

## LEGIBILITY: BRIDGET RILEY AND RACHEL WHITEREAD

As indicated above, Griselda Pollock has laid out the problematic of the intersection of modernist painting and feminist practice, preparing the ground for further analysis. Two recent articles by other women have begun to address the materiality of paint (and in one work discussed, plaster) in a manner that works at undoing phallomorphic understandings of paint and of writing about paintings. Instead, they suggest new possibilities for women engaging with the practice of painting, either as subjects who paint or as subjects attending to paintings. Joan Key's 'Unfold: Imprecations of Obscenity in the Fold'(Key 1997) attends to an experience the writer had of seeing Rachel Whiteread's *Untitled (Airbed)* (1992) and Bridget Riley's *Arrest II* (1965) exhibited together, the only two artworks in a gallery space. Alison Rowley's 'On Viewing Three Paintings by Jenny Saville: Rethinking a Feminist Practice of Painting' (Rowley 1996) also takes as its starting point (as the title suggests) a gallery experience. I was struck by the way in which both these articles (each written by a painter) attended to the experience of being in the same space as the artworks and to the presence, substance and make-up of the works they were discussing. Both writers attend to the particular medium of paint or plaster as if they were sites through which Irigarayan mediation is occurring (although neither writer theorises the materials in this way); both attend through sight – seeing the works – 'which is after all, the only place where a painting can be experienced by the viewer' (Rowley 1996: 97); but both are acutely aware of the significance of touch in producing what they see: 'a highly tactile sensation, not only the desire to press, but a response to that pressure, to be pressed back: a sensation that hints of desire and relation in excess of the contemplative utility of art' (Key 1997: 194).

Rachel Whiteread's *Untitled (Airbed)* is a plaster-cast of the space above an inflated airbed. Bridget Riley's *Arrest II* is an acrylic on canvas painting of black, grey and white wavy lines. Key tells us that the curator had no reasons for exhibiting the two works together other than superficial resemblance; he considers them to be utterly different historically, intentionally and conceptually. She says that this 'suggests an excess of "pleasure" over reason or "function", and not the appropriate workings of "judgement"' (Key 1997: 197). While she is suspicious of this, she identifies a space of dialogue that has thus been created between the two works, uncluttered by any gallery interpretation other than a label for each work with the artist's name, a title and date, a space 'for intense study of traces, residues, minute details, in suspension of awareness of the indications that would permit judgement' (Key 1997: 196). Here there is room to contemplate surface, fluidity, skin, absence, closure, openness, masking.

Key's description of the two works betrays a discernment of conflicting morphological structures. In the work by Whiteread:

> ... the plaster retains its pristine self, straight from the mould. It is not modified with the touch of handiwork, but displays the unquestionable authenticity of time and imitation that inheres to the mechanics of casting. This permeates the work and reproduces intimately the surface of inflated fabric and its internal structural dynamic. The sense of liquid origins in the slight signs of pouring and bubbling transforms these physical references. They also refer to the lost container/matrix [...] the hidden sign of the fragmented nature of the casting process. (Key 1997: 186)

This work does not claim authenticity by indexing the artist through her gestural trace. Rather, any claim to authenticity rests in its indexing of the technical process of its making – in particular, the once-liquid state of its material (plaster), and the flexible nature of its matrix (the airbed).

Bridget Riley's painting is in contrast to this:

> Riley's paint is flat: it's original fluidity may be residually referenced in the flowing pattern of the drawing, but now it lies in a fine layer across the picture in an even continuous film, its own texture subordinated to a plastic ideal of

> perfectly smooth consistency. Phenomenal painterly content is totally rationalized into a predetermined scheme: the flawless surface seems to have arrived through automatic procedures. Paint is literally a skin, divided by sharply delineated streams of black/grey/white. The closure of their edges is absolute: not a layering but a suffocating continuity in the surface. The perfection of the skin reveals and reproduces the hidden structure of the underlying support, a surprising reference to cloth, evenly woven, stretched but elastic, subject to pressure: an estimated depth of movement paralleled in the imaginary depth of the undulation of the painted pattern. The image, in the design of a wave pattern, suggests continuity, duration and distance. However, Riley's pattern is cut at a random edge, and brought up close by its unvarying ratio. Like the patterning of textile or wallpaper, it implies the function of a cover or a blanket/obliteration. (Key 1997: 187)

Knowledge of the original fluidity of its materials (paint and canvas) is suppressed. Any trace of the gesture of the artist's hand has been removed to provide a perfect closure: the smooth, flat skin of the paint surface. The canvas is stretched taught; its trace in the finished painting seems incidental to the artist's intention, but will prove crucial. Rather than index its fluidity of material or of process, the work instead has fluidity simulated within it, in the image it carries.

Alongside these differences between the works is another set of qualities which resonates between them. Both employ what was originally a fluid medium that has, in particular ways, coagulated to form a pristine surface. Both artists employ techniques that suppress any signatures in mark-making, but both use techniques that make the works instantly recognisable as being by that particular artist. Both works contain imagery of waves – the painting in the pattern painted, the sculpture in the undulations of the bed. 'Both works suggest themselves as whole, while, unsettlingly, they turn out to be fragments; both have an area of unseen content that is powerfully present yet invisible' (Key 1997: 187).

The morphology informing each begins to differentiate them, and to form their differing significatory process in the Symbolic. The painting has a surface which is closed, suffocating, described in a manner which suggests that it was produced with a maintenance mimesis of a phallomorphologic. The sculpture is more ambiguous, asserting its presence through processes of reversals – the bed and its absence; authentic presence with no visible trace of the artist; apparent solidity displaying originating fluidity and so forth. More ambiguous still is the 'reserve' of each work, that which is always already there during any configuration of the works as being informed by a phallomorphologic: the potential presence of a morpho-logic of the mucus. In both works this can be found in cloth and the artist's touching of cloth through the once-fluid medium of paint or plaster. Key does not use this terminology at all, but her description of the works allows for such a reading:

> Both the Whiteread and the Riley share a reference to the potentially mobile surface of cloth. In both the sculpture and the painting this reference seems to have the status of an incidental detail, but it imposes on their form with unexpected force, since in both, the image of the cloth is embedded in another surface (plaster or paint) to the point where it nearly disappears. (Key 1997: 191)

This 'incidental detail', if one cares to look for it, can be perceived as a determining detail for the attentive audience of the two works. Even though the flow of plaster and paint is stilled (closed), the memory of it is carried in the material of the plaster as (to use terminology from an earlier chapter) an hysterical reserve, and in the material of the differently tinted paint as masquerade, finery, *parure*.

There is another element in this: the encountering of the two works by an attentive audience. The way Key has written her essay is through a series of folds; episodic, it does not demand a linear reading, and indeed (with the exception of the initial paragraph) encourages both circular and non-linear reading, each episode touching upon others. While not formless, it does not have a traditionally academic form. What is of particular interest in this context is what Key discerns, not only within each work, but in the third term they create between them, the work they do together; traces of which they each, in their particular ways, bring individually to the encounter:

> This is a continuous folding and unfolding that is out of the spectator's control: a simultaneous display of two positions, so that there is a perpetual relay between two opposed visual messages. This process puts the content of the fold on display, returning its hidden nature to a surface which cannot settle into place and immediately hides it again. This refusal to keep still leaves the spectator with literally 'nothing to hold on to', deflecting the spectator's gaze through the permanent defeat of closure to a surface that seems always on the verge of opening up, an unconscious movement of logarithms and numbers, not to be controlled by conscious design. (Key 1997: 192)

In this we can discern a non-phallomorphic logic at play between the materiality of the artworks and their imagery – and between the artworks and Key. Nowhere does she capitalise the fold: though she does tell an amusing anecdote (courtesy of Joan Copjec) which suggests how a phallomorphologic might do so. The tale of psychiatrist, Gaetan de Clérambault, could be interpreted as on the one hand an instance of hysteroscopy, and on the other, a castrating refusal to see. De Clérambault ran, at the École des Beaux Arts, a course on drapery and folds which was peremptorily closed down by the authorities: 'the recoil they felt it necessary to make, in order to disassociate themselves from that very concern with FOLDing, demonstrated the degree of their embarrassment. It was important to mark not just disapproval, but the stronger emotion of disgust, a visceral revulsion' (Key 1997: 192–193). It is in Key's discernment of the never-completed, never-completable folding and unfolding of cloth in the reserve of the two works and in the work they make together that the phallomorphic 'scandal' of their interaction can be found: a morpho-logic of 'the lips' and of the mucus.

## LEGIBILITY: JENNY SAVILLE

Alison Rowley's essay allows us to concentrate more closely upon the manner in which the handling of the material substance of paint and the configuration of imagery in paint touch upon each other. Her shifting of terminology from 'formal' qualities to 'technical' procedures (Rowley 1996: 92) would seem initially to hold the two apart; but in fact the term 'formal' insists that issues arising from the relationship between the image on the canvas and anything which lies beyond the canvas be discarded in favour of abstract discussions of, for example, 'composition'. Distinguishing technical procedures from configuration of imagery (and by extension, matters of representation) allows us to attend anew to their touching upon each other.

As with Key's essay, Rowley's contains a memorable passage of writing which is more than descriptive of the artwork under discussion – Jenny Saville's *Plan*. Because it is not only pertinent to the discussion of the morphology of the relationship between the audience and the artwork, but also suggestive of how this morpho-logic may be signified through the writings of the art critic or theorist, I will quote the paragraph in full:

> At my height of 5′ 7″ if I stand at painting distance from the canvas (by the size of the marks this is closer than arm's length as these are manipulations of the brush by fingers and wrist, not swings from the shoulder), I have in my focused vision a group of oblongish marks of flesh tones modulated to simulate the play of light over a smooth but slightly uneven surface. Into this surface break some small brownish black curved marks of raised paint which I can imagine as have been made by gently laying a fine, long-haired brush loaded with colour onto the surface of the canvas and quickly lifting it off again. The memory

> from my own experience of manipulating paint, of the controlled combination of amount of paint, weight of hand, movement of fingers needed to execute marks like these is very pleasurable. At this distance from the canvas I'm lost in the memory of the tactile pleasures of paint application. And literally lost in the space of the canvas with nothing to locate myself, I cannot see any whole shapes or the edges of the canvas. How does this area of painted marks relate to those on the rest of the canvas, and to construct what? To find out, I have to pull a good way back from touching distance before I have the whole canvas within my field of vision and can see that what the marks make is where the pubic hair peters out into the smooth skin of the stomach. But at this distance my memories are of another order, in another register: they are memories of other images of women without clothes, from other paintings and photographs with which I begin to compare *Plan*. By moving back to hold the whole canvas within my view so that I can see how the marks coalesce into the bounded shape I look for as standing for the human figure in the conventions of Western painting, I have to forfeit the tactile pleasure of an imaginary application of marks to the surface of *Plan*, the memory of my own body in contact with a canvas. But I can move in and back again at will. (Rowley 1996: 92)

Sight, informed by knowledge and bodily memory of touch making what is seen; movement between proximity and distance; identification with the woman painter; identification of a body sexed female in representation; these are experienced as moments of pleasure. I detect a hint of a more ambivalent consideration of the representation in relation with other representations in the memory.

In a long and complexly layered essay, Rowley compares Saville's technical choices (in particular, handling of paint, viscosity of paint, size of canvas and figure-ground scale) with those of Helen Frankenthaler and Dorothea Tanning. This is done against a background of analysing of the context into which Saville's work was placed, and how she was represented by newspaper critics at the time of her 1994 Saatchi Collection exhibition, when she was compared with Lucien Freud, with any feminist intent at best acknowledged and then ignored. Colour and (interestingly, in relation to Joan Key's article) 'sensitivity to the quality of canvas as material ground' (Rowley 1996: 102) are noted as spatial devices in Frankenthaler's work, and as being under-utilised in Saville's. Rowley quotes Hubert Damisch on the image in a painting being characterised 'by a surplus of *substance*, from which would come its weight, its charge, its title of painting, and which would produce, under that title, an effect of pleasure specific to it' (Rowley 1996: 103). This leads to an identification of a problem with Saville's work: her 'reliance on paint to simulate flesh produces, like all simulations, a sure, disappointing and wearying foregrounding of its falling short of that which it attempts to simulate. This is surplus paint, and highly unpleasurable' (Rowley 1996: 106).

In Rowley's essay Freud's work is evoked as highly problematic, but not given the close reading afforded Saville, Frankenthaler, Tanning or Spence.

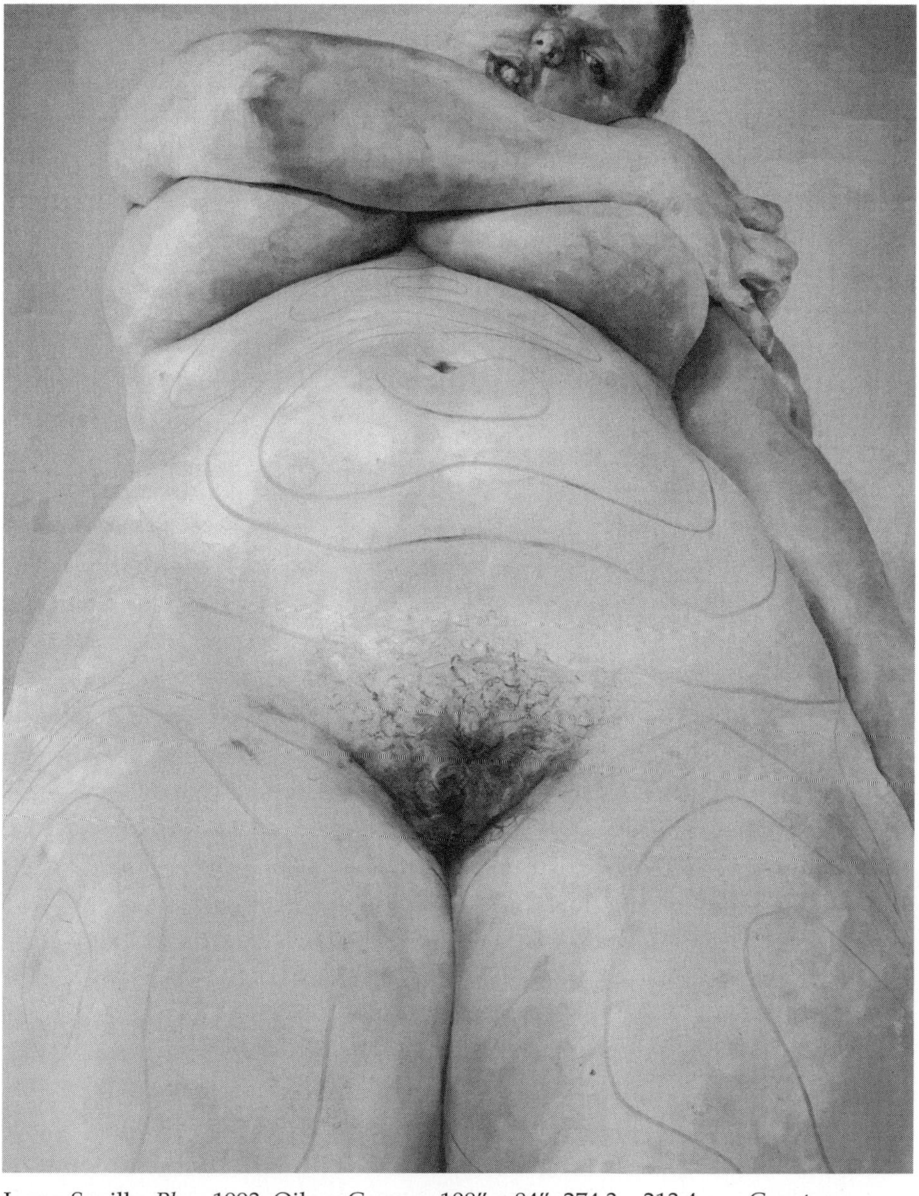

Jenny Saville, *Plan*: 1993. Oil on Canvas, 108" x 84"; 274.3 x 213.4 cm. Courtesy Gagosian Gallery.

While this could be greeted with relief, its absence means that certain possibilities in Saville's painting could be missed. I am trying to create from memory an imagined space for an encounter between works by the two. What I find is a number of instructive differences between the two, both at the level of technical procedures and of configuration of imagery. Few of Freud's paintings are as large as many of Saville's; the figures imaged in them are not only thus relatively smaller, but in addition the relation of the scale of the figures to the size of the canvas is usually more conventional: they 'fit' into the picture. In terms of figure-ground relation, they are more bounded. Their object-like status is increased by the view-points most often used by Freud, higher than the seated or lying person, and at a distance from a standing person. In Saville's work we are frequently given a view-point of the figures whereby we are looking up at them, and from a position of closeness. Thus we are invited into an intimate relation with their flesh, both by the scale of the figures (and the potential 'loss' of the boundaries that Rowley suggests) and by the way the scale of the figures butts up against the size of the canvas: they fill and exceed the field of vision in the painting, thus provoking memory of a necessary closeness in order to make sense of the image. Even when we are at a distance from the canvas, beyond touching distance, the memory is of being within touching distance: a memory indicated by Irigaray as crucial to intersubjectivity: 'The memory of touching? The most insistent and the most difficult to enter into memory. The one that entails returning to dues whose beginning and end cannot be recovered' (Irigaray 1984: 197–198. Translation modified; 1993d: 215).

It would be hard to reproduce in front of a Freud painting the 'loss' of mastery of the figure that Rowley described when close to the Saville painting, or the 'memory of flesh [...] which has not yet been born into language' evoked by Irigaray (Irigaray 1984: 197–198; 1993d: 215). Freud's paint work (particularly in his painting of skin) may look creamy from any distance, but it is also usually shiny, with a hard, repulsing surface, giving us phallomorphic closure and rigidity in the shiny paint surface. In his painting of limbs and bodies, large brush strokes (though usually small on the face) while 'moulded' in effect, often appear to work against the architecture of skin, muscle and bone. It is an activity which I read as displaying a fear or hatred of, or revulsion from, flesh, and which certainly resists intersubjectivity or any mediation of the other's subjectivity. In that close-up activity of painting, I extrapolate Freud interrogating his models visually, delineating the object on canvas – the over-production of the object at the expense of subjectivity identified in the last chapter. As Irigaray asks, 'is the memory of touching always disguised by senses that forget where they come from? Creating distance through a mastery that constitutes the object as a monument built in place of the subject's disappearance' (Irigaray 1984: 197; 1993d: 214–215).

Saville's paint work differs. Her paint has a matt, but not 'dry', surface; her brush is not large, nor are her brush strokes; and in relation to the scale of the figures imaged, both brush and strokes could be considered very small. When close up to the canvas, she is not delineating the object; its borders are not in her visual control. She is, through a series of touches, building the image: multiple tiny touches and strokes touch upon touch upon touch to think and image flesh. From Rowley's account, we can imagine the patience with which she does this, 'urging it to unfold without a show of force' (Irigaray 1984: 197; 1993d: 214–215). There is also, as Rowley indicates, an identification between Saville and the body she is painting, whether as self-portrait or not: the image of the woman she paints can thus never fully be her object.

While I agree that simulation of flesh is problematic and can easily fall back into a maintenance mimesis, I think something else is happening here, something akin to love, which it is important not to miss. Rowley quotes Saville as saying 'I'm not painting disgusting, big women. I'm painting women who've *been made to think* they're big and disgusting, who imagine their thighs go on forever…I haven't had liposuction myself but I did fall for that body wrap thing where they promise four inches off or your money back' (my italics). Rowley then wonders 'Does Saville, then, worry about her own size?' (Rowley 1996: 95). But Saville's comment was in the past tense, not the present: I read her act in painting as she does as a gesture of attending to the interrelation of subjectivity and body, and of restoring touch to sight, through the mediation of paint. Rather than being 'surplus paint, and highly unpleasurable' or using paint as a 'modelling material' in simulating flesh (more likely to be found in a Freud painting), Saville is restoring beauty to that *which has been regarded* as surplus substance[7] by returning through the imaging of that body and that subjectivity; making a gift-space/object necessary for intersubjectivity and for mediation between women. Once again, there is a non-phallic morpho-logic at play between the technical applying of the paint and the deferral between the surplus substance of the paint and the surplus substance of the image, which pivots upon the qualities that Saville has required of the paint and the countless touchings.

What these two articles by Key and Rowley achieve is to alert us not only to practices of using the materiality of fluid media as artists, but also practices of attending to the implications of this materiality as an audience. Irigaray wrote in an early work 'now if we examine the properties of fluids, we note that this "real" may well include, and in large measure, a *physical reality* that continues to resist adequate symbolisation and/or that signifies the powerlessness of logic to incorporate in its writing all the characteristic features of nature' (Irigaray 1977a: 105; 1985d: 106–107). As we have seen, this has developed into the suggestion that we need to think through the mucus – not only to 'think it through' as a political and theoretical necessity, but also to 'think through it' as a means of achieving an appropriate syntax and the possibility of mediation in intersubjective relationships. Key and Rowley evoke what we could refer to as the hysterical reserve of the Whiteread sculpture, the *parure* of the Riley painting and the touching-upon within Saville's painting. Further, we can read the two writers as alerting us to a particular morpho-logic at play and beginning to be productive of its Symbolic syntax. It is a morpho-logic which is discernible in the *différance* between the technologies selected and the imagery produced; in the traces (implicated in this *différance*) of the material fluidity of cloth and of the plaster and paint; and in the gaps between the three artworks and the two essays. It is discernible also through attempting to develop a practice of thinking through it: attending to the possibility of mediation through the morphology of the mucus and 'the lips'.

# 4

# Gesture

## GESTURAL PROCESSES

In her essay 'Gesture in Psychoanalysis' (Irigaray 1987e, 1993g), Irigaray explores the gestures commonly found in the psychoanalytic scenario (the encounter between analysand and analyst) and the gestures that informed some of Sigmund Freud's crucial thinking. In her approach to this and her analysis she provides us with an opportunity to rethink the concept of 'gesture' as it is used with reference to modern and contemporary art. Doing so produces new possibilities for understanding gesture as it is embodied in the artwork, remaining as a trace of the artist's engagement with materials in the processes of making the work. This comes from her attention to gesture as a way of thinking about the relation between the psychic subject, the sexed subject and a practice.

In the essay Irigaray explores two sites of gesture from her experience (as a practising psychoanalyist) of the psychoanalytic scenario: the gestures which are particular to that scenario, and gestures which originate beyond it, but which she has uncovered within and through it. She begins her paper with a long discussion of the gestures and gender-specific experiences of the classic analytic scenario and their significations. Irigaray exposes how, in the arrangement of the scene, the gestures involved are as dramatic as any (Irigaray 1987e: 107; 1993g: 93). This is a situation where gesture is ostensibly repressed and neutered in favour of speech. In this practice as it was developed by Freud the analysand, who was usually a woman, lies down. The analyst sits behind the analysand, out of her sight. These gestures are decidedly not neutral in their implications – the laying down of a person, usually a woman, by a man who then assumes a position sitting where he will be unseen by her. This has the effect both of disrupting social etiquette, and of betraying a socially gendered norm of power and voyeurism by confirming phallocular patterns: he will be able to see that she does not have it. Irigaray wonders if this is generally considered to be an a-sexual, neutral or neuter practice in part because the analysand is infantalised through it or reduced to what she calls 'childedness [*l'enfantinage*]' – a term she has coined. As she points out, the noun 'child' is neuter in Freud's language, German: 'already the child is considered to be neuter or neutered before he or she begins to speak! What a loss of freedom in the imaginary, the symbolic, the gestural!' (Irigaray 1987e: 108. Translation modified; 1993g: 94). Apart from being a tragedy for the development of children's subjectivities, this marks a failure of Freud's, and a failure within subsequent Freudian psychoanalytic practices.[1]

Irigaray's original contention that the analytic scenario is a gendered experience readable through body language is then expanded when she points out the gestural sex-specificity in 'the scene that, according to Freud, marks the entry into the symbolic order' (Irigaray 1987e; 1993g: 95). In *This Sex* she had already stated, in relation to a syntax appropriate to women, that 'I think the place where it or she could best be deciphered is in the gestural code [*gestualité*] of women's bodies' (Irigaray 1977a: 132; 1985d: 134). Here she draws upon gestures from beyond the analytic scenario but which contiue to have implications within it. This crucial scene observed by Freud was that of his grandson, Ernst, playing with a cotton reel and string. Ernst's gestures in this game were interpreted by Freud, says Irigaray, as 'an action designed to master' the absence of his (Ernst's) mother (Irigaray 1987e: 110; 1993g: 96). Much of Irigaray's argument in 'Gesture in Psychoanalysis', in counterdistinction, derives from her exploration and understanding of the daughter / mother relation, of the specificity of the daughter's relation to the absence of her mother, and in particular from her insight into the ways in which the little girl comes to terms with the trauma of experiencing her mother's absence. Most pertinently, Irigaray indicates how this is mediated through the syntax of the girl's gestural codes.

Little Ernst's game was one of repeatedly throwing the reel away (into his mother's bed), then retrieving it with the string, accompanying this with noises that Freud interpreted as 'fort' and 'da' – 'far' and 'near'. Irigaray stresses that Ernst is a boy, and that nowhere does Freud question the gender specificity of the event, or suggest that a girl might act in the same way.[2] If we refuse to consider children as gender-neutral, then the responses of girls to the absence of their mothers must merit some separate attention, and there are significant reasons for doing this:

> My hypothesis is that it couldn't have been a girl. Why? A girl does not make the same gestures when her mother goes away. She does not play with a string [*un fil*] and a reel symbolizing her mother, because her mother is of the same sex as she is and cannot have the object status of a reel. The mother is of the same subjective identity as she is. (Irigaray 1987e: 111–112. Translation modified; 1993g: 97)

Here, the deliberate play on the word '*fil*', the plural of which ('*fils*') also means 'son', reminds the reader to consider again the 'double syntax' of the Symbolic and the morphology informing both the gestures of little Ernst and Freud's reading of them. The little girl doesn't have to create her mother as 'other of her same' and as her object in order to understand her relationship to origin or to attain her subjectivity. She will not have to accommodate difference as well as loss.

Irigaray indicates three significant reactions from a little girl when she misses her mother. Firstly, 'she throws herself down on the ground in distress, she is lost, she loses the power and the will to live, she neither speaks nor eats, totally anorexic' (Irigaray 1987e: 112; 1993g: 97). As the little girl and her mother are 'of the same subjective identity', when they are parted the little girl loses a transcendental model for her subjectivity. This is unlike the little boy, who instead has to come to a realisation of himself (or achieve a sense of his subjectivity in separation) as differing from the subjective identity of his mother. Thus the little boy may try to 'master' his mother's absence by symbolising her as an object – in the instance of little Ernst, with a reel. The little girl, however – who has no reason to think of her mother in terms of subjective difference, and who has therefore lost part of 'her' subjectivity – is bereaved. She begins to show symptoms of hysteria. Irigaray elsewhere made a closely related link between the hysteric and her loss of her mother as a subject, when she referred to this moment of desire in the hysteric for her mother as an aspect of the hysteric's reserve: 'Yet there is a revolutionary potential in hysteria. Even in her paralysis, the hysteric exhibits a potential for gestures and desires. A movement of revolt and refusal, a desire for/of the living mother who would be more than a reproductive body in the pay of the polis, a living, loving woman' (Irigaray 1991f: 47–48).

The second reaction of a girl who is missing her mother, Irigaray tells us, is that:

> She plays with a doll, lavishing maternal affection on a quasi subject, which allows her to organize a kind of symbolic space; playing with dolls is not simply a game girls are forced to play, it also signifies a difference in subjective status in the separation from the mother. For them, the mother is a subject that cannot

easily be reduced to an object, and a doll is not an object in the way that a reel, a toy car, a gun, etc., are objects and tools used for symbolization. (Irigaray 1987e: 112. Translation modified; 1993g: 97)

So if the mother cannot be symbolised as an object (such as the reel) by the little girl, then she has to be symbolised differently: with the quasi-subject of the doll (and dolls are overwhelmingly girl-dolls made for girls to play with).

This suggestively aids our perception of what is at stake in the ways some women approach the making of their artworks. The possibilities for different understandings of this process lie in the girl's organisation of 'a kind of symbolic space', the 'subjective status' of the relationship which leads to play, and the fact that the thing played with 'is not an object' in the way that the boy's toys are. The doll is not in an 'either/or' relation to objecthood, so we might instead consider it as a non-capitalised object for the little girl who is playing with it. This also echoes the earlier indication of the need for women to develop the gift-space/object as a means of mediating their subjectivity to themselves and to others. In this image of the little girl and her doll, Irigaray is offering an approach where process can be stressed without process in and of itself being the meaning; where the importance of the art object as object is fundamentally compromised; and with it the notion of mastery. Instead, this approach favours a perception of the artwork as a non-capitalised space/object of mediation for the subject.[3] This insight concerning the little girl and her doll is one Irigaray gained from psychoanalysing women. It pertains to a practice which is pivotal in the engendering of an 'appropriate' femininity in girls, but which 'is not simply a game girls are forced to play': it also reflects and makes manifest the girl's psychic accommodation of the absence of her mother through gestural codes in body and imaginative space. As the little girl plays with the doll, she gains comfort; through repetition, the play gains signification: it produces signifiers of the little girl's subjective identity and the means of possible mediation for that subjectivity.

Thus through the structure in Irigaray's argument we can propose for the subjects, women, a potential relation to the artworks they make that is both gendered and yet variable among women. It is a relation which could be manifested materially in particular practices. The practices of play (their processes and effects) are embedded in and understandable through social practices. Thus the embodiment of such practices of play in art practices may well be discernible, but this is by no means inevitable. This is a reading which might, therefore, be appropriate for practices of some women which sit uneasily in current discourses of the art object, yet it is a reading which also resists any simplistic collapse back into an essentialist discourse. It is an insight, moreover, through which we can begin to account for the desire of many women artists to work with representations of the female body or 'bodiliness', if you like; an understanding which would refute charges of narcissism, and instead attend to the gift-space/object, a non-capitalised symbolisation which is of the same subjective identity as the artist.

## PERFORMATIVITY

A third way in which girls cope with the absence of the mother is through dance, and in particular a whirling or spinning dance. Irigaray focuses on the gestures of the girl's dance:

> She dances and thus makes for herself a vital subjective space open to the cosmic maternal world, to the gods, to the present other. This dance is also a way to create for herself a territory of her own in relation to the mother. […]
>
> Among women, the relationship to sameness and to the mother is not mastered by the *fort-da*. The mother always remains too familiar and too close. In a way, the daughter has her mother under her skin, secreted in the dampness of the mucous membranes, in the most intimate of intimacies, in the mystery of her relationship to gestation, to birth, and to her sexual identity. Furthermore, the basic sexual movement of the female is linked more to gyration than to the gestures of throwing and pulling back of little Ernst. The girl then tries to reproduce around and within her an energetic circular movement that protects her from dereliction, immediate breaking into, depression, loss of self. Spinning round is also, but in my opinion secondarily, a way of attracting [*séduire*]. The girl describes a circle while calling and refusing access to her territory. She plays with this gestural territory and its limit. There is no object here, in the strict meaning of the word, no other that has had to be introjected or incorporated. On the contrary, girls and women often set up a defensive territory that can then become creative, especially in analysis. (Irigaray 1987e: 112. Translation modified; 1993g: 97–98)

Here, Irigaray opens an analytic site through which we can account for some performative aspects of women's art practices – actual making and doing, gestures in the studio, the physical negotiation of the work by artist and viewer alike.

It is important at this point not to collapse the term 'performative' back solely into the category of 'performance art' as it might be commonly understood in a visual art context, though it is of course useful in analysing such practices. An understanding of a woman performance artist 'calling and refusing access to her territory', a territory she has described with her body, could well begin to account for the resistant position many women performers feel themselves to be in with regard to the male gaze. For example, Carolee Schneemann wrote in 1968 that in the absence of further discourse she had been labelled as 'an image, but not an Image-Maker, creating my own self-image', and that 'the life of the body is more *variously* expressive than a sex-negative society can admit. I didn't stand naked in front of 300 people because I wanted to be fucked, but because my sex and work were harmoniously experienced I could have the audacity, or courage, to show the body as a source of varying emotive Power' (Schneemann, in Lippard 1990: 103). However, it is more productive to remember that the performativity of the gesture of the little girl, as Irigaray describes it, has a function as particular to her as Ernst's was to him: the production of subjectivity in the face of the traumatic absence of her mother – who is of the same subjective identity. The gestural process of the spinning dance is a struggle for a life, one of signification. The subjectivity of the little girl is developed through her performativity, including that of bodily gestures that can develop signification and legibility in the Symbolic – an example of a developing legibility in an appropriate syntax.

Feminist cultural theory has concentrated much energy upon analysing how both the body and image of woman is structured as object of the (male) gaze. This can be found in strands of feminism as diverse as, on the one hand, the anti-pornography movement, in its activist form (Dworkin 1981); and on the other hand, psychoanalytic film theory, particularly the line of enquiry engendered by the highly influential paper by Laura Mulvey (Mulvey 1975). Feminist art practice across different media has often incorporated an exposure of, or resistance to, a voyeuristic and phallocentric gaze at the image of a woman, and attempted to construct non-phallocentric ways of looking at women.[4] In 'calling and refusing access to her territory', the stress is on the creation and assertion of the territory: her subjectivity as signified in an appropriate Symbolic syntax that involves the spatialisation of female subjectivity and its desire for and distance from the mother. The work of Jo Spence is just one example: not only is such resistance and reconstruction visible in her photographic work, but she has also charted her struggle towards it in her writings. Her visual works include *Mother and Daughter Shame Work: Crossing Class Boundaries* (with Valerie Walkerdine; 1988); *Mother and Daughter Work: Saying Goodbye to my Introjected Mother* (with David Roberts; 1988) and a large number of works with Rosy Martin, such as *My Mother* (1985). Of this last collaborative photographic partnership with Martin, Spence wrote:

> I feel I am no longer an onlooker or critic of patriarchal theory, but have become a participant within developing aspects of feminism in relation to the theory and practice of psychotherapy … Out of the broken pieces of the self will come a subjectivity that acknowledges both the fragmentation process and the 'part work', but which encompasses and embraces such parts and allows them to have a dialogue with each other. (Spence 1995: 155)

The way we understand the word 'gesture' is also crucial. Irigaray associates it with the idea of being in some way performed (whether that performance is the reason for the gesture's being, or whether the performance of the gesture is considered pragmatic, or a means to an end). This is a specific usage through which we can assess the gestures of women artists in their studios, certain gestural structures they build into their work, their approach to the spaces in which their work is made public, and the manner in which it is made public. In short, it suggests a space for analysis of *what, where and how* the performative gestures of women artists *are* in their practices. As I resisted above a reductive reading of 'the performative' as performance art, so too 'gestural' should be read as literally 'of the gesture' in the manner in which Irigaray charts the gestures of lying or sitting in the analytic scenario, and emphatically *not* reduced to its traditional usage in art criticism in relation to, for instance, Abstract Expressionism. This particular distinction is crucial, given the naming and over-determination of a particular form of gesture within the area of visual art discourse, and how it is redolent of patriarchy, modernism and genius.[5]

Griselda Pollock has analysed Abstract Expressionism as:

> … a form of painting that specifically staged a kind of primal gesturing, an intentionally informal relation between the body of the painter and the things with which the painter works to create a trace of being in that body by its movements in space – both literal and mapped on canvas. If, at a certain level, abstract painting took to its logical conclusion, as Greenberg argued, the fundamentals of the activity – paint, a surface, and, add from Rosenberg, an active, but also acting painter – we have the gesture as the articulating sign of that process we call subjectivity. (Pollock 1996b: 256)

This identifies the role of gesture granted by Abstract Expressionism. However, it is the morphological structure through which these moments in the process relate to each other which differentiates their manifestation in Abstract Expressionism and their potentialities if understood through Irigaray's work. Pollock again:

> Abstract Expressionism is a celebration of the 'expressivity' of a self which is not to be constrained by expressing anything in particular except the engagement

> of the artistic self with the processes and procedures of painting. Thus 'painting' is privileged in modernist discourse as *the* most ambitious and significant art form because of its combination of gesture and trace, which secure by metonymy the presence of the artist. These inscribe a subjectivity whose value is, by visual inference and cultural naming, masculinity. (Pollock 1996b: 142)

Here Pollock exposes the phallic morphologic at work within the critical discourses of Abstract Expressionism. A clear hierarchy of practices is set up by these discourses. A concept of 'painting' is the most privileged by them, and is constructed as a metonymic trace of the artist, who is then valorised for his mastery of the medium. Thus, readings are produced wherein the medium does nothing but get mastered. This mastery by a (male) subject is all it mediates, and indeed is read as the artist's 'I am'. The gestural traces in the medium are capitalised by these discourses; the finished paintings are capitalised; the artist is capitalised for (as Irigaray might put it) 'creating distance through a mastery that constitutes the object as a monument built in place of the subject's disappearance' (Irigaray 1984: 197; 1993d: 214–215). Irigaray describes a different process of entering language for girls: 'Girls do not enter language in the same ways as boys. [...] They enter language by producing a space, a path, a river, a dance and rhythm, a song... Girls describe a space around themselves rather than displacing a substitute object from one place to another or into various places' (Irigaray 1987e: 113; 1993g: 99).

Any approach to painting as mediation in a process of intersubjectivity – a co-creation of a signification through gestural practices between a subject artist and a subject attentive audience – would not be recognised by the phallic morphologic which informs the presently dominant critical structures of Abstract Expressionism.

## LOUISE BOURGEOIS'S *CELLS*

If the loss of the mother leads girls to a distinct relation with the thing that signifies the mother in her absence, covering or displacing the fear of her loss; if it leads them to particular delineation and definition of space – space which is both a defensive space which speaks of the experience of loss, and a display at the same time; and if this is articulated through gestures which are gendered, sexualised even, an enunciation which invests in process rather than object through which to construct its syntax – then I think we have a set of concepts which can facilitate a developing analysis of aspects of Louise Bourgeois's practice. We have to return to Bourgeois's relation to her mother.

For the 45th Venice Biennale (1993) the USA selected the French-born artist Louise Bourgeois as their representative. An exhibition was mounted in the US pavilion consisting of 13 sculptures, dating from 1984–1993. Four of these were large works each given the title *Cell*, with further individual titling supplied in brackets: *Cell (Eyes and Mirrors)* (1989–1993); *Cell (Choisy)* (1990–1993); *Cell (Glass Spheres and Hands)* (1990–1993); and *Cell (Arch of Hysteria)* (1992–1993). The catalogue for an expanded version of the exhibition held at the Brooklyn Museum in 1994 also included *Cell II* (1991); *Cell III* (1991); *Cell IV* (1991) (plate 18); *Cell (You Better Grow Up)* (1993); *Cell (Three White Marble Spheres)* (1993) (plate 20). Also documented in the Brooklyn catalogue are *Cell I* (1991); *Cell V* (1991); and the related *Precious Liquids* (1992). Anything between 3′8″ and 14′ wide and between 7′ and 12′ high, the sheer bulk and number of these works, produced when the artist was in her late seventies and eighties, spoke of the importance to her of this development in her work; and indeed she had a continuing interest in this sculptural structure for many years after this exhibition, both with further *Cells* and, through the 1990s, with a series of *Spiders*, also very large, and related in structure. The Venice and Brooklyn exhibitions, however, were the first times that a large number of the *Cells* were brought together.

The *Cells* are best described as creations of interior spaces. They are bounded by 'walls', made from old warehouse window frames, with some of the glass still in place, from steel grilles, from sheet metal, old doors, wooden planking. In the 'walls' are door- or window-type entrances through which the audience can sometimes walk, or sometimes only look. Contained within the walls, various elements, found or made by the artist, are placed in juxtaposition. The objects inside vary widely: old furniture, mirrors and objects seemingly scavenged from waste sites – an industrial saw, bottles, a desk-guillotine. There are glass spheres and phials, and marble sculptures with a mix of rough-hewn stone and highly polished, smooth, exact finish. The details fascinate, yet none seems superfluous. The spaces pull the gaze into and around them; the 'walls' both cage and house their contents.

Richard Serra is quoted in the Brooklyn catalogue: 'the meaning [of the works] evades me: discursive analysis, conceptual terms fail. All tracking leads to dead ends. Imposition of formal logic and conjectures of academic language do not resolve the content' (Eckman 1994: 80). The *Cells* do not fit into any categories of art, even the broadest: they resist terms of figuration or abstraction, modernism or post-modernism. In this categorisational void in the discourses around the work has been inserted the biography of the artist. Since the early 1980s, criticism has constructed, theorised and made famous a 'Louise Bourgeois' who makes work stemming from her feelings about her father (Storr 1995: 29). In our eagerness to hear another version of the Freudian 'family romance'[6] – in this case, a charming, philandering, autocratic and ultimately intolerable father, whose mistress is not only the daughter's nanny and governess, but is also moved by the father for a number of years into the marital home – it becomes easy to focus on the daughter-to-father emotion; the anger, the desolation of the daughter, the young Bourgeois. It becomes manifest in the work. Indeed, at times, it is explicitly of great importance. Bourgeois herself helps us focus on this through her own words, providing a moving, at times devastating account of her autobiography – 'My father betrayed me by not being what he was supposed to be... It is just a matter of rules of the game, and in a family the rules of the game are such that a minimum of conformity is expected' (Meyer-Thoss 1992: 182). 'My father provoked in me a continual loss of self-esteem' (Meyer-Thoss 1992: 187).

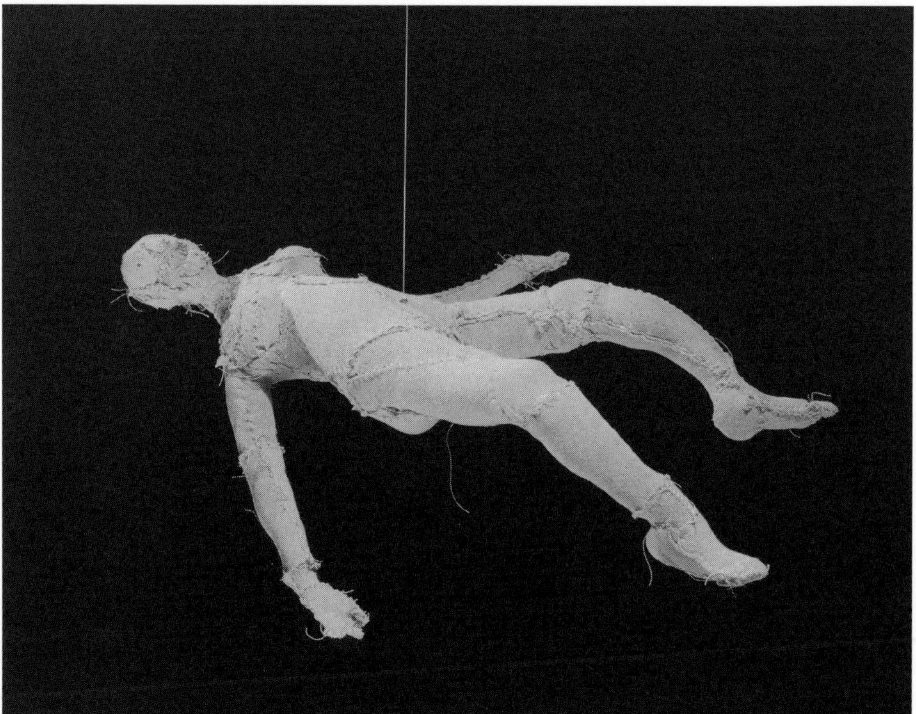

Louise Bourgeois, *Arch of Hysteria*: 2000. Hanging Piece: Pink Fabric 5 " x 17" x 11"; 13.9 x 44.4 x 27.9 cm. Courtesy Karsten Greve, St Moritz. Photo: Christopher Burke.

She has also stated that when her mother died, her father ridiculed her grief (Wye 1994: 18).

But this dysfunctional father–daughter relationship has functioned as a 'suitable' subject for critical voyeurism. In the literature on Bourgeois it is the lack of discussion of her relationship with her mother that becomes apparent. Donald Kuspit, however, does develop an argument about the importance of Bourgeois's mother:

> Bourgeois's entanglement with her mother, not her father, is becoming clear as the inner content of her work. She has filled the void of mother/artist in spirit as well as substance, an Oedipus replacing the mother instead of the father, a sphinx whose secret is that a story about a relationship to a father is really a story about a relationship to a mother. (Kuspit 1987: 121)

This is the conclusion, rather than the starting point, of his article, and is a theme which has not been taken up by anyone else. Maybe a girl's relation with her mother is seen as having less potential for scandal and tragedy, less glamour, and less scope for critical voyeurism; or maybe it is a relationship which remains largely unvalued because, as Irigaray argues, it is unseen in women's gestures (Irigaray 1977a: 132; 1985d: 134).

Bourgeois herself, however, gives us plenty of prompting to take her relationship with her mother seriously. To give just three examples:

> These titles are informative. 'Blind Vigils' is like 'Blind leading the Blind'. Blindness came from the blush I experienced at the side of the people around me, everybody. As I say, my father was promiscuous. I had to be blind to the mistress who lived with us. I had to be blind to the pain of my mother. (Kirili 1986: 71)

> When I was afraid of my mother dying, a challenge I could not meet, the warding off of her death, not to let her disappear, I made a vow. I swore to myself, if my mother survived that morning I would give up sex. (Meyer-Thoss 1992: 187)

> The material was there taking all that room and bothering me, bothering me by its aggressive presence. And somehow the idea of the mother came to me, This is the way my mother impressed me, as very powerful, very silent, very judging, and controlling the whole studio. And naturally this piece became my mother. At that point, I had my subject. I was going to express what I felt toward her… First I cut off her head, and I slit her throat… And after weeks and weeks of work, I thought, if this is the way I saw my mother, then she did not like me. How could she possibly like me if I treat her that way? At that point something turned around. I could not stand the idea that she wouldn't

> like me. I couldn't live if I thought that she didn't like me. The fact that I had pushed her around, cut off her head, had nothing to do with it. What you do to a person has nothing to do with what you expect the person to feel toward you… Now at the end I became very, very depressed, terribly terribly depressed. (Nixon 1995: 87)[7]

I find it interesting that Bourgeois's comments have surfaced in recent years, and I would like to link them to a strand in her work which, although it can be traced back, has also emerged in a particularly notable manner over the past decade in the *Cell* works and other related pieces. In these we can find Bourgeois's embodiment, through particular manipulation of space through materials, of an earlier interest (manifested in a more straightforwardly representational manner) in the spiral and circling movement. We also find a blurring of subject/object relations: the *Cells* are not easily containable 'art objects' as such, and neither are the 'objects' comprising them clear in their object status to either the attentive audience or to Bourgeois herself. However, in order to make any tracing between Bourgeois's work and her comments on her mother, it is necessary to problematise the 'Freudian family romance' provided in the present critical analysis. Constructing this 'romance' through the father–daughter relationship alone is clearly insufficient for the structure of the Bourgeois household from little Louise's viewpoint. It is arguable whether the Oedipal son/mother relation can simply be reversed to 'fit' a daughter/father relation; and it is apparent that the relationship of little Louise with the displaced Mme Bourgeois is crucial. My aim, however, is not to displace the father with the mother in this particular family romance. Nor do I wish to read the works for metaphors of the relationship between mother and daughter, its events and emotions. Such an approach would close the work down, restrict its meaning and significance to being simply a form of therapy for the artist. Instead I wish to move away from the specificity of that to try to make legible the processes and methods – the very gestures at play in the making of the work.

## LOUISE BOURGEOIS'S GESTURES

Coming to terms with the trauma of her mother's loss is part of the structure of separation for the little girl. In 'Gesture in Psychoanalysis', Irigaray is not referring to particularly notable or extreme case studies; rather she is attending to a structure of inevitable separation. Bourgeois would have experienced such loss, as have all daughters. But for the little Louise the trauma of losing her mother would have been drawn out: Madame Bourgeois was displaced from her position as mother within the family as a result of her husband's introduction of his mistress into the house. She no longer had a structural position in her family which was clear and comprehensible to little Louise. There was also no longer clarity in the structural 'mother'/daughter relationship, as the mistress was also tutor to the girl, *in loco parentis* in more ways than one. Madame Bourgeois was still physically present; but her position *as mother* was displaced; the nature of her presence spoke of her loss of position of 'mother'. It is this removal, this loss, that caused such pain, anger and anxiety in her daughter. The anger is expressed towards her father for doing what he did; and towards her mother for not being all she should have been. It is notable that in this story the father's position as patriarch of the family remains intact: in this respect he was still structurally what he should have been, although personally flawed and unethical in his relationships with these three women.

Bourgeois has frequently referred to her life history as the cause of her impulse to work. For example, Deborah Wye quotes her as saying of some earlier works that they 'had nothing to do with sculpture, they meant physical presences. That was an attempt at not only re-creating the past, but controlling it' (Wye 1982: 19). While her biography, as indicated above, has been repeated many times by critics, it remains of necessity a fairly perfunctory literary exercise that can confound as much as it can aid any legibility to the works. There is no overt narrative content to the works, and in the attempt, detective-style, to seek one or impose one – whether it is one drawn from the words of the artist or from those who speak about her work – we are in severe danger of forgetting that the significance of all art forms and artworks is not reducible to any singular overt narrative. On the other hand, as this present text is arguing, the specificity and subjectivity of the artist has to be respected. Drawing upon the insights offered by Irigaray, I would like to propose that the period starting in the early 1990s during which Bourgeois has been articulating in interviews the intensities and complexities of her feelings towards her mother, has also been the period in which she has articulated this relationship through her work. Further, if we identify a correspondent morpho-logic informing the gestural practices of the little girl traumatised by the loss of her mother, and the gestural practices embodied in Bourgeois's *Cells*, then we can open a space of mediation between the two which can suggestively enrich our readings of both.

Irigaray indicated that the girl missing her mother will (among other things) organise a symbolic space around herself. She produces a territory through gestures of spinning, sexuate, gender-specific circular movement. This performs three main functions for the girl: it protects her from abandonment, depression, attack, loss of self; it attracts; it refuses access. It is also a process in which there is no clear object – no capitalised object – produced by the subject. The little girl also plays with objects which are of the same subjective identity as herself, and which therefore remain uncapitalised in the significatory syntax constructed through that play. These are precisely the processes I think Bourgeois has performed in making the *Cell* pieces.

Referred to by critics as 'installations' (Morgan 1996: 56), the *Cells* are, however, unusual for installation work as they delineate a self-determined, architectural, material description of the artist's own psychic space, rather than an artist making manifest his or her psychic (or intellectual or aesthetic or whatever) space within the architectural terms provided in a pre-existing environment. The mapping and embodying of space performed by Bourgeois is thus autonomous to a degree not usually found in installation artworks, which tend to be architecturally reactive. The role of the work in protecting the artist from her childhood abandonment and loss of self is apparent from her own statements. Little in the work is reducible to object-status; things in the works are never treated in a manner where they can be identified as symbolic objects, but retain an ambivalent status. Thus, for instance, marble 'sculptures' such as that of the hands on the table in *Cell (Glass Spheres and Hands)* and that of the leg in *Cell III*, referring in both their material and its working to a well-established tradition of object-making, are placed in space or juxtaposed with other materials or things (respectively in these instances, old chairs and stools, and old taps and a table guillotine) in a manner clearly compromising that tradition. Likewise, 'found objects' in the works are not placed to emphasise their surreal nature or their usage as universal symbols, nor to encourage a reading of them as fetish objects; rather they are used as visual material through which an idiosyncratic narrative is being articulated; non-capitalised objects, with which we have to work to create meaning. As Terrie Sultan has written, 'one of the defining characteristics of Bourgeois's work [is] the great care the artist takes to ensure that as viewers we are left to make our own attachments to her forms' (Sultan 1994: 38). We have to read the spaces between, as with the picture-puzzles mentioned above in an earlier chapter:

> pictographs in which the hunter and hunted, and their dramatic relationships, are to be discovered between the branches, made out from between the trees. From the spaces between the figures, or stand-in figures. Spaces that organize the scene, blanks that sub-tend the scene's structuration and that will yet not be read as such. Or not read at all? Not seen at all? Never in truth represented

or representable, though this is not to say that they have no effect upon the present scenography. (Irigaray 1974: 171; 1985c: 137–138)

Viewers are attracted in to the *Cells*, but at the same time kept at bay through Bourgeois's delineation of this, her signifying space. She does this sometimes literally, by making us peer in, while refusing us clear physical or visual access; sometimes she does this through her imagery and the 'spaces that organize the scene', with what can be for the viewer a baffling lack of didacticism for such precisely selected or made things and such rigorously articulated space. As Mieke Bal observes, 'Like abstract signs, the *Cells*, though not at all abstract, refuse to represent. Instead they address. They beckon' (Bal 2001: 112).

But this struggle with legibility is the moment at which an engagement with a gestural syntax as articulated through a morphology appropriate to women can begin to provide us with a site of difference through which to read the work and construct critical discourses around it. The significance of the dimensions of the *Cells* provide one instance for this discourse of difference.

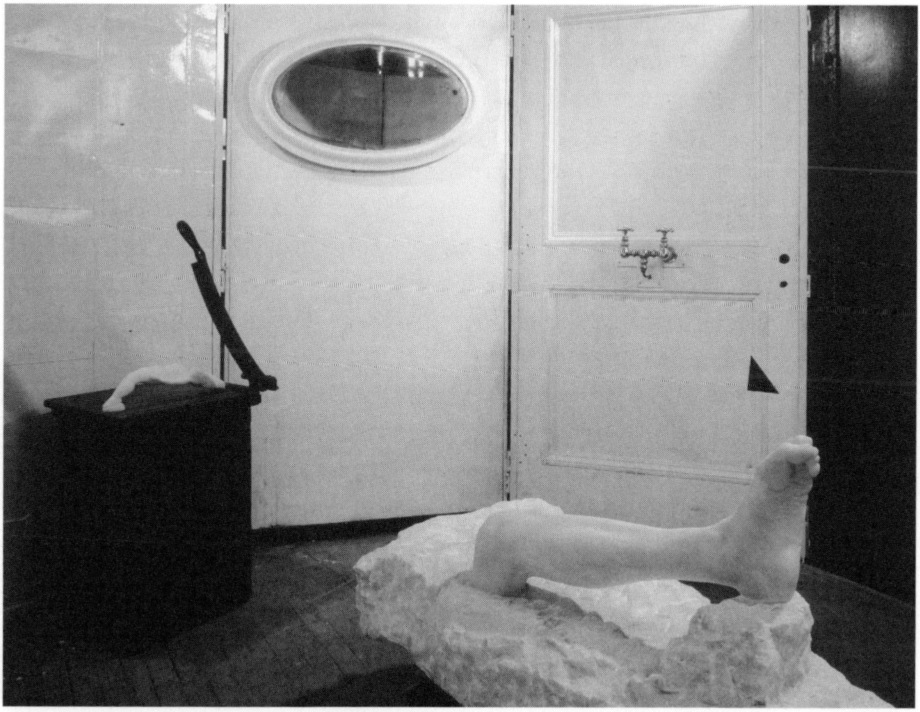

Louis Bourgeois, *Cell III*: 1991. Mixed media. 111″ x 130″ x 165. 1″; 281.9 x 331.4 x 419.4 cm. Collection Ydessa Hendeles Art Foundation, Toronto. Photo: Peter Bellamy.

There is here an engagement with what Irigaray calls 'gestural territory and its limits', and a spatial relationship to the human body. Their generic title, *Cells*, recalls on the one hand cells both of incarceration and of contemplation, with their connotations of spatial relation to body size; and on the other hand, evocations of the cells of the body, and implications of literal incorporation of experience. Bourgeois has said 'since the fears of the past were connected with the functions of the body, they reappear through the body' (Meyer-Thoss 1992: 195). She does indeed produce in these works 'a space, a path, a river, a dance and rhythm, a song'. One can almost imagine her performing the dance that Irigaray has identified, circling or spinning around, arms outstretched, to find the dimensions that are appropriate for each piece – dimensions which will thus vary from piece to piece. The gestural territory will exceed the immediate dimensions of the static body. The artist-subject reaches, turns, steps and twists to establish the appropriate space/object relation, delimitation and articulation through a material signifying practice. As established above, Bourgeois marks out her imaginative space through her working practices and processes, as well as those gestures being evoked in the deployment of materials: hence the articulation of space with signifying 'objects'. The *Cells* (their limits, materials, spaces and 'objects') can thus be read as a gift-space/object mediation by the subject of a process of *différence* between the little girl and the mature woman.

Bourgeois has made many comments about the signification in her work of spiralling, in a manner which resonates with Irigaray's notion of spinning – for instance: 'There are a lot of spirals ... but they are not automatic. The spiral is a vacuum ... It represents something ... the void, the anxiety void, the void of anxiety' (Meyer-Thoss 1992: 72–73). and: 'The spiral is the beginning of movement in space. As opposed to the rigidity of the monolith, the subject is exploring space' (Kirili 1986: 74).

The spiral and the spinning figure can be found as a theme in many works earlier than the *Cells*. There it is in sculptures such as the *Spiral Women* of the late 1940s and early 1950s; *Life Flower I* (1960); *Spiral/Summer* (1960); and *Spiral Woman* (1984). This last has a slate disc of some three foot wide placed on the floor; hanging above it, at about head height, suspended on a wire and able to turn, is a small bronze of a female figure. Her torso and head are surrounded by a thick coil of bronze; her limbs are positioned as if she were twirling round. In the terms of this discussion this appears to be possibly a transitional work, somewhere between on the one hand the earlier projection onto materials of what it is to spin and spiral, as in the earlier, more literal, *Spiral Women*; and on the other hand, in the subsequent *Cell* works, a creation of a symbolic space

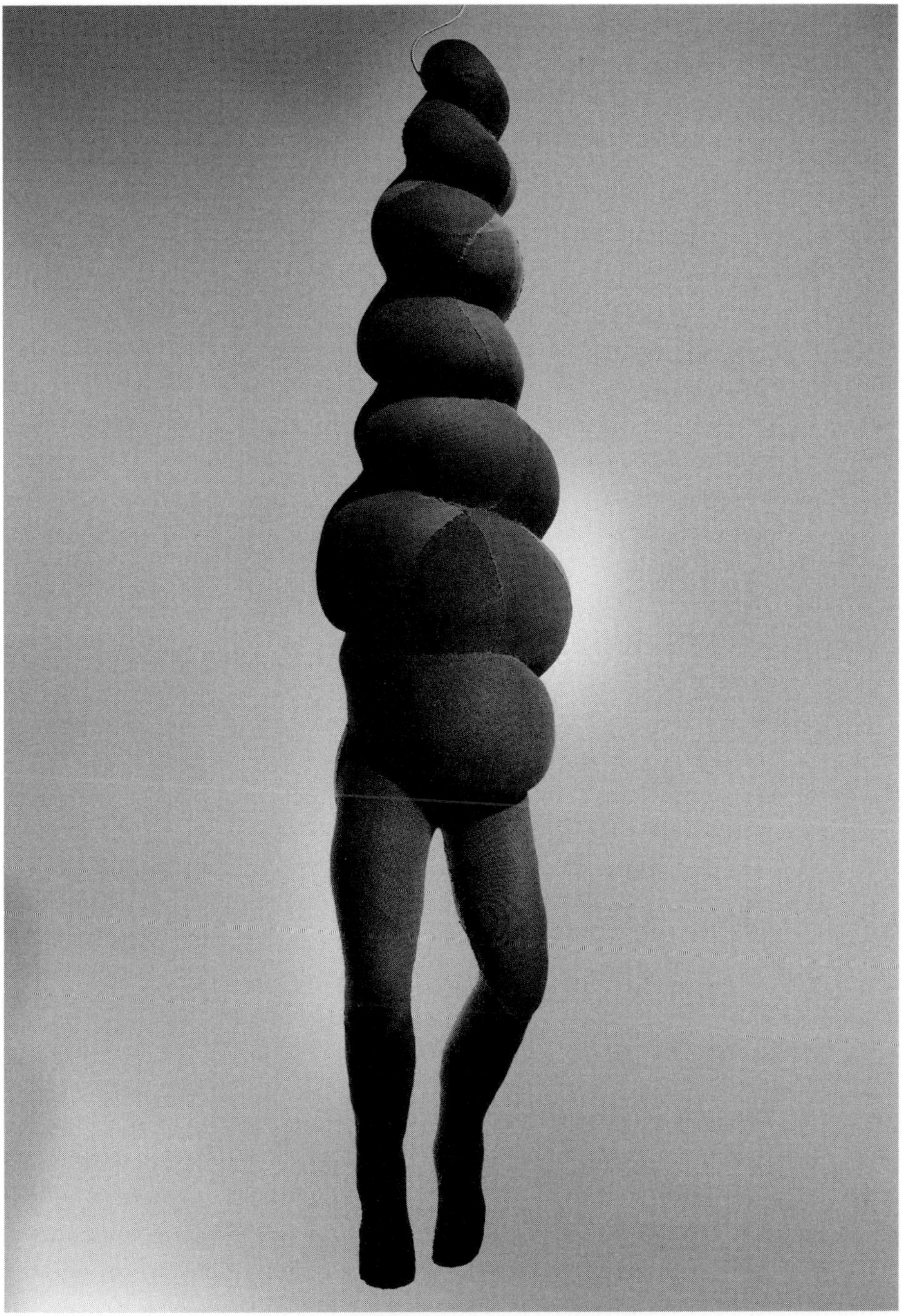

Louise Bourgeois, *Spiral Woman*: 2003. Fabric, hanging piece. 69″ x 14″ x 13″; 175.2 x 35.5 x 34.2 cm. Collection of the Artist, courtesy Cheim & Read, New York Photo: Christopher Burke.

*through the gestural manipulation of materials*, producing a site of mediation for that spinning, its causes and indeed its comforts and pleasures.

Possibly. But the *Spiral Woman* recurs in 2003. This time the work is not bronze, but stitched and stuffed blue fabric, a pair of legs and a round belly morphing into a lumpen twist, and covered with stitched and stretched fabric. This work relates to a shift that started in the *Cells* in the late 1990s, where Bourgeois started introducing women's clothing into the works, for example, *Cell (Clothes)* (1996); *Cell XXV (The View of the World of the Jealous Wife)* (2001). The dresses, blouses and other garments are hung on hangers or on dummies, layered, draped, stuffed and / or stitched. This use of clothing to evoke presences continued outside of the *Cells* in works like *Pink Days and Blue Days* (1997) where a camisole, a coat and other garments are hung from hangers or from ox bones suspended mobile-like from a central steel pole, or *Untitled* (1996) where a padded-out orange house coat has sprung a long tail and is counter-balanced with a hanging bronze double twist.

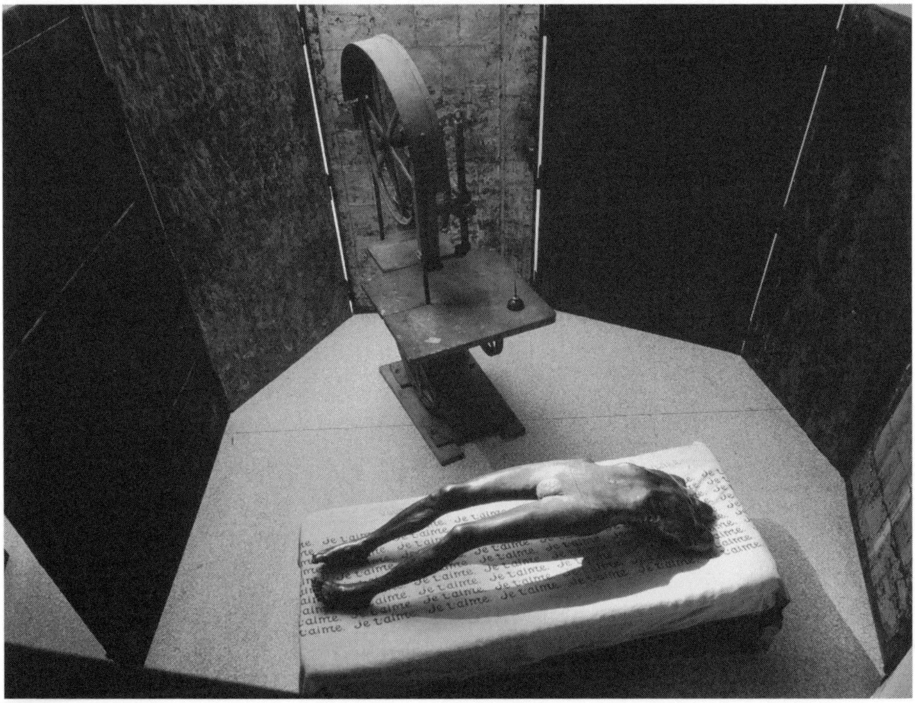


Louise Bourgeois, *Cell (Arch of Hysteria)*: 1992–1993. Steel, bronze, cast iron and fabric. 119" x 145" x 120"; 302.2 x 368.3 x 304.8 cm. Collection Centro Andaluz de Arte Contemporaneo, Seville. Photo: Peter Bellamy.

At the same time that this use of clothing was introduced, so too were constructed stitched and stuffed figures. *Couple II* (1996) shows two copulating torsos, headless, life-sized, made from stitched stuffed dark blue fabric and presented in a glass cabinet. From that date, this method of working has become increasingly prevalent in Bourgeois's work, and was the focus of the exhibition *Louise Bourgeois: Stitches in Time* at the Irish Museum of Modern Art, Dublin, 2003. Usually either life-sized or 6″–18″, sometimes in a cell or in a glass cabinet, these works show figures often embodying extreme states of being. A number revisit earlier themes in Bourgeois's work. *Femme Maison* (2001) is a life-sized female torso in a glass cabinet. Made from off-white, soft fabric, a house is sprouting between her breasts and her pubis. *Femme Couteau* (2002) is a torso in a hessian or heavy linen fabric, with a hinged contraption emerging from her chest with a knife poised, threatening the genitals and belly. *Arch of Hysteria* (2000) is a complete female figure about 18″ long, made from pink fabric very roughly stitched together. The figure is suspended from a wire attached just below the belly button. The arms and legs fall back and downwards, while the head and neck are in a straight line with the spine, eyes wide, mouth open. The related *Arched Figure* (1999) is life-sized, presented in a glass cabinet. This figure has no arms and her head falls back, the legs seem stiff with the toes pointed. A mirror is positioned to show and enlarge the face with its open mouth and closed eyes.

The viewer of these works can experience a wide range of emotions and states – fear, horror, humour, the sublime, ecstasy – while also feeling a disquiet, almost an embarrassment in the encounter. It is instructive to note the contrasts between the works that revisit older themes and their antecedents. The imagery is fundamentally similar. Arched figures, for example, bend backwards, may be missing limbs, may be in cell structures or alone, may be suspended from wires attached near the belly button. But there is a distancing mechanism that helps the viewer retain a certain comfort that is missing with the fabric pieces. The earlier arched figures are generally made of highly finished bronze, a substance and method that connotes a long tradition of figurative sculpture. Even if it can be hard for critics to align Bourgeois's work with particular movements as indicated above, we know we are safely in the realm of Art when looking at her figures in bronze or marble.

Something different happens with the stitched figures. It is not simply that some of them are rawly made, roughly stitched, with threads from the stitching. After all, some of Bourgeois's bronzes show highly finished surfaces next to raw materiality in the original from which the piece was cast, and some of her marble carvings juxtapose highly finished passages of carving with raw stone.

This is an approach that can be traced back though sculptors such as Rodin and Michelangelo. Rather, the disquiet starts with the turn towards fabric and stitching by hand. While the environment for this work, and some if its presentational methods, are strictly within the visual codes for museum-based fine art – the steel and glass cases for example, and certainly the curatorial contexts – the gestures and methods of production of these fabric figures are at the furthest remove from those of high art practices. They are unmistakably gendered and classed, and allude to a particular position in the hierarchy of creative endeavour. The connotations here are not of Art, but of the domestic sphere, of furnishings, of dressmaking, patchwork, make-do-and-mend, of an activity passed from mother to daughter, where rawness tells of skills not yet acquired rather than purely aesthetic choices – where stitching at its highest level is either invisible or decorative. Further than this, these works speak of skills that are not used in relation to the creation of human figures other than in one instance: the making of dolls. We are in the realm of the little girl learning to stitch through making dolls, or of the rag doll made by a mother for her daughter: the 'quasi subject' though which the daughter's symbolic space can be organised. But these dolls are adult figures: they are not baby dolls, and they are far more adult and womanly than the smoothed-over bodies of a Sindy or Barbie. They have open mouths and open genitals; the pains and pleasures described through their forms are all too adult; the life-size figures make spaces for the audience to identify bodily with the subjectivity they represent; the smaller figures provoke memories of playing with dolls and create space for fantasies of caring and of the projection of subjectivity onto these non-objects. Herein lies their ability to disturb: they cannot be distanced as objects; they only gain legibility as vital and present mediations of an insistent subjectivity.

Robert Storr has looked back to what he calls 'the whirling dervish figure' in plate 4 of Bourgeois's print sequence *He Disappeared into Complete Silence* (1947):

> When she [Bourgeois] comes round it is never to close the circle but to re-inscribe its course with a new emphasis, widening or narrowing its scope as she proceeds [...] The animating force of her formal language and a self portrait, that figure is the direct spatial expression of an insatiable need. She is the spiral-woman, seeking but never finding the absolute core of her being, always advancing even when she seems to be retracing her steps, always restless because she has not reached her outer limits. Nothing in the psychic or aesthetic economy of Bourgeois's obsessions has altered these terms. (Storr 1995: 31)

But Storr, for all his acute perception in his essay, also forgoes any account of Bourgeois's relation to her mother, despite mentioning both her father and his mistress. In this he also demonstrates the effect of this lack, by suggesting that the artist is 'seeking but never finding the absolute core of her being'. In missing the mother, and the little girl's loss the mother, the void is, rather, in the centre of *his* discussion of Bourgeois: a void that represents in a phallocentric structure 'the horror of nothing to see' (Irigaray 1977a: 25; 1985d: 26). His discourse around Bourgeois is struggling with the limits of phallomorphic logic and its syntax, and therefore his comments are unable to make that imaginative leap into reading, across difference, the syntax appropriate to women as it is embodied in this particular site of enunciation. What is missed, then, is that the mother of the woman is central to her morphologic and her self-representation:

> Woman always speaks *with* the mother, man speaks in her absence. This *with her* obviously takes different shapes and it must seek to place speech *between*, not to remain in an indissociable fusion, with the women woven together. This *with* has to try to become a *with self*. Mother and daughter turn around each other, they go up and down while encircling themselves but they also delineate the two entities that they are: in the lips, the hands, the eyes.
>
> The girl-subject does not exert mastery, except perhaps in her silence, her becoming, her overflowing. The girl-subject does not have objects as the boy does. It splits into two in a different way and the object or the goal is to reunite the two by a gesture, to touch both perhaps so the birth is repeated, so that no unconsidered regression occurs, so that the self is kept whole or, sometime, upright. Women do not try to master the other but to give birth to themselves. (Irigaray 1987e: 113–114; 1993g: 99)

In *Endless Pursuit* (2000) the head and shoulders of a woman emerge from a sphere. The fabric this is made from is blue, the colour that in the West denotes space, sky, water, infinity and female divinity. The circle around the figure could be one measured by her bodily limits. Her breasts rest upon the surface of the sphere: she is not being swallowed by it so much as defining this space. The sphere attracts, delineates and forbids the audience access. The woman appears to be singing.

Mediation between mother and daughter, two subjects of the same subjective identity, and mediation of the woman to her self, will spring from the same morphologic, and are necessary to produce intersubjectivity and avoid the reduction of the one into the other. If we accept the importance of the morphology of the mother–daughter relationship, and the birth of the subjects, women, through an appropriate syntax, we can assess in Bourgeois's *Cells* and in her stitched figures a signification which otherwise remains unacknowledged. In so doing, we also test the structures of gesture proposed by Irigaray. Each woman's work augments the legibility of the other's.

# PART 3

# Women's Genealogies

The premise is that women cannot see [illegible] beauty, [illegible] they cannot see their beauty outside a syntax that is appropriate for their

# 5

# Divine Beauty

At present, argues Irigaray, 'we are still not *born women*' (Irigaray 1987c: 78; 1993b: 66). We have not attained our full subjectivity, or found our syntax in the Symbolic; we struggle to achieve the creation of objects of mediation between ourselves. We have not become women because we have no horizon corresponding to our morphology, nor do we have our genealogies. Women's genealogies (which I understand as the culture in an appropriate syntax passed from woman to woman through the generations) have been utterly disrupted by patriarchal social, sexual, legal, cultural and religious structures; we have no sense of our potential for divinity according to our morphologics, no appropriate transcendental, no universal which allows us an horizon towards which we can move, no sense of our beauty. We see that this structure grants our mothers no respect, and without an horizon of possibilities leading us to do otherwise, we reproduce those structures. Mother to daughter, in a state of immediacy, we are not in position to become the subjects, women.

In this chapter I will follow through Irigaray's analysis of the structures necessary to allow us to become women and to reassert woman-to-woman genealogies. This includes the need for an appropriate horizon of possibilities in the ideal realm of the spiritual: a divine, a transcendent and a universal sufficient to allow those born female to become women, to realise our beauty. The premise is that women cannot become beautiful, cannot create beauty and cannot see their beauty, outside a syntax that is appropriate for their morphology. It is impossible without forms that allow for full subjectivity. As part of this, discussions of various artworks will be brought in to discover how this might be developed or made legible.

## BEAUTY

Irigaray begins her essay 'How Can We Create Our Beauty?' by positing her argument in words which are a challenge to many of us who are involved with contemporary art practices. This terminology can even appear naive for a number of reasons; in some instances it is either not used in contemporary criticism or, if it is, then with a different meaning. Most of us making or working with art will have taken on board, for instance, Adorno's discussion about the impossibility of lyricism after Auschwitz; or the way an avant-gardeist principle of 'épater les bourgeois' has disintegrated into post-modernist horror-chic; or a feminist-realist impulse to 'tell it like it is'; or possibly even the desire for catharsis which can only be achieved at the resolution of a certain order of narrative. Irigaray appears either to ignore or be unaware of the impact of each of these for contemporary art practice. She writes:

> Very often, when looking at women's works of art, I have been saddened by the sense of anguish they express, an anguish so strong it approaches horror. Having wanted to contemplate beauty created by women, I would find myself faced instead with distress, suffering, irritation, sometimes ugliness. The experience of art, which I expected to offer a moment of happiness and repose, of compensation for the fragmentary nature of daily life, of unity and communication or communion, would become yet another source of pain, a burden. (Irigaray 1990b: 121; 1993h: 107)

Irigaray outlines in four main points why she thinks women make images of pain, and how women could create beauty. First, she puts herself into the discussion by pointing out that she too deals with pain in her work, but states that she attempts to do so in what she calls 'a literary style' to cushion any potential sense of dereliction in the reader. At the same time she will look for a positive – something for which women, 'who have a tendency to identify only with what they lack, their shortcomings', sometimes criticise her. She says that showing the negative:

> ... is positive and necessary given that it was meant to stay hidden. The portrayal of suffering is, then, for women an act of truthfulness. It's also akin to an individual and collective catharsis. [...] Daring to manifest publicly individual and collective pain has a therapeutic effect, bringing relief to the body and enabling them to accede to another time. (Irigaray 1990b: 122; 1993h: 108)

The effect of this representation of anguish is then likened to the masked figures subjected to fate in Greek tragedy.

Irigaray's second point is that having children is a most wonderful creativity. However, within the 'male social order' there is a particular obligation to do it; and further, a distinction is made between creation, which is reserved for men, and procreation, which is deemed of a lesser order. She suggests that 'there would seem to be confusion now between the beauty of the work [of childbirth] and its definition within a between-men civilization in which women no longer have a recognized right to engender spiritual values' (Irigaray 1990b: 123; 1993h: 109).

The third point is stated bluntly: 'as women, we have thus been enclosed in an order of forms inappropriate to us'. In order to exist, we must break out of these forms. This may have one of three consequences: first, it may destroy us: 'instead of being reborn, we annihilate ourselves'. Second, it may show us what flesh, and therefore what colours, we have left: 'I think colour is what's left of life beyond forms, beyond truth or beliefs, beyond accepted joys and sorrows. Colour also expresses our sexuate nature, that irreducible dimension of our incarnation'. The third possible consequence is that women may rediscover their identity and forms, forms which are 'always incomplete, in perpetual growth, because a woman grows, blossoms and fertilizes (herself) within her own body' (Irigaray 1990b: 123–124; 1993h: 109–110).

The fourth and final main point of 'How Can We Create Our Beauty?' concerns the representation of a 'female divine'. As we have seen earlier, the between-men culture disallows women's expression of meaning. Just as a child is not an abstract or arbitrary sign, so too for women 'meaning remains concrete, close, related to what is natural, to perceptible forms' (Irigaray 1990b: 125; 1993h: 110). In what is called pre-history, women participated in civil and religious life and were represented as woman goddesses (not only as mother goddesses). Today, lack of divine representation leaves women in a state of dereliction, without means of designating or expressing self, identifying and respecting mother–daughter genealogies.

From this essay, then, there are three salient points for discussion: 1) the very broad issue of flesh, body, their representation and female morphology; 2) the nature of female creativity, and in close relation, subjectivity; and 3) the representation of what Irigaray terms the 'female divine' and its inevitable adjuncts, 'universality' and 'transcendence'. Running through these discussions, as they fold out into Irigaray's wider writings, are two others: the necessity for productive acknowledgement of female genealogies (two-way interchange between mother and daughter, and its concomitant, exchange between women) and, in very close relation to this, a notion of fulfilment or 'becoming' for women. Without any of these, women's beauty is not possible: indeed, these in conjunction would be productive of and allow for the performativity of women's beauty. It is thus clear that anything approaching 'an Irigarayan aesthetic' will not be found in the reproduction of certain methodologies in the studio, or adherence to one or another 'style' of imagery. Irigaray's discussion of beauty therefore, and my discussion here, is *not* about defining a new aesthetic, *nor* is it an essentialist notion of a female aesthetic which has been overshadowed by a male aesthetic, and which only requires a light to be shone on it in order to become visible. For Irigaray, 'beauty' for women is a potential state of being which can only come about as a result of rethinking political and cultural discourse. Her discussion of beauty is about making possible an order of discourse which would in and of itself, and inevitably, be productive of beauty. It is a discussion which requires the reader to think differently: to rethink what might be productive of beauty, and what might constitute the transcendental and the universal.

## IDENTITY

Achieving an appropriate subjectivity for women, rather than the sensibility assigned us by the patriarchy, is a point of political and cultural struggle:

> It is a matter of demanding a culture, of wanting and elaborating a spirituality, a subjectivity and an alterity appropriate to this gender: the female. It's not as Simone de Beauvoir said: one is not born, but rather becomes, a woman (through culture), but rather: I am born a woman, but I must still become this woman that I am by nature. (Irigaray 1992b: 168; 1996: 107)

Being born physically female does not determine sensibility: girls are assigned an identity through the culture, one deemed appropriate because of their physiology. It is precisely because identity is produced through a play of *différance* within cultural assignations to physiology that it can be shifted. This is true of both men and women; and it spreads the realm of the political, and of political responsibility, into the site of consciousness. Attention to the socio-political has to be informed by attention to the subjective-political: Irigaray argues for an ethical relation between each woman's attention to her conscious being (her self-knowledge) and her attentive intersubjective relations, including the most broadly social.

The term 'identity' should be differentiated from subjectivity: it refers here to those traits within a subject which would mark him or her as behaving in a manner appropriately (for example) 'manly' or 'womanly' for a culture; traits of which the subject is or can become conscious and upon which he or she can 'work'. Irigaray's argument for a radical practice of psychoanalysis would form one strategy of doing this work. In refusing models of identity that others try to impose upon her, one strategy that a woman could follow might be to embrace 'capriciousness, dispersion, the multiplicity of her desires'; this however, would lead to further loss of identity, rather than a discovery or establishment of identity. Conscious development of identity would involve a woman instead in 'gather[ing] herself within herself in order to accomplish her gender's perfection for herself, for the man she loves, for her children, but equally for civil society, for the world of culture, for a definition of the universal corresponding to reality' (Irigaray 1992b: 53; 1996: 27). Only if political work is undertaken on identity appropriate to gender can individuals achieve their subjectivity, and so allow the other gender to begin to recognise the limits of their own gender and subjectivity.

Thus, self-consciousness has its role in developing subjectivity: 'It would be a matter of setting into motion a passive and retroactive intentionality: to become aware of being a woman or a man, and wanting to become one. It is by recognizing this that I am able to bring my intentions in line with my reality.' This is a reality which will have no imposed origin: 'My project is regulated on the basis of my natural identity. The intention is to assure its cultivation so that I may become who I am. Equally, it is to spiritualize my nature in order to create with the other' (Irigaray 1992b: 71–72; 1996: 39). The term 'natural identity' here can be problematic within many extant theoretical frameworks as it evokes a conflation of woman and nature. I understand it instead as another example of Irigaray re-entering a 'site of exploitation' in order to wrest it away from a phallocentric syntax. As she points out, 'The word "nature" is a quite recent, abstract and ambiguous term because it has so many meanings. It doesn't exist for the Greeks, for whom it would rather correspond to: "coming to appear" – to be born in a certain sense – growing' (Irigaray and Lotringer 2000: 95). 'Natural identity' is not one suited to bolstering the identity of another gender according to its partial and exclusive configuration of the world, nor is it an essential identity, as we might most commonly and colloquially use the term 'nature' today. Rather, it is the site of potentiality appropriate to each gender, and, therefore, a site of resistance to current configurations of gender – which are in themselves a disruption to possible appropriate realisations of the gendered self. Fidelity to one's gendered identity will produce a gendered spirituality – a gendered transcendental – and thus provide a site for ethical intersubjective relations. This is what is 'natural'. In order to achieve this 'natural' it is thus necessary to establish positive discursive relationships through woman-to-woman genealogies – particularly the mother–daughter relation – and a female divine. Irigaray places the two in a radical and challenging relationship: 'It is impossible to ask a woman to be holy, absolved of blame, as long as she is unable to recognize the potential holiness of her own mother' (Irigaray 1994a: 77).

## THE DIVINE

Following the earlier discussion, we can understand relationships between women as only practicable when they are faithful to women's morphology. It has been long recognised by feminism that even at the most publicly social level (for example, in most Western cultures, in the passing down of family names) mother–daughter relations have been utterly disrupted by patriarchy; but the potentially positive impact of configurations of the divine upon this has not always been appreciated. Gayatri Chakravorty Spivak has indicated the wide-reaching significance of this, and why it is important for Western feminists to recognise the political and methodological work necessary to remedy the neglect:

> Given the connection between secularism and imperialism, there is almost no way of getting to alternative general voices except through religion. And if one does not look at religion as mechanisms of producing the ethical subject, one gets various kinds of 'fundamentalism'. Workers in cultural politics and its connections to a new ethical philosophy have to be interested in religion in the production of ethical subjects. There is much room for feminist work here because Western feminists have not so far been aware of religion as a cultural instrument rather than a mark of cultural difference. (Spivak 1992: 192)

While many women have rejected dominant religions because of their patriarchal structures and their misogyny, feminist spiritual or theological movements have often been regarded as a bit of an embarrassment, or the potential for a dynamic importance of spirituality for women has been ignored, simply not discussed. Yet patriarchal notions of the divine (Irigaray is talking mainly about the dominant Western religion, Christianity, though the argument could be extended into some other religions) are far from appropriate for women:

> Man has sought out a unique *male* God. He has created God out of his gender… He scarcely sets limits within Him and between Him: he is father, son, spirit. Man has not allowed himself to be defined by another gender: the female. His unique God corresponds to the human race, which we know is not neuter or neutral from the point of view of the difference of the sexes. (Irigaray 1987d: 74. Translation modified; 1993e: 61–62)

The morphologic of men-among-themselves, of the Same, has left female sexuality without its spirituality and without representation in terms of the divine because this morphologic 'denies transcendence in the feminine. Everything that is of the feminine gender is thus less valued in this logic because it lacks any possible dimension of transcendence' (Irigaray 1992b: 115; 1996: 67). Without this sense of the divine and of transcendence, women can only repeat the representations of themselves constructed by a phallo-morphologic. But, as elsewhere in Irigaray's thinking, a notion of surface equality is spurious: 'A theology of women's liberation establishes as its priority not equal access to the priesthood, but rather an equal share in the divine. This means that what I see as a manifestation of sexual liberation is God made a couple: man and woman and not simply God made man' (Irigaray 1994a: 74) – a structure of the divine as always already multiple that echoes the structure of the Symbolic established earlier.

For a believer, the notion that God is purely a product of man's morphologic could be highly problematic: God would then be seen to be 'the space of an empty sign' (Jones 1995: 65), a mere mirror-construct made by man, and therefore all belief would have to be suspended. Another problem could be that this God would be understood as something approaching flesh made God, rather than (in part) God made flesh – which would be an heretical interpretation. In this understanding of God as 'God made a couple: man and woman and not simply God made man' resides an answer. God has been represented by man in his (man's) own image, according to the same morphologic that has produced the representation 'woman'. This rethinking of the phallomorphic structure of God requires that God is understood as couple and not as The One, nor as the 'bisexual', one God transcending gender by being interchangeably both, which also reasserts, at the end of the day, a singular, hence phallomorphic God. To put it another way, if God is understood as always already plural, rather than He or She or S/He, then believers might be able to find a structure flexible enough to allow for different morphologics as are appropriate for them as gendered subjects; a structure, 'god', that pre-exists man and woman and their syntaxes of representation.

## THE TRANSCENDENTAL

If a woman is to become woman (to achieve her subjectivity) and thus be born into a knowledge of her limits and of intersubjective relationships, she must have a sense of a transcendent that can be recognised through the structures of her morphology. Intersubjective relationships depend upon the irreducibility of the other subject: 'Between us there is always transcendence, not as an abstraction or a construct […]: I will never be you, either in body or in thought' (Irigaray 1992b: 161–162; 1996: 103–104). This transcendental is experienced in difference between one subject and another. It is what Irigaray terms a 'sensible transcendental' (Irigaray 1985a: 300, and elsewhere; 1991d: 112): that is, a transcendental which resolves any split between the material body and the spiritually ideal as it is informed by appropriate morphologies. The ideal for each sex, in the sensible transcendental, corresponds to its morphologic and thus recalls in part the material body; and the morphologic of the material body can be recognised in the ideal to which that subject can aspire:

> Transcendence is thus no longer ecstasy, leaving the self behind toward an inaccessible total-other, beyond sensibility, beyond the earth. It is respect for the other whom I will never be, who is transcendent to me and to whom I am transcendent. Neither simple nature nor common spirit beyond nature, this transcendence exists in the difference of body and culture that continues to nourish our energy, its movement, its generation and its creation. (Irigaray 1992b: 163–164; 1996: 104–105)

If Irigaray's configuration of the transcendental insists upon the material real for each gender – a transcendent which is at one with the morphologic of the subject and in which man will transcend woman and woman will transcend man – then the same initial analysis informs her configuration of the universal. She critiques the movements which demand equality (rather than her politics of respect for difference) as resulting from the same morphologic as do our present structures of the universal – equality meaning sameness and thus ultimately (particularly in the case of gender) death: 'an ideal aimed at universality, totality, the absolute, and essence by reducing distinctions and dissimilarities' (Irigaray 1992b: 155; 1996: 99). Phallomorphologic, in producing a concept of equality as singularity, totalising universality and sameness, has produced something which (to pick up an earlier point) goes against nature. Neither nature nor its content are universal – not even its basic elements, such as air, which is variable 'and is not, therefore, universal matter as such even though without it there can be no universal' (Irigaray 1992b: 68–59; 1996: 37). Sexual difference is the constant reminder of the impossibility of a singular universal: 'The universal has been thought as *one*, thought on the basis of *one*. But this *one* does not exist' (Irigaray 1992b: 65; 1996: 35). Some notion of non-singularity, limit and irreducibility therefore exists throughout the living world, to the extent that sexual difference itself is the only globally appropriate *content* for the concept of the universal (Irigaray 1992b: 84; 1996: 47). Other differences for the subject, including racial difference, will be recognised and confronted after sexual difference. Mostly, the little girl or little boy will produce their gendered identity through a recognition of sexual difference before they produce a racial identity through recognition of racial difference.[1]

In this way we can see that the universal is paradoxically not one but is at least two; and that it is related to a redefined 'natural' which, as indicated above, is the potential for an order respecting difference. Through this natural universal of sexual difference a sexuate culture can be developed; and across its nature of difference irreducible to one we have to establish ethical mediation. Mediation, therefore, can be seen as a secondary characteristic of the universal: 'language is the *tool* of the universal. Yet it is not the universal. Anything associated with nature is immediately universal; that which passes through articulation is only mediately universal' (Irigaray 1987d: 127; 1993e: 111–112). Mediation, as we have already seen, is sexuate.

What this means for the individual sexuate person, man or woman, is that there is a morphological relationship between their particularity and the universal – a second seemingly paradoxical element of this understanding of universality:

> With generic identity, there is no longer an opposition between particular and universal in the sense that the universal is already within me and does not have to be constructed outside of me. Of course, I am still subject to a historical particularity. But no longer is there any contradiction between the singularity of that history and a neuter(?) universal produced by a culture, a spirit. That tension is resolved within the horizon of belonging to a universal as generic identity. I no longer have any reason to estrange myself from myself so as to meet up with the absolute in a for-itself existing outside of me. Rather, I have to fulfil myself as what and who I am: a woman. This woman I am has to realise the female as universal in the self and for the self as far as she is able during the period of History in which she finds herself and given the familial, cultural, or political contingencies she has to overcome. (Irigaray 1992b: 225–226; 1996: 144–145)

Particularity, the universal, mediation, the divine, the natural and the transcendental, once they are (re)thought through a sexuate morphology, can be understood as being in harmony with and for our respective genders, and as elements through which we can achieve our gendered subjectivity. They would no longer be riven with splits and exclusions, as they are in our present configuration of them. What we see now in a patriarchal culture as paradoxes could be understood as coherent in a different morphologic.

## ABSTRACTION AND 'THE BEAUTIFUL OBJECT OF CONTEMPLATION'

Thanks to her structuring of morphology and its effects, Irigaray's re-conceptualising of the divine and the transcendental remain rooted, non-abstract. For her, the abstract is a human product which none the less is completely arbitrary in its relation to the human body. This is expounded upon in most detail in 'Flesh Colors' which starts with an examination of the psychoanalytic scenario, where sound (the spoken word) is prioritised over light. The gestures and colours within that scenario are spoken of only when the spoken word fails – for example, the gestures of the hysteric are only commented upon because of her muteness. Because sound moves more slowly than light, 'psychoanalytic practice becomes an exercise in patience' (Irigaray 1987a: 167; 1993f: 153), a soporific experience, where the subject risks sinking into a colourless demented language of arbitrary forms. Lying down increases this risk, as the subject no longer needs a sense of balance, encouraging an artificial, arbitrary – abstracted – reality. For women, she suggests, being rooted in the non-abstract is particularly important; for them, 'meaning remains concrete, close, related to what is natural, to perceptible forms. It also develops like our bodies, those of our children, of our sexual partners, of those that belong to the living world' (Irigaray 1990a: 125; 1993i: 110). The effects of abstraction reach from the body through culture, with links discernible between writing, gender, figuration and abstraction.

In an interview about her practice of writing Irigaray suggests that our present alphabetical writing is not part of a syntax in the Symbolic which is appropriate for women, but at present it is what we have to work with: 'I use it to communicate even if I think this method is limiting to what I have to say, especially as a woman. [...] Indeed, alphabetical writing is linked historically to the civil and religious codification of patriarchal powers' (Irigaray 1990a: 59, 61; 1993i: 51, 53). This she traces back to 'pre-history' – an era loosely identified as being pre-alphabetical writing as well as pre-phallocentric, 'when women participated in civil and religious life [and] written signs were still partially figurative, non-abstract' (Irigaray 1990a: 125; 1993i: 110). The limits of alphabetical writing are a result of its abstractness: 'writing has difficulty translating colors, sounds, bodily identity, the chromo-soma... All the civilizations that give priority to nonfigurative writing, arbitrary forms, and formal codes, move away from color and from tonality as qualities of flesh, gender, genealogy' (Irigaray 1987a: 174–175; 1993f: 160). The stress of our culture upon an abstract system for a primary method of communication impacts upon the Symbolic at all levels – and indeed is implicated in Philosophy itself, the discourse of discourses. Frequently the abstract is posited as the realm of rationality, but this is a delusion, begging the question why rationality should be based upon abstract logic, rather than 'a culture of experience, including sensual experience?' (Irigaray and Lotringer 2000: 73). In close relation is the linking of the abstract with objectivity – also a delusion:

> This abstractness and the loss of that concrete, sensual immediacy that was always Hegel's point of departure block the passage from subjective into objective, from objective into subjective. Hegel sought to keep faith with nature but to do this one must pass through that question of sex and the spirit. The increase in so-called objective cultural effects produced by an inadequate dialectic of subjective and objective risks burying us under its spiritless shell, overwhelming us with its pestilential waste products. (Irigaray 1987h: 156; 1993k: 142)

This model is one that echoes across all of Irigaray's work on writing, on the abstract and the arbitrary, and that informs her thinking about the cultural, social, political and religious roles accorded the body.

Alphabetical writing is fundamentally implicated in the valorising of the (phallocentric) abstract, she argues. It developed as cultures shifted from women-goddesses to mother-of-sons-goddesses, from goddesses to gods, from oral histories to written histories, from living with nature to hierarchical domination of nature, and as financial systems were developed. Underlying this is a phallocentric structure which sees woman not as different but as other of the same – in itself a form of abstraction. As a result our culture is constructed from 'resemblances, abstracted from the body instead of expressive of it, that form a system of mimicries that allow me to say that I am like the other sex without in fact there being any correspondence with the same living forms, the same relations to sounds, to colors' (Irigaray 1987a: 174; 1993f: 160).

One of the sites in which we can see the significance of such abstracted resemblances is in the representation of goddesses. The notion that this imagery is abstracted from the body rather than being expressive of it can, I think, begin to explain (and help us understand) representational shifts that in turn signify a shift from the representation of women-goddesses to mother-of-sons-goddesses:

> During the period when there were female goddesses, the woman's sexual organs always appear in the representation of the bodies of women, particularly goddesses, and not merely in the form of the triangle indicating the womb, but also in the form of the labia, an inscription which will later be erased. The cult of goddesses who are exclusively mothers, and mothers of sons, is a late episode

> in the history of women. In the symbolism of social exchanges, it is accompanied by the representation of the woman's sexual organs as the figure of the triangle representing the womb and standing as a symbol of the maternal function. (Irigaray 1991d: 178)

The triangle/womb alone represented women reduced to mothers; the representation, 'woman', without her ontology recognised, without her relation to origin or her sexual pleasure and desire represented. The triangle/womb plus the line/labia, in distinction, remains expressive of the body, faithful to it: it represents the woman-goddess and, through this concept of the woman-goddess, the possibility of transcendence and mediation for the subjects, women. Neither of these representations could be confused with Realism, and it becomes clear that decrying abstraction is not necessarily to suggest that we return to forms of Realism in art. That which is expressive of the body, after all, has to be a form of mediation, not a form of illusion. Considered this way, the rigid structures of two-dimensional, illusionistic Realism could be considered as resemblances that are abstracted from the body, and far from expressive of it.[2]

In an often-quoted paragraph Irigaray links the visual at all levels – and particularly in its seeing/not seeing and representing/not representing women's sex – with phallocratic logic:

> Within this logic, the predominance of the visual [*regard*], and of the discrimination and individualization of form, is particularly foreign to female eroticism. Woman takes pleasure more from touching than from looking [*du regard*], and her entry into a dominant scopic economy signifies, again, her consignment to passivity: she is to be the beautiful object of contemplation [*à regarder*]. While her body finds itself thus eroticised, and called to a double movement of exhibition and of chaste retreat in order to stimulate the drives of the 'subject', her sexual organ represents *the horror of nothing to see.* A defect in this systematics of representation and desire. A 'hole' in its scoptophilic lens. It is already evident in Greek statuary that this nothing-to-see has to be excluded, rejected, from such a scene of representation. Woman's genitals are simply absent, masked, sewn back up inside their 'crack'. (Irigaray 1977a: 25–26; 1985d: 25–26)

At the centre of this passage is representation in the visual. The phallocratic economy is predominantly scopic; there is the question of the relation of touch and the visible; the representation, 'woman' is the object of visual contemplation; her genitals are not only 'nothing-to-see', but they *represent* 'nothing-to-see'. Thus, her genitals are excluded from 'such a scene of representation' as the realm of 'art' – that other production of beautiful objects of contemplation.

There is a paradox here, that this exclusion of women's genitals from 'art' should exist alongside what Irigaray has called 'hysteroscopy':

> Yes, man's eye – understood as substitute for the penis – will be able to prospect woman's sexual parts, seek there new sources of profit. Which are equally theoretical. By doing so he further fetishises (his) desire. But the danger of the mystery remains, however large a public has been recruited of late for 'hysteroscopy'. (Irigaray 1974: 180 Translation modified; 1985c: 145)

This appears to be a useful way of negotiating the difficulties which British feminism encountered in the 1970s when employing psychoanalysis in order to understand the phenomenon of pornography. Before images of women's genitals were routinely presented in 'high street' pornography, the concept of fetishism was used to account for the stylised and prop-laden imagery available in both pornography and art. Lisa Tickner wrote that 'whilst the image of woman as fetishised object, repository for male sexual fantasies and fears, is "acceptable" in our society, the image of the vulva itself which the fetish seeks to displace, is "obscene"', (Tickner 1978: 243) going on to say that such an analysis was not available in cultures such as the Japanese Ukiyo-e tradition, where directories of courtesans included portraits of their faces and vulvas. Laura Mulvey wrote: 'it is man's narcissistic fear of losing his own phallus [...] which causes shock at the sight of the female genitals and the fetishistic attempt to disguise or divert attention from them' (Mulvey 1973: 15). John Ellis argues that Mulvey, working from a Freudian model, analyses fetishism as 'a disavowal of woman's lack of a penis, and therefore should always involve avoiding the direct sight of the female genitals' (Ellis 1980: 99). Such analyses of fetishism – widely interpreted as concluding that the fetish replaces the sight of woman's 'castrated' genitals – were bound to require re-evaluation upon the proliferation of images of women's genitals, alongside fetishistic props, in pornography in the UK from the late 1970s on. As John Ellis indicated in 1980, Laura Mulvey's 1973 position 'seems to be unable to account for and analyze the ways in which current visual pornography is obsessed with women's genitals' (Ellis 1980: 98). If we follow Irigaray's analysis of phallocentrism's 'blind spots', and allow that the phallocentric gaze, rather than refusing to look at the 'horror' of women's genitals, instead *does not see what is there*, then such imagery can be more fully understood. John Ellis summarises this as '"I know (woman has no penis), nevertheless (she has, through this fetish)"' (Ellis 1980: 100). Fetishism 'completes' women's genitals for the phallic gaze, rather than replacing, or displacing, them. Fetishistic discourses of representation, as Griselda Pollock has said, produce 'terms of a hierarchical difference premised on assigning a lack to a perfectly whole body' (Pollock 1991: 219). Women's genitals are thus 'seen' in as much as they are looked at, but 'seen as' (and thus signify her as) lacking. Such a 'hysteroscopy' as we have experienced in pornographic imagery, rather than contradicting the fetishistic structure as outlined by Laura Mulvey, will constantly reinforce (in the phallocentric gaze and mind) woman's lack of ontology, that she is other of man's same, and confirm man in his hom(m)osexuality, the auto-erotics of phalloculologocentrism.

If 'woman' is the phalloculocentric representation of the subjects, women (who of course cannot be 'seen' as subjects in that regime), and one of the ideal manifestations of this representation, 'woman', is 'the beautiful object of contemplation', then this is what phallocentric man will re-reproduce, as the ideal, and a carrier of his meaning, in his 'art'. If women's genitals and their significance – that the subjects, women, have their own relation to origin, and a potential appropriate syntax – cannot be 'seen', then they will not be shown. If what phallocentric man sees when he sees women's genitals is the 'horror of nothing to see', then they can have no place in his *re-representation* in 'art' of 'woman' as 'the beautiful object of contemplation'. If they did, there would be an intolerable tension between his attempt at an act of contemplation and, on the one hand, the representation, 'woman's' loss of status as a passive object, and on the other the continually anxious investigation by his hysteroscopic gaze. The two are, of course, contiguous; one will signify the other, and one cannot exist without the other. In understanding their interdependence, phalloculocentric man may well *name them* as the virgin and the whore, rather than seeing them both as his / the representation, 'woman': once again seeing and naming without reflecting upon the sources of that act of seeing.

It is in relation to this interdependence being made manifest in works by artists from Courbet to Kitaj that we find many examples of high anxiety in comments by art writers. Kenneth Clarke, writing on Boucher's painting *Miss O'Murphy*, shows an awareness of the contiguity between the representation, 'woman', and hysteroscopy. Nonetheless he sees, names and omits to reflect upon the source of that act of seeing to the point of absurdity:

> Freshness of desire has seldom been more delicately expressed than by Miss O'Murphy's round young limbs, as they sprawl with undisguised satisfaction on the cushions of her sofa. By art Boucher has enabled us to enjoy her with as little shame as she is enjoying herself. One false note and we should be embarrassingly back in the world of sin. (Clarke 1956: 140)

This omission includes: neglecting to reflect upon the material practices of composing a painting (*her* choice of pose?); the generally known material realities of Louise O'Murphy's life as the teenage daughter of an emigrant

Irish cobbler, whose sisters were prostitutes and who was herself 'the King's mistress' (*her* cushions and sofa?); let alone desire, whether imagined (*her* desire?) or provoked (enabled *who* to enjoy her?) or represented (*whose* lack of shame?); and the construction of 'undisguised satisfaction' in this painting, commissioned by the King for his private delectation.

When the interdependence of hysteroscopy and the beautiful object of contemplation is made explicit by a woman, however, then the reaction, rather than anxiety to accommodate, can be one of anger or censorship. One example of this would be the general critical denigration of the untitled installation by Zoe Leonard in the 1992 *Documenta*, in Kassel, Germany, described in chapter 1. For example, Peter Schjeldahl wrote of her 'furious intervention' that 'with flabbergasting literal-mindedness, Zoe Leonard invaded a collection of [...] paintings. [...] It was a gesture of blasphemy – an offense that, unlike heresy, is open only to believers' (Schjeldahl 1992: 96). Another example would be the reaction of the Arts Council of Great Britain to Suzanne Santoro's artist's book, *Towards New Expression*.

In the short text in this image-based work, Santoro's words resonate with Irigaray's slightly later comments on the excision of women's genitals from the scene of representation in phallocentric 'art'. The text first discusses a graffito on a wall in Rome of a penis, a vulva and drops of semen being collected in a cup:

> The penis and the semen were drawn with force and the cup for the care and preservation of the semen was given great importance. On the other hand there was the subordinate and mystified presence of the female genitals, the usual crack-hole, hole-crack. [...] When I saw how this subject had been treated in the past, I realized that even in diverse historical representation it had been annulled, smoothed down and, in the end, idealized. [...] We can no longer see ourselves as if we live in a dream or as an imitation of something that just does not reflect the reality of our lives. [...] The substance of expression is unlimited and has no established form. Self expression is a necessity. Expression begins with self assertion and with the awareness of the differences between ourselves and others. (Santoro 1974)[3]

Santoro's aim through the bookwork is (as the title suggests) to begin to work towards what we might call a syntax appropriate to women. She does this through the delicate and spare selection, editing and juxtaposing of photographic images in this intimately scaled book (each page is approximately 16 cm x 11 cm). The images are of the vulva; the labia; the clitoris; of women's genitals seen from the front, with the outer and inner lips visible above the 'Y' formed by the tops of the thighs; of shells; of flowers; of Greek statues; and of the 'Y' as represented by artists such as Cranach and

Raphael, missing the representation of the lips, in the same fashion as the triangle mentioned earlier as presenting the mother goddess omitted the line indicating them also. Santoro makes explicit her aim of encouraging women towards expression through an appropriate significatory system:

> The placing of the Greek figures, the flowers and the conch shell near the clitoris is a means of understanding the structure of the female genitals. It is also an invitation for the sexual self expression that has been denied to women till now, and it does not intend to attribute specific qualities to one sex or the other. (Santoro 1974)

Notoriously, the Arts Council of Great Britain (as it was then called) removed *Towards New Expression* from an exhibition of artist's books touring Britain in 1976–1977, after it had been selected and included in the published catalogue. In an article written about the affair, Rozsika Parker contrasts this censorship with the inclusion of Allen Jones's artist's book *Projects* (Parker 1977). It was about Jones's work that Laura Mulvey had expounded her theory of fetishism (Mulvey 1973), and Parker cites this in order to analyse why the ACGB felt able to include the Jones book while excluding Santoro's. She quotes Robin Campbell of ACGB justifying the exclusion 'on the grounds that obscenity might be alleged'. Obscenity per se was clearly not the issue, however, as the ACGB was 'willing to defend obscenity on the grounds of artistic excellence'. The ACGB's problem was that Santoro's book did not merely image the 'obscene' but was in and of itself 'obscene' because 'the avowed intention of the book was primarily a plea for sexual self expression' (in Parker 1977: 44–45).

Bypassing the skewed logic of this (as Parker points out, presumably Santoro's work was artistically excellent enough to merit its initial selection), and the vexed question of the definitions of 'obscenity' in a patriarchal legal system,[4] I think we can expand Parker's understanding of the censorship as resulting from phallocentric man's need to remove women's genitals from his sight. It is notable that Jones's work, which takes its imagery from fetish and bondage magazines, *does not* image the female genitals. Drawing from Irigaray's insights about hysteroscopy on the one hand, and the need to develop women's sexuate subjective identity (as the subjects, women) and the necessary concomitant, a Symbolic syntax appropriate to women on the other, we can see Santoro's work as being part of that broader, cultural and ontological threat to phallocentric man which Irigaray identifies. It is this not because it images women's genitals, but because it is a strategic response, developed from within the political, collective site of the women's movement (Parker 1977: 44), to what Irigaray identifies as the 'need [...] to work out an art of the sexual, a sexed culture' (Irigaray 1987f: 15; 1993c: 3); 'an art of the sexual that respects the colors, the sounds, and the forms proper to each sex' (Irigaray 1987b: 179; 1993f: 165).

## GODDESS IMAGE: CYNTHIA MAILMAN AND YOLANDA LÓPEZ

Irigaray has expanded upon the differences in the representations of women-goddesses and mother-goddesses (the triangle plus labia, or the triangle), and the signification of this different form of imagery: 'Their divinity doesn't depend upon the fact they can be mothers but upon their female identity, of which the inter-enter-opening of the lips [*l'entre'ouverture des lèvres*] are an affirmative expression (Irigaray 1990a: 125. Translation modified; 1993i: 111). Such representations of goddesses resist reduction to being representations of mother-goddesses: the womb is not represented in isolation. A concept of the divine in a syntax appropriate to woman is not located in its representation of her ability to be a mother, but in its representation of her *as a woman*.

It would be easy to assume that the kind of artworks that might be a contemporary development of this form of representation would include many of the goddess images produced from the 1970s onwards as a result of the

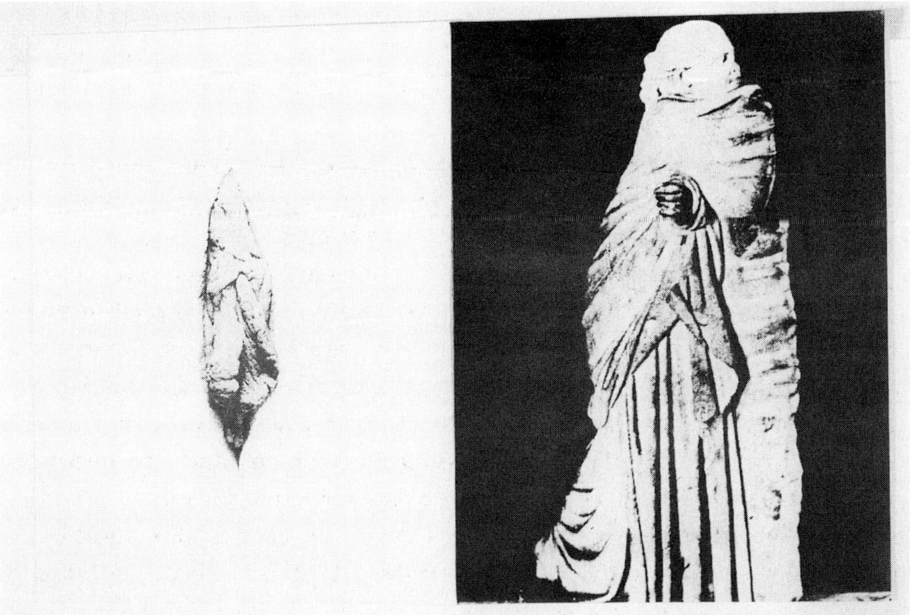

Susanne Santoro, *Towards New Expression*: 1971–1972. Detail from artist's book. Courtesy of the artist.

women's movement. Painters such as Monica Sjöö, performance artists such as Mary Beth Edelson, and countless women wishing to reassert a female divine produced such images not only in formal artworks, but also as graphics for feminist journals and as jewellery. However, interrogating the visual representations of divinity and conceiving them anew is far from straightforward, and a large number of these images enact a simplistic reversal upon the phallic languages we have been taught. This is a more general trap, of which Irigaray is aware:

> From a feminine locus nothing can be articulated without a questioning of the symbolic itself. But we do not escape so easily from reversal. We do not escape, in particular, by thinking we can dispense with a rigorous interpretation of phallogocentrism. There is no simple manageable way to leap to the outside of phallogocentrism, *nor any possible way to situate oneself there, that would result from the simple fact of being a woman*. (Irigaray 1977a: 157; 1985d: 162–163)

Images produced simply under the banner of 'women' or 'sisterhood' will not suffice. I will indicate in a brief examination of two artworks how some artists, in attempting a feminist development of goddess imagery, have assumed that there is a 'simple manageable way to leap to the outside of phallogocentrism', and how others have attempted to locate a reserve in our cultural imaginary, and to work towards a differing syntax.

A work such as Cynthia Mailman's *Self Portrait as God* (1974) falls into the former category. A painting 9′ high, the centrally placed figure is well over life-size. Painted naked in a symmetrical standing pose and using a perspective that illusionistically increases the height of the figure, the effect is of an all-powerful being who literally and metaphorically looks down upon the viewer. We see the lips of her vulva, as in the woman-goddess images Irigaray cites, but any disruption of the viewer's relationship to a phallomorphic construct is immediately undone by the pose, the perspective and by the style of painting. Flat areas of colour are articulated with hard-edged borders and use of line. The overall effect is of a phallic goddess, the one who knows, sees and judges all, and who maintains a fixity of position; the viewer too has to maintain a fixed (subordinate) position in order to be in relationship with her. (I can't help feeling also that there is displayed here by the artist – in what is after all a self-portrait – at best an over-weening ambition.) Irigaray has warned about how we explore goddesses or reinvest in their images and significations today:

> I am far from suggesting that [...] we have to regress to siren goddesses, who fight against men gods. Rather I think we must not merely instigate a return to

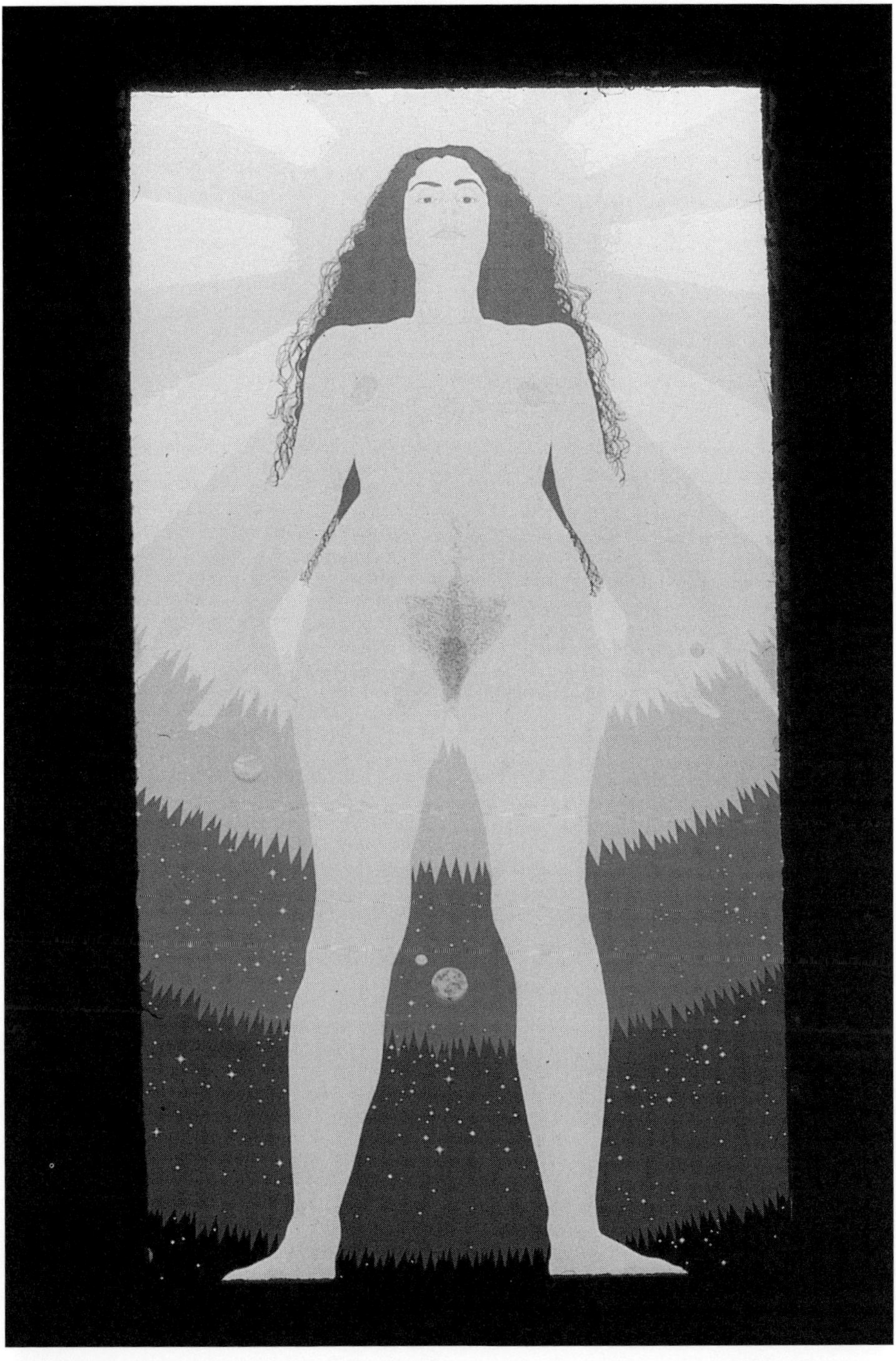

Cynthia Mailman, *Self Portrait as God*: 1974. Acrylic on Canvas, 60″ x 108″ Courtesy of the artist.

the *cosmic*, but also ask ourselves why we have been held back from becoming *divine women*. [...] But all this must be done in the context of entering further into womanhood, not moving backwards. If we resist hierarchies (the man/woman

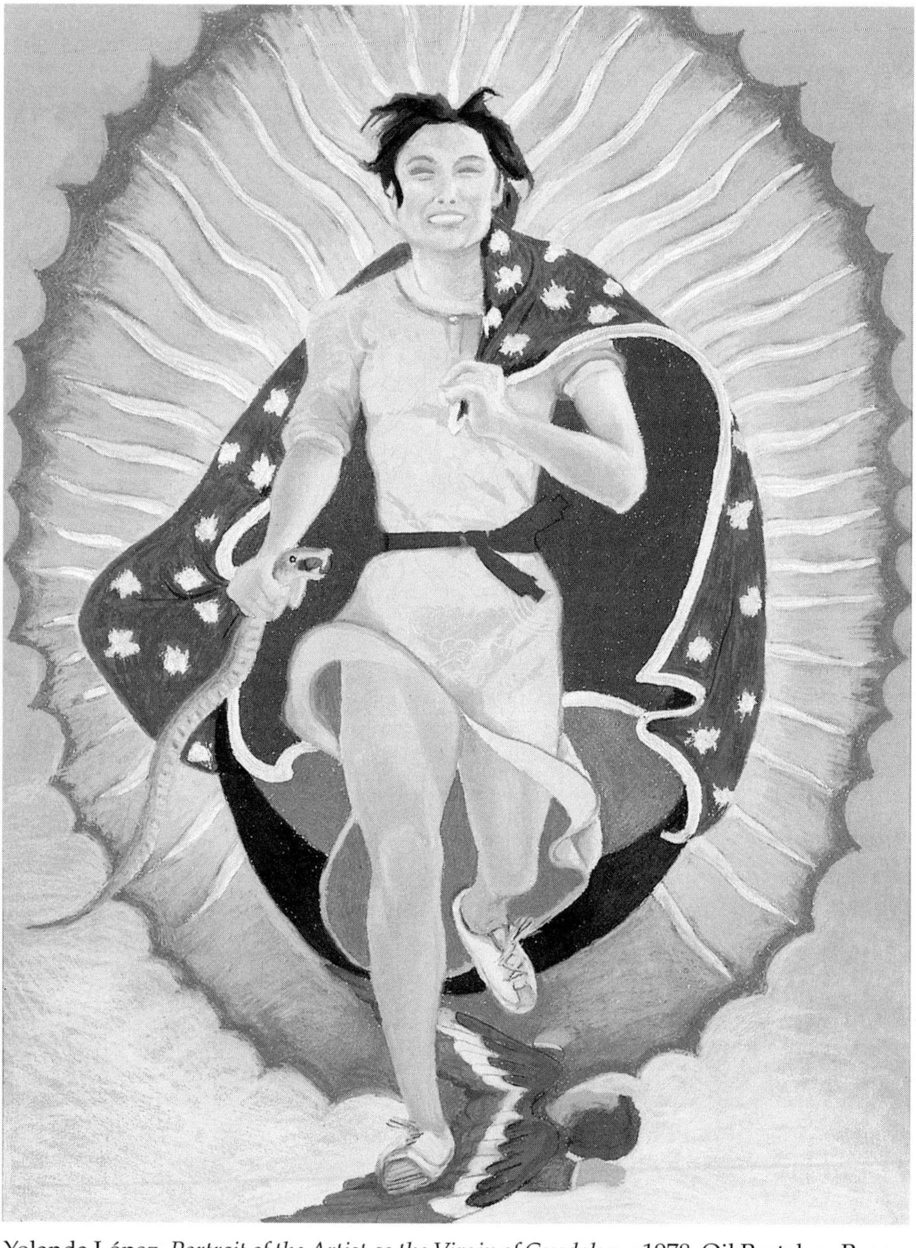

Yolanda López, *Portrait of the Artist as the Virgin of Guadalupe*: 1978. Oil Pastel on Paper, 22″ x 32″. Courtesy of the artist. Collection of the artist.

> hierarchy, or state/woman, of a certain form of God/woman, or machine/woman), only to fall back into *the power* [*le pouvoir*] of nature/woman, animal/woman, even matriarchs/women, women/women, we have not made much progress. (Irigaray 1987c: 72–73; 1993b: 60)[5]

Mailman in this painting has fallen back into these retrogressive power structures. In attempting to retrieve a powerful female deity, she has created an image where there is no space for mediation between the subjects, women and her/their divine; there is no intersubjectivity, no reassertion of female genealogies. We have here an equivalent to a Zeus, or a Christian representation of an Old Testament God, in a woman's body; a maintenance mimesis of phallocentric structures of representation and patriarchal structures of religion.

Yolanda López's *Portrait of the Artist as the Virgin of Guadalupe* (1978) forms an interesting contrast as it has some strong similarities with Mailman's painting: both are two-dimensional works, both self-portraits, and in both the figure is centrally placed, frontally posed and against a background which represents infinite space. The López, however, is an oil pastel drawing and just 22″ high; the outlines are necessarily a little fuzzy because of the pastel; and the figure carries a cloak-like cloth which billows around her, giving a sense of dynamic interrelation with space. Importantly, the figure is seen straight on (rather than illusionistically towering over the viewer), and active: she runs out of, or through, or is creating as she runs, the energy field which encircles her. Her eyes are partially closed by her very human grin, so the viewer is not fixed by her gaze into a spatially or emotionally static relationship with her.

Chicanas (women of the Mexican diaspora) regard The Virgin of Guadalupe as a symbol of cultural identity, while Mexicans have her as a national symbol. In herself – the Virgin Mary as a Mexican – she begins to undo some of the Euro-centrism of Catholic symbolism; but she is still very much an interceder, and is maintained in a particular position in the Catholic patriarchy-hierarchy of imagery. The patron saint of Mexico, and with the skin colour of an Indian, she is much loved, and was used as a symbol by the independents during the Mexican revolution (Warner 1985: 302–303). None the less, she is used as a means of policing the behaviour of Mexican women. López has commented on the influence Guadalupe has as a powerful visual image and problematic role model for Chicanas, and indicates the productive mimesis she was attempting on this image:

> Essentially she is beautiful, serene, passive. She has no emotional life or texture of her own. She exists within the realm of magical mythology sanctified

> as a formal entity by religious tradition. [...] Because I feel living, breathing women also deserve the respect and love lavished on Guadalupe, I have chosen to transform the image. Taking symbols of her power and virtue, I have transferred them to women I know. My hope in creating these alternative role models is to work with the viewer in a reconsideration of how we as Chicanas portray ourselves. It is questioning the idealized stereotype we as women are assumed to attempt to emulate. (López in Goldman 1991: 199)

By representing herself as Guadalupe, López asserts her own Chicana cultural identity; by representing Guadalupe as a physically and spatially dynamic contemporary women, López discards the role of interceder; by showing her holding a snake, López refers back to and across cultures, to pre-Columbian religion and to the Cretan snake goddess; by then placing this image as the centre of a triptych which also images her mother and grandmother with the familiar starred cloak of Guadalupe, López asserts a genealogy which also modulates across time and space, both within each image and across them, wresting the imagery away from the Catholic Church in an exploration of the matrilinear and the divine. Not a 'simple manageable [...] leap to the outside of phallogocentrism', López's work suggestively interrogates a phallocentric divine, finding a reserve of representation that is faithful to her Chicana genealogy, and which begins to configure anew a syntax of the divine.

## REFLECTING (ON) BEAUTY

In 'Divine women', after quoting Ludwig Feuerbach as saying 'God is the mirror of man', Irigaray comments:

> Woman has no mirror wherewith to become woman. Having a God and becoming one's gender go hand in hand. God is the other that we need absolutely. In order to become, we need some shadowy perception of achievement; not a fixed objective, not a One postulated to be immutable but rather a cohesion and a horizon that assures us the passage between past and future, the bridge of a present *that remembers*, that is not sheer oblivion and loss, not a crumbling away of existence, a failure simply, to take note. (Irigaray 1987c: 79; 1993b: 67)[6]

Feuerbach's comment adds to the complexity of the structure which rests upon a fundamentally simple premise: phallocentric structures build man's subjectivity upon his 'seeing' everything around him as other of his same. Most importantly for this discussion, it means that he has constructed the representation, 'woman', and projected it upon women. But it also means that, certainly in patriarchal, Western, Judeo- or Helleno-Christian cultures, man can create God in his own image. This other, 'idealised', other of his same (as distinct from the 'malformed' other of his same, the representation, 'woman') then functions as the horizon of his possibilities, that necessity for a 'becoming' into subjectivity. For patriarchal man, the other of his same functions for his subjectivity as a mirror. But if women do not have an horizon of possibilities, an enunciative divine/position from the burning mirror, then one of the things that is needed is a movement the other way:

> The impotence, the formlessness, the deformity associated with women, the way they are equated with something other than the human and split between the human and the inhuman (half-woman, half-animal), their duty to be adorned, masked, and made up, etc, rather than being allowed *their own* physical, bodily beauty, their own skin, their own form(s), all this is symptomatic of the fact that women lack a female god who can open up the perspective in which their flesh can be transfigured. (Irigaray 1987c: 76; 1993b: 64)

As well as a move towards recognising the potential for a representation that is an horizon of possibilities, we need also to move from this to its necessary corollary: a representation that is 'in the real life of the senses' that allows for such an horizon; a self-image in a real-life mirror and elsewhere. There are clear implications here for art practices (representational practices) by women; not only how women image themselves, but how they image each other, how they image womanliness and femininity: becoming a woman. In following this argument through, without being proscriptive about the nature of practice, Irigaray offers indicative analyses of the structures by and through which women represent themselves in the broadest sense (initially to themselves, but not exclusively).

In her account of women's relation to their own self-image in the mirror, and to their beauty, found in the essay 'Divine Women', Irigaray performs a move from an horizon of possibilities in the divine to one in the spirit *through* the body: 'Women have rarely used their beauty as a weapon for *themselves*, even more rarely as a *spiritual* weapon. The body's splendour has rarely been used as a lever to advance self-love, self-fulfilment' (Irigaray 1987c: 76; 1993b: 64). Without being able to see their self-image as beautiful (to represent it to themselves as beautiful), there is no potential for women to recognise/develop a representation which is an horizon of possibilities appropriate for them. Such an horizon would necessarily include a possibility of beauty for women, a female soul and a female divine. Following this point, over the subsequent couple of pages, Irigaray works through the problems of self-image for women in a patriarchy, and the credible potential for self-representation. (I distinguish here between women's relation with self-image, by which I mean in particular the visual image in the mirror, and self-representation in the broad sense indicated above, and including how women mediate that self-image to themselves: how they see the image, allow for and develop its potential as an horizon.) I shall follow these arguments through, taking Irigaray's discussion in five sections.

*Section one.*

> Maternal beauty has been glorified in our religious and social traditions, but womanly beauty for centuries has been seen merely as a trap for the other [*que séduction pour fair tomber l'autre chez la femme amante*]. The transfiguration of a female body by beauty, the active share that the woman can have in that transfiguration, are today often misunderstood. Perhaps they have been forgotten. Beauty is not presented or represented as the spiritual predicate of the flesh. Yet, it is not impossible to imagine that a body can be, can above all become, intelligent or stupid, that our relation to corporal love can be actively aesthetic or passively abject, reduced: for example, to a pseudoanimality (animals themselves are beautiful in their sexual displays; bestial is an animal quality negatively attributed to man), or to motherhood, with its associations to bodily deformity and the link often made between it and chastity. (Irigaray 1987c: 76–77; 1993b: 64–65)

Beauty in women, as it is understood in Western patriarchal culture, is found in the two extremes of the representation, 'woman': the/his mother and the/his mistress, the virgin and the whore, the beautiful object of contemplation and the woman subjected to hysteroscopy. This has been well charted, not least through feminist research and works such as Julia O'Faolain and Lauro Martines' *Not in God's Image*. They have collected such passages from the early teachings of the Church as this from Tertullian:

> And so a veil must be drawn over a beauty so dangerous as to have brought scandal into heaven itself, so that before God, in whose eyes it is guilty of the angel's fall, it may blush in the presence of the remaining angels and give up the licence to show itself and hide even from the eyes of men. (quoted in O'Faolain and Martines 1979: 144)

Mary was the model of beauty for women, but as mother and virgin, not as woman. Mothers were encouraged to emulate her as much as was possible. Marina Warner includes in her eloquent charting of the mythic figurations of Mary the following modern prayer for girls: 'Most blessed Virgin Mary ... your life of faith and love and perfect unity with Christ was planned by God to show us clearly what our lives should be ... you are the outstanding model of motherhood and virginity' (Warner 1985: 68), while Olwen Hufton has collected a seventeenth-century French prayer recommended by the church for women in labour which begins: 'Oh Mother of the holiest one of holies who approached nearest to his divine perfection and so became mother to such a son' (Hufton 1995: 183). But to place women as mothers by creating an ideal who is figured as a mother rather than as a woman is to reduce women; and to structure an ideal of motherhood which has bodily failure built in to it (Mary conceived without sex, and did not die but was taken body and soul into heaven) is to reduce still further any possible sense of this figure aiding women in becoming subjects. As it is, and with this impossible ideal, the motherly body is often considered deformed (and thus shameful in its relation to the ideal?)[7] and has to remain chaste (the closest approximation to the patriarchal definition of Mary's virginity?).

The language that Irigaray uses in her discussion of female beauty and women's self-images in the mirror intertwines terminology of corporeality with that of Christianity, particularly Catholicism. While exposing the maintenance mimesis expected of women in Western patriarchy, she performs an act of productive mimesis upon this terminology in order to work towards a sense of spirituality or the divine for women, which issues from a sense of female beauty. A sense of womanly corporeal beauty is part of this, and thus so too is a woman's comprehension of beauty in her self-image. In this introductory passage, Irigaray talks of 'the transfiguration of the female body by beauty' and the possibility that beauty can be 'the spiritual predicate of the flesh'. We already consider other emotional and intellectual aspects of the body; why, then, is it impossible to think of the spirituality of the female body?

*Section two.*

> Female beauty is always considered as *finery* [*parure*] ultimately designed to attract the other into the self. It is almost never perceived as a manifestation of, an appearance of, a phenomenon that speaks of interiority – whether of love, of thought, of flesh. We look at ourselves in the mirror to *please someone,* rarely to interrogate the state of our body or our spirit, rarely for ourselves and in search of our own becoming. (Irigaray 1987c: 77. Translation modified; 1993b: 65)

Feminine beauty is *une parure* – that most feminine of finery, a word used in France in relation to (for example) the frivolity of food trimmings, bridal wear and the innate floweriness of spring. Innate, frivolous, up for consumption and feminine, it is both a trap – indicative of intentionality and concealment – and surface, not speaking of the profundity and interiority of body and spirit. We are back in the realm of the two dimensionality of the phalloculologocentric representation, 'woman': surface, with an illusion of depth. The relationship that women *as* the representation, 'woman', have with the mirror at present is one *of* maintenance mimesis of the representation, 'woman': to please, to reproduce the allure that the other has in the eyes of the same. We cannot become subjects in this representational economy; we cannot become women. When we look at images of ourselves, in the mirror and elsewhere, *we look at ourselves as* the representation, 'woman'. We *represent ourselves to ourselves as* the representation, 'woman'. The Symbolic does not have a syntax for articulation and representation of a woman's subjectivity (the hole in its scopophilic lens). So, caught in a representational economy which can only recognise the phallocentric representation, 'woman', we cannot yet see, read, understand or create our self-image in a different syntax, as subjects, women.

*Section three.*

> The mirror almost always serves to reduce us to a pure exteriority – of a very particular kind. It functions [*il intervient*] as a possible way to constitute screens between the other and myself. In a way quite different from mucuses or skin, living, porous, fluid differentiations and the possibility of communion, the mirror is a weapon of frozen – and polemic – distancing. I risk only my double to love. I do not abandon or give myself as body, flesh, as immediate – and geological, genealogical – affects. The mirror signifies the constitution of a fabricated (female) other [*d'un(e) autre fabriqué(e)*] that I shall put forward as an instrument of seduction in my place. I seek to be seductive and to be content with images of which I remain the artisan, the artist. (Irigaray 1987c: 77. Translation modified; 1993b: 65)

As we have seen, in the dominant ways of seeing in Western culture the flat mirror structures representational and interpretive possibilities. As guarantor of 'the subject' (man), it is also guarantor of the other of his same. A screen for projecting onto, it maintains this 'otherness', it maintains a distance without a possibility of mediation and disallows the play of couples. Thus the representation, 'woman' is fixed, frozen: the mirror is *la glace* – the ice-glass-mirror – not *la psyché*, the soul-mirror, or the *miroir ardent* – the burning glass. A woman, always already elsewhere than her double, the representation, 'woman', can never enter fully that play of the couple, can never, as the representation, 'woman', fully risk love. How can she when her subjectivity is elsewhere? The representation, 'woman', created by patriarchal man, is re-created in a process of maintenance mimesis by women. This is her stake in the patriarchal game of representation: to create the seductive *parure*. As with the hysteric and her mimesis (as we saw earlier), this is her art. How can there be room here for her to make anything else as art? This does not mean that she will not make 'art': but that the 'art' she makes will embody aspects of the representation, 'woman', and not her subjecthood, her subjectivity.

*Section four.*

> I have yet to unveil, unmask, or veil myself *for me* – to veil myself for self-contemplation, for example, to retouch myself with my gaze so as to limit my exposure to the other, but also to again be in touch with my own gestures and garments, thus to re-nest (into) my vision and contemplation of myself. Which is not a kind of cold narcissism, but rather a way that I can supply extra help and assistance, as an adult, to the different houses, the different bodies that have borne me, enveloped me, rocked me, embraced me, wrapped themselves around me... The mirror, and indeed the gaze, are frequently used as non-tactile weapons or tools, which break off the fluidity of touch, including that of the gaze. (Irigaray 1987c: 77–78. Translation modified; 1993b: 65)

If *la parure* is a covering of finery and trimmings for the representation, 'woman', then the subjects, women, must have garments which are different and with a different relationship to the gaze. In 'The Poverty of Psychoanalysis' Irigaray describes the function of the dance of the veil:

> In many traditions [it] is the sexual and religious rite *par excellence*, a dance with a mystery and a cosmic reality that is at once prior to and beyond any already-constituted subjectivity. The scene is played out by the goddess mother or the woman-lover, the gods and the universe. It does not cover nothingness; it attempts to pass through illusion towards the act/gesture of creating or begetting the world. (Irigaray 1985b: 261. Translation modified; 1991c: 87)

This leads me to understand the use of the word 'veil' in the prior passage as indicating in two directions ontologically: not merely a choice of being clothed or not. 'I have yet to unveil, unmask' I see as an acknowledgement of having yet to remove the covering that is *la parure*, the representation, 'woman', the masquerade required within patriarchy: to remove the surface plan/e or screen of the mirror. With 'I have yet to [...] veil myself *for me*' a difference in the veil is indicated: note that she says 'veil' and not 're-veil' after the unveiling. This indicates towards, among other things, clothing oneself with the vestments that are the syntax of one's subjectivity, and thus to have a screen/veil of mediation, whether of the subject with herself or of intersubjectivity. This is a veil that allows the self-contemplation of the subjects, women; and it also sets limits on that subjectivity and choice about marking those limits. It is a veil which allows touch to return to the gaze, rather than one which retains the gaze as abstract specularisation. This is not the frozen auto-erotics projected onto the representation, 'woman', by an economy of the same, but a subjectivity *to* which amorousness, touch, vision and history have been returned, and *in* which they are returned to each other.

*Section five.*

> Though necessary at times for separating, the mirror – and the gaze when it acts as a mirror – ought to remain a means and not an end to which I yield. The mirror should assist, not undermine my incarnation. Generally it reflects back nothing but superficial, flat images. There are other means that generate volume better than specular reflection. To work at beauty is at least as much a matter of working at gestures as the relationship to space and to others as it is a matter of cross-examining, usually with anxiety, your mirror. The mirror freezes our becoming breath, our becoming space. Our becoming bird, perhaps? Though it may at times help us to emerge, to move out of the water, the mirror paralyzes our energies, our movements, our wings. What protects me from the other and allows me to move toward him or her is more often the plotting out of a space of air rather than the interposition of mirrors and ice glasses [*glaces*] whose cutting edge always threatens to turn against me. After the totally enveloping *waters* of our prenatal time, we have to construct for ourselves, bit by bit, an envelope of *air* for our time on earth – air in which we can breathe and sing freely, in which we can spread our appearances and movements. Once we were fishes. We are destined to become birds. This will not happen without opening and mobility in the air. (Irigaray 1987c: 78. Translation modified; 1993b: 65–66)

Irigaray is not discarding mirrors. A sense of immediacy is intensely problematic for women, who have not had an appropriate syntax through which to mediate themselves and their subjectivity. Then, a sense of separation is necessary, and mirrors can assist. But assist they must, not hinder: at present, they do not assist women's becoming and their subjectivity. As we have seen, in phalloculologocentric structures, they fix women as the representation, 'woman', freeze them into an anxious, speculative relationship with their own self-imagery. Irigaray suggests that beauty is to be found in our gestural relationships with space, with other subjects. Space – air – is necessary for breath, life and movement. Beauty does not reside in the anxious relationship of the representation, 'women', with her image as the representation, 'woman', in the mirror; caught in a closed circuit, a maintenance mimesis of the phalloculologocentric gaze. Beauty – divinity, body, art – will be found in our becoming the subjects, women, for which air and space is necessary.

# 6

# Mother–Daughter Genealogies

> Patriarchy has disrupted mother-daughter relationships through an act of matricide. As patriarchy reduces women to their relationship to motherhood (reducing them to mothers, or as sub-categories, potential mothers or non-mothers), the woman-mother and woman-lover, 'a creator who has a specific desire and who fights for her desire', is erased in favour of the mother-reproducer (of the male): 'One sees this matricide at the beginning of our culture; our culture has been founded on it. When the fathers took power, they had already annihilated the mother. This can be seen in mythology, in Greek tragedy'. (Irigaray in Baruch et al. 1988: 156)

This chapter will explore how women artists are engaging with the disruption of women's genealogies and reasserting productive genealogies, ultimately represented in new attention to and representation of mother–daughter relationships.

## WOMAN–WOMAN GENEALOGIES

If women are reduced to mothers from their status as women in order to 'fit' the identity the patriarchal culture provides for them, then this has a devastating effect upon mother-to-daughter genealogies. We have seen in the previous chapter how, if a daughter cannot imagine her mother partaking of the divine, then she will have no divine of her own. There will be no horizon for her on which is situated an ideal feminine. But as well as this, in the site of a particular relationship between a mother and a daughter, 'given the exploitation that she submits to on the part of her father/husband, given her exclusion from social and creative activity, [a mother] reproduces the oppression to which she is subject' (Baruch et al. 1988: 156). Irigaray has confirmed this through analysis of mother–daughter conversations (Irigaray 1992b: 203–204; 1996: 130–131).

The antidote to this, the strategic response for disrupting the disruption of this relationship, is twofold. Initially the strategy would be of attending to the subjectivity of the mother, who alienates and cannot give a subjective identity to her daughter precisely because she herself has no subjective identity as a woman: 'The mother has to find her identity as a woman and from that point, she would be able to give an identity to her daughter' (Baruch et al. 1988: 157). Finding her identity as a woman involves a further strategic move: the development of an appropriate syntax, and with it, the establishment of objects of mediation and intersubjectivity. A key element of the patriarchy would be effectively unpicked, not through head-on collision, but through establishing respectful and amorous relationships between women: a potentially revolutionary move:

> In a sense we need to say goodbye to maternal omnipotence (the last refuge) and establish a woman-to-woman relationship of reciprocity with our mothers, in which they might possibly also feel themselves to be our daughters. In a word, liberate ourselves along with our mothers. That is an indispensable precondition for our emancipation from the authority of fathers. In our societies, the mother/daughter, daughter/mother relationship constitutes a highly explosive nucleus. Thinking it, and changing it, is equivalent to shaking the foundations of the patriarchal order. (Irigaray 1991f: 50)

Daughters need to identify with their mothers as women in an intersubjective relationship as a result of recognising their same subjective identity. Only then is it possible to establish objects of communication between the two which perform the presently tricky task of not reducing either subject to object-status in the eyes of the other. Again, there is a potentially revolutionary effect here, this time in language, which would impact upon both genders: 'But if mothers could be women, there would be a whole mode of a relationship of desiring speech between daughter and mother, son and mother, and it would, I think completely rework the language that is now spoken' (Irigaray 1991f: 52). An indication of how this might develop can be gleaned from attending to the present words of little girls when they say things to their mothers: 'in the words, whether real or imaginary, that the little girl addresses to her mother, there are always two persons speaking to one another and they are represented as doing something together. Rarely is there an object circulating between them, except an object of communication' (Irigaray 1992b: 203; 1996: 130).

At this point it is useful to reflect upon Irigaray's suggestions about the public and domestic display of images of mother–daughter couples. These are found in passages in *Thinking the Difference* and in *Je, Tu, Nous*; books which have a more polemic tone than much of her other work. The first concern the public environment:

> To anyone who cares about social justice today, I suggest putting up posters in all public places with beautiful pictures [*belles images*] representing [*figurant*] the mother-daughter couple – the couple that bears witness of a very particular relationship to nature and culture. Such representations are missing from all civil and religious sites. This is a cultural injustice that is easy to remedy. There will be no wars, no dead, no wounded. This can be done before any reform of language, which will be a much longer process. This cultural restitution will begin to redress women's individual and collective loss of identity. It will cure them of some ills, including distress, but also rivalry, and destructive aggressiveness. It will help them move from the private sphere to the public, from their family to the society in which they live. [...]
>
> Putting up images – photographs, paintings, sculptures, etc, not advertisements – of mother-daughter couples in all public places today would show respect for the social order. The social order is not made up of mothers and sons, as patriarchal culture represents it. (Irigaray 1989: 27–28, 30. Translation modified; 1994c: 9–10,12)

The image of the mother–daughter couple is evoked by Irigaray as a matter of social justice, of redressing and re-addressing a social order, and with recollection of the relation to nature outlined in the last chapter. The language used here is very direct, straightforward, with cause and effect clearly plotted out, which suggests that this advocacy of placing such images in public is verging on the propagandist. Irigaray's aim, however, is not so much didactic as healing. Images can be extraordinarily effective in effecting change, while developments or shifts in linguistic habits can take not only years but decades to achieve. The more serious problem in this passage to my mind is that visual signifiers need careful attention, at least as much as do verbal signifiers – something of which Irigaray seems not fully aware. Certainly she does not attend to this. Yet it is clear from the earlier chapter on morphology that the subtleties of visual representation are just as delicately poised as the subtleties of verbal language in respect to women's venture towards a cultural reserve yet to come, towards an appropriate syntax and towards mediation. We know that it is possible to produce fluently phallomorphic visual representations in the name of women. But at the same time there is something highly attractive about this strategy for the simple reassertion of women's genealogies.

Similar problems occur in the second passage. This attends more to the family and domestic space, rather than the public space:

> In all homes and all public places, attractive [*belles*] images (not involving advertising) of the mother-daughter couple should be displayed. It's very damaging for girls always to be faced with representations of mother-son, especially in the religious dimension. I'd suggest to all Christian women, for example, that they place an image depicting Mary and her mother Anne in the communal rooms of their homes, in their daughter's rooms, and in their own rooms. There are sculptures and easily reproducible paintings of them available. I'd also advise them to display photographs of themselves with their daughter(s), or maybe with their mother. They could also have photographs of the triangle: mother, father, daughter. The point of these representations is to give girls a valid representation of their genealogy, an essential condition for the constitution of their identity. (Irigaray 1990a: 53–54. Translation modified; 1993i: 47–48)

This also presents problems of an apparent disregard for the morphologic which may be at play in the visual language of an image. The other major problem here is a surprising lack of interrogation of Christianity and the production of the representations 'Mary' and 'Anne' by the patriarchy of today's Churches.[1] However, if we read this in the light of its presentation in her most polemical book as one of six 'practical suggestions for the development of mother-daughter relationships' (Irigaray 1990a: 53; 1993i: 47) and understand it as a short-term strategy which is amplified by other strategic actions, then it can make more sense. It is again a simple and straightforward strategy, accessible to all who have a camera in their family, as well as to those who are able and prepared to do some art-historical research for such images.

It can also make more sense when considered in relation to an earlier passage in the same book, where Irigaray describes an encounter she had with a work of art:

> In May 1984, after a conference at the Venice-Mestre Women's Center entitled Divine Women, I went to visit the island of Torcello. In the museum there is a statue of a women in the position of Mary, Jesus's mother, sitting presenting the child who sits on her knee, facing those who look at them. I was admiring this beautiful wooden sculpture when I noticed that this Jesus was a girl! That had an effect on me, which was perceptual, mentally significant, and of jubilation. I felt freed from the tensions of that cultural truth-imperative which is also practiced in art: a virgin-mother woman and her son depicted as the models of redemption we should believe in. Standing before this statue representing Mary and her mother, Anne, I felt returned calmly and joyously into my body, my affections, and my woman's history. I was facing an aesthetic and ethical figure that I need to be able to live without contempt for my incarnation, for

that of my mother and other women. (Irigaray 1990a: 25–26. Translation modified; 1993i: 25)

This was certainly a profound experience. The sculpture itself is indeed beautiful. About four feet high, wall-mounted, it dates from the fifteenth century and is now a little battered. If one did not look closely it would be easy to assume it was of Mary and Jesus. There is a light and open quality given to the features of both woman and girl, and despite the relatively formal composition, an affectionate gesture passes from mother to daughter. With similar faces and postures, the daughter encompassed but not swamped by her mother's body, they look out on the world together with pleasure. Irigaray does not analyse these elements, but had the sculpture been comprised of elements which jarred with a positive reading of the mother–daughter relationship, then the experience of seeing it must have been different. As it is, it becomes significant that Irigaray is able to contemplate the sculpture in its own terms as a representation of a divine mother–daughter couple, and not through any re-mediation through the patriarchal structures of the Church.

St Anne does not appear in the New Testament, nor in other primary sources of late antiquity, so she has been described as a constructed saint (Ashley and Sheingorn 1990: 6). The construction, which developed into the cult of St Anne, clearly was one aimed at ironing out inconsistencies in the biblical writings and their interpretations. For example, the existence of Jesus's brothers is inconsistent with Mary's continuing virginity. From the ninth century on in the Western Church Anne is presented as the matriarch of a large and holy clan, referred to as the Holy Kinship. The mother not only of the Virgin, but also of Mary Cleophas and Mary Salome (by two further marriages) she is the grandmother of Jesus, James the Less, Joseph the Just, James the Great and John the Evangelist – whose close relation to Jesus can then explain their description as brothers. But as a constructed saint, she was also able to reflect the ideologies and teachings of the times in which her cult flourished. The earliest known image of St Anne shows her holding the infant Mary (Santa Maria Antiqua, Rome, c.650 *AD*). So from the start she was represented in her role as a mother; and indeed through the height of her cult in the late Middle Ages is hardly ever shown without her daughter, the Virgin Mary (Ashley and Sheingorn 1990: 11–12).

An important representational trope of St Anne and the Virgin Mary was the development of the trinity of Anne, which became particularly popular in the fifteenth century (Ashley and Sheingorn 1990: 25). It showed Anne, Mary and Jesus together, sometimes with Mary as a child and Jesus as an infant; or with Anne holding both; or Mary on Anne's lap and Jesus in turn on hers. This image of sitting on the lap can evoke the caring of infants, or in some more symbolic cases indicate the place of the womb (Sautman 1990: 84).[2] The matrilineal trinity is sometimes shown in conjunction with the patrilineal trinity of Father, Son and Holy Ghost. In the early Middle Ages genealogical accounts traced both male and female lineages. However, as patrilineage became socially more important during the eleventh century, images of The Tree of Jesse began to appear. This represents Christ's male lineage and was common by the thirteenth century. In contrast, 'Holy Kinship images deliberately focus on women as progenitors of the sacred' (Sheingorn 1990: 173); these images begin to appear around the same time as the Tree of Jesse images, possibly as resistant images to the male lineage, or as commentary upon the biblical fact that Jesus's patrilineage was spiritual, not human. By the late medieval period, images of the Holy Kinship have Anne in the background and stress the fathering roles of her husbands and the husbands of her daughters (Sheingorn 1990: 190).

It is wholly possible that the carving that Irigaray encountered in Venice was originally a trinity of Anne, Mary and Jesus: there is some damage that could suggest loss or removal of the further detail of the infant Jesus on Mary's lap. However, images of the two women, or the woman and the girl, alone, were also common during the Middle Ages. Particularly widespread in the devotional context were images of St Anne teaching Mary how to read. Just as St Anne herself was a constructed saint, so too this image of her teaching Mary to read 'flourishes in spite of a virtual, if not total absence of textual sources' – a most unusual occurrence (Sheingorn 1993: 70–71). While many images of saints depict them carrying books as an attribute, these are usually closed, whereas Anne and Mary actively read their books: they signify 'book' as an object rather than 'reading' as an activity. One school of thought suggests that in these images of Anne and Mary the girl is here learning her destiny. Another interpretation is provided by Pamela Sheingorn who has pointed out that the growth in number of such images occurred at a time of growing literacy among both men and women, and that they could both function as a reflection of, and advocacy for, the education of girls of different classes: such images were found in expensive illuminated psalters for the nobility and on the walls of parish churches (Sheingorn 1993: 75–77).

While books and reading could be used to inculcate behaviour desired by the dominant ideology among girls and women, the literate person is not as controllable as the illiterate. Anne, in teaching Mary to read, was passing on power and knowledge:

> Yet we should not forget that another possible consequence of literacy is to foster criticism and commentary, and that there were literate women in the

> Late Middle Ages, most notably Christine de Pisan, who employed her literacy to construct a devastating critique of the ideology of patriarchy. Although we cannot predict the end to which it will be used, we can agree that literacy is power. Through the pictorial arts, Anne empowers her daughter and encourages other mothers to follow her example. (Sheingorn 1993: 78)

Other than these images of Anne teaching Mary to read, the image of the woman teacher is rare. Women were forbidden to teach by the fathers of the Church, who often cited the example of Eve to demonstrate why this would be a bad thing. St Paul said 'But I suffer not a woman to teach, nor to usurp authority over the man, but to be in silence. For Adam was first formed, then Eve. And Adam was not deceived, but the woman being deceived was in the transgression' (I Timothy 2:12–14); St John Chrysostom followed in the fourth century AD with 'The woman taught once, and ruined all. On this account... let her not teach. But what is it to other women that she suffered this? It certainly concerns them; for the sex is weak and fickle'(O'Faolain and Martines 1979: 141–142). Both these men followed their strictures by saying that the compensation for women was to be found in child-bearing. Learning, as well as teaching, is here implicitly also a masculine activity, though 'If they [women] will learn anything,' St Paul writes elsewhere, 'let them ask their husbands at home: for it is a shame for women to speak in the church' (I Corinthians 14:35). It is then doubly subversive to have an image of a woman teaching and another woman learning. It represents a genealogy of women's knowledge being passed through the generations, actively taught and learned, beyond the control of the Church and of husbands (and fathers) within families.

The earliest known image of a woman artist with female pupils (Borzello 1998: 82) is the magnificent *Self-Portrait with Two Pupils, Mlle Marie Gabrielle Capet and Mlle Carreaux de Rosemond* (1785) by Adélaïde Labille-Guiard, now in the Metropolitan Museum of Art, New York. The artist has painted herself nearly life-size, seated in her studio before a large canvas that is turned away from us. She is dressed resplendently, but appropriately for her age and social standing, in grey silk and a hat with ostrich feathers. Her left hand holds palette, brushes and mahlstick; her right hand holds a single brush, poised over the palette. She is at work – on this very self-portrait it seems: she looks up and out with a steady gaze as if pausing to check the image in the mirror before applying the paint to the canvas. Behind her stand her two pupils, more modestly dressed. The gaze of one echoes that of her teacher, out towards the supposed mirror; the other looks at the canvas. Both appear engrossed. In the background of the studio are a bust portrait of Labille-Guiard's father, and a statuette of a vestal virgin holding an eternal flame.

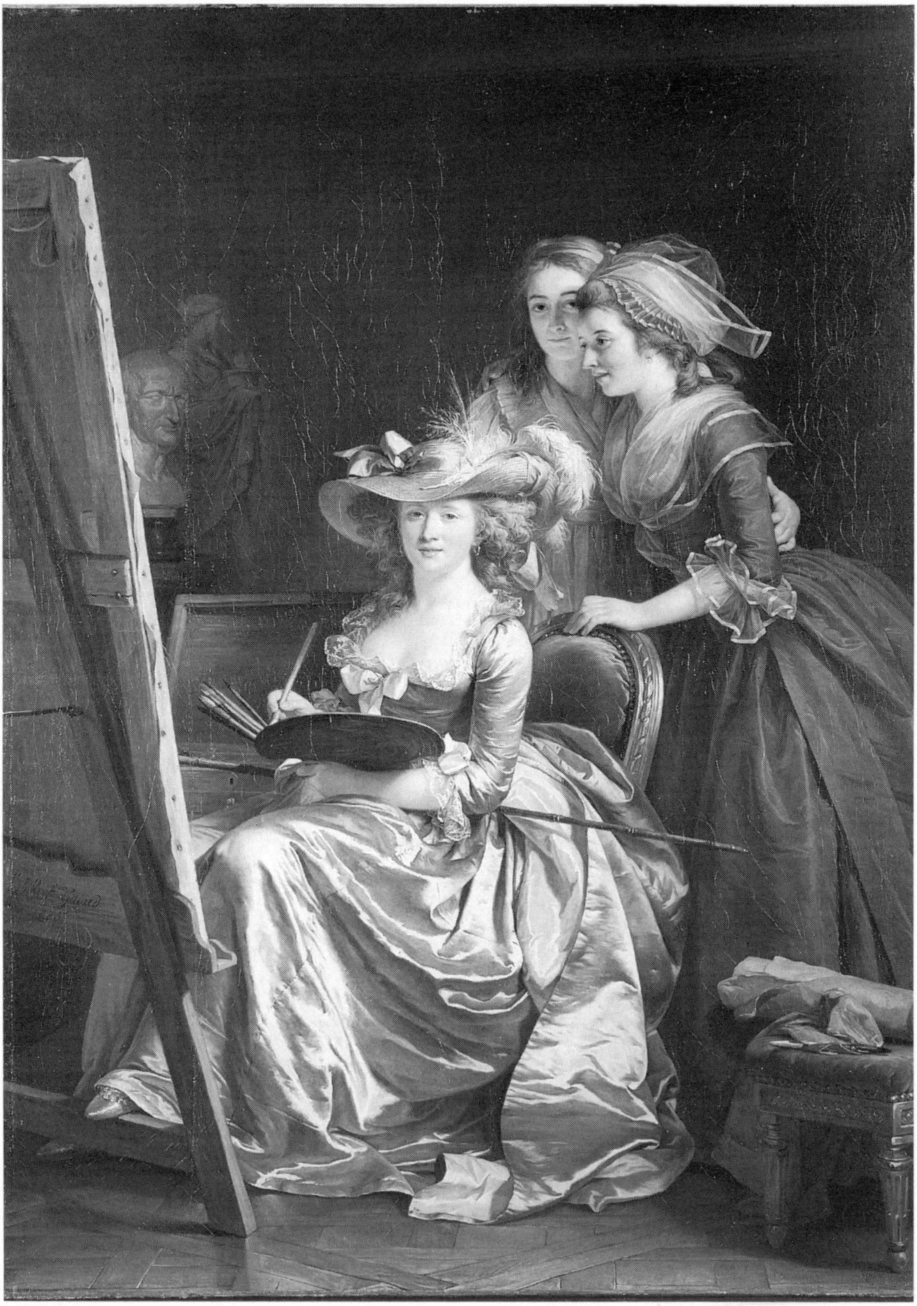

Adélaïde Labille-Guiard, *Self-Portrait with Two Pupils, Mademoiselle Marie Gabrielle Capet and Mademoiselle Carreaux de Rosemond*: 1785. Oil on Canvas, 83″ x 59 1/2″; 210.8 x 151.1 cm. The Metropolitan Museum of Art, Gift of Julia A. Berwind, 1953. Photograph © 1980 The Metropolitan Museum of Art.

Like the images of Anne teaching Mary, this is also a subversive and indeed a political, feminist painting, produced for the salon two years after Labille-Guiard had been admitted to the Académie. That same year, 1783, Elisabeth Vigée-Lebrun, just six years her junior, had also been admitted, thus completing the complement at that time of just four places granted women. The differences between the two women's approach to their activity as artists are interesting. Vigée-Lebrun's work was much softer in style and approach, and was often dubbed more 'feminine'. She married and was the mother of a daughter, and as well as making self-portraits of herself alone she produced a number of portraits of herself with her young daughter in close embrace, such as the 1786 and 1789 portraits. In both these paintings, mother and daughter have arms passionately around each other, and look out at the audience with a slightly breathless air. It is a manner of imaging mothers and daughters that had been popularised and supported by other artists at that time, such as Greuze. Teaching, however, she found 'irritating' and she soon gave it up. Labille-Guiard, who married, divorced and re-married, had no children. Her self-portraits are less romantic in approach, and other than in the 1785 painting they show her alone. She enjoyed teaching: indeed, in the Exposition de la Jeunesse of 1783, there were works by nine of her pupils – all women (Greer 1981: 265). At the time of the revolution, she planned an art school for women, which never came to fruition, but she did fight successfully for the limit of four female members of the academy to be lifted. The statuette of a vestal virgin painted in the back of the 1785 self-portrait indicates chastity: both women had to contend scurrilous rumours about their sexuality, but also about who had actually produced their paintings. Labille-Guiard, who was often given the 'compliment' at the time that she painted like a man, had to go so far as to paint portraits of male academicians in order to prove that she, and not a man, had produced her paintings. Significantly, she has signed the 1785 self-portrait 'Labille Fme Guiard', where 'Fme' stands defiantly for 'femme' – woman.

The only male element is the portrait of her father; apart from that, the 1785 self-portrait is a cyclical image that addresses women, and pulls in the female audience. The composition does not exclude the male audience however: the frontal self-portrait is very common and one reading of the narrative in this painting could be that the lesson provided by the teacher demonstrating to her pupils has been interrupted by us, the audience: hence the gaze turned to us by two of the three women. But this painting also makes a specific and subtle address to a female audience. The gazes of Labille-Guiard and her students re-enforce the perception that the artist is at work on the very painting at which we, the audience are looking. These three gazes, which cross each other in the painting, draw us back to the acts of looking involved in making this painting. The gaze of the young woman at the back, who is also the middle and the highest figure, is directed straight out of the canvas. Her companion's profile overlaps her face, slightly lower and to the right in the painting. She gazes at the image on the canvas that is being worked on by Labille-Guiard and is unseen by us. Then, below these two but in the foreground and slightly above the centre point of the picture, is the appraising gaze of the artist herself. The final part of the cycle is the supposed mirror

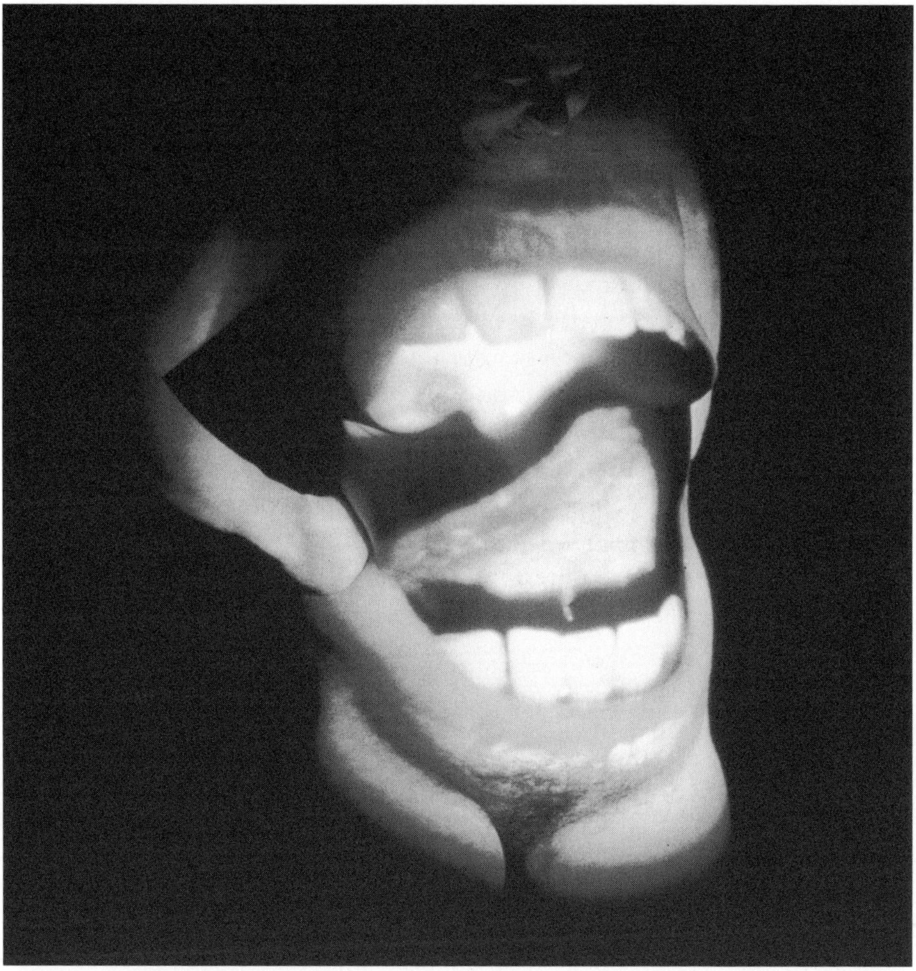

Pauline Cummins and Louise Walsh, *Sounding the Depths* (detail), 1992. Cibachrome print from a collaborative mixed media installation. Collection: Irish Museum of Modern Art. Courtesy of the artists.

into which she and her student are gazing. If this is indeed that canvas at which she is at work – and most of the elements in the composition of the painting suggest that it is[3] – then both she and her student, in gazing at us, the audience, are gazing at their own image. There is a direct invitation here to the female audience to identify with both the teacher and the student, and to meet the subjectivity of the artists – teacher and student – in the space set up in the canvas that reaches beyond it to our gaze: the reserve space of the imagined mirror.

The sculpture of Anne and Mary that Irigaray encountered showed that couple in harmony facing the world. While produced from a Christian story, and therefore part of a structure that is ultimately patriarchal (Father and Son) it has nonetheless provided for an experience of the transcendental and the divine – provided an horizon of possibilities – which can aid a woman in fulfilling her subjectivity. Representations of this mother–daughter couple come from a reserve in the Christian story, and this particularly powerful example of the transfiguring effect of the mother–daughter couple can provide a model for rethinking their representation in other cultural and political contexts. Its morphology can be felt in the Labille-Guiard self-portrait which also represents a harmony in the mediation of knowledge and affection between the generations. Nancy Spero has indicated how this mediation can work through this painting to today's generations of artists who are women. She has said of this painting:

> Normally I wouldn't react to a work of this period, considering my esthetic. But I saw a woman painting, looking beautifully, perfectly dressed, not a spot of paint on her, with these two women assistants, and I was immediately drawn to the picture. We are all looking for a heritage. It may be narrow to think this way, but artists do have a gender, they come from a milieu and it helps to recognise that.(Kimmelman 1996: C5)

## ESSENTIALISM

The 'heritage' that Spero is looking for in conjunction with the 'milieu' in the present she identifies is the 'generic identity' described by Irigaray, in which:

> there is no longer an opposition between particular and universal in the sense that the universal is already within me and does not have to be constructed outside of me. Of course, I am still subject to a historical particularity. But no longer is there any contradiction between the singularity of that history and a neuter(?) universal produced by a culture, a spirit. That tension is resolved within the horizon of belonging to a universal as generic identity. (Irigaray 1992b: 225; 1996: 144)

In this subtle structure of having both a specific history and context, and being of a universal within a culture, we have an engagement with the still knotty problem of essentialism. In the context of this discussion of women's genealogies (the culture passed from woman to woman, mother to daughter, through generations), if women are starting from places of difference (differences of history, of culture, of politics, even of subtle and crucial differences of language and concepts of womanliness and motherliness), then they will produce differing representations of women's genealogies and objects of inter-subject mediation as a result of their exploration of appropriate strategies to deal with that position of difference. This will have little to do with embracing or maintaining a fundamentally essentialist position according to English or US criteria, and indeed the structures of the essentialist representations of women will themselves differ within different contexts.[4]

I was prompted to consider the cultural specificity of women's genealogies in relation to the structures of essentialism when *Sounding the Depths* (1992), a collaborative installation by Pauline Cummins and Louise Walsh at the Irish Museum of Modern Art, was described to me by a prominent English critic as 'essentialist'. This description seemed to me not to be possible if the work was read within the specific contexts of the history of Irish visual culture. Approaches to figuration and representation of women's bodies have developed among Irish women artists in a manner which is quite distinct from that seen in Britain, Europe or the USA as a direct result of specific cultural and political structures, including a complex post-coloniality and tangential relationship to modernism, the specific structures of Catholicism in Ireland, and an engrained intertwining of the image and concept of 'woman' with that of 'mother', and both with the image and concept of 'Ireland', as not only land but also state. As Gerardine Meaney has indicated, 'in Ireland, sexual identity and national identity are mutually dependent. The images of suffering Mother Ireland and the self-sacrificing Irish mother are difficult to separate. Both serve to obliterate the reality of women's lives.'[5] These structures have allowed for the development of a feminism and a related women's culture of representation and difference distinct from those developed in England and the USA. Anglophone feminist art criticism has found the work made in this space hard to acknowledge: it rarely features in feminist books on art.[6] But it is against this background that the successes and failures of Irish women artists should be measured. To dismiss the work of women from Ireland as essentialist is in itself an essentialising judgement: it ignores the specificities of Irish cultural history, as if essentialism were universal not only in its structures but also in its effects and symptoms.[7]

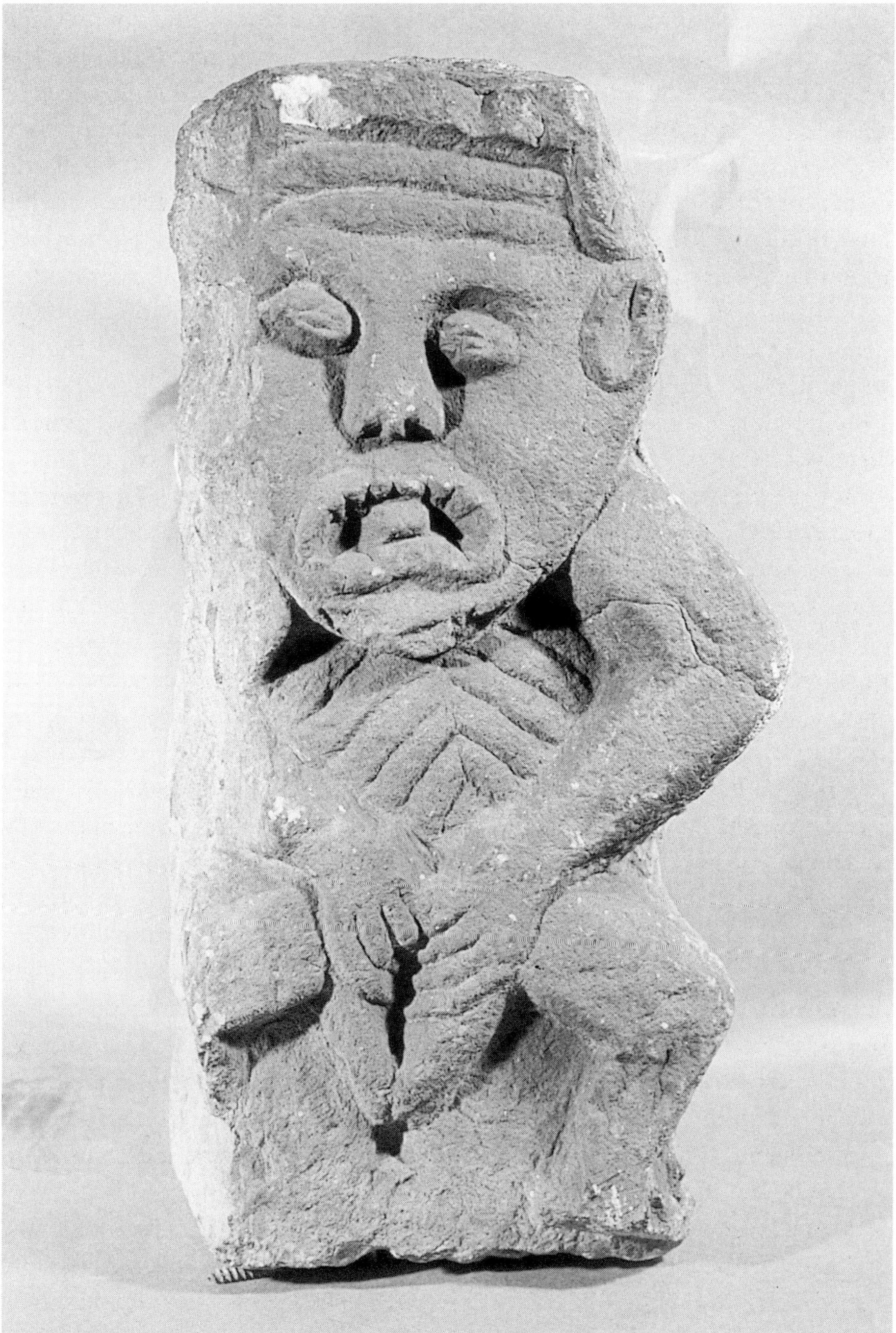

Síle na gig, Lavey, Co Cavan: Courtesy of the National Museum of Ireland © National Museum of Ireland.

The main section of *Sounding the Depths* was a darkened room with black walls. Focused spot-lighting illuminated a series of large photographs. The artists had taken slide images of mouths, grinning, grimacing, teeth clenched or open. These slides had then been projected on to the bodies of the two artists, who gestured in relation and reaction to the images across their torsos. Photographs were then made of this, and it was these images that were seen in the final installation. Thus the images were of the bodies of mature women which were inscribed with and incorporated a means of enunciation in a manner that carried a strong visual morphological resonance with síle na gig figures.[8]

Síle na gigs are medieval and Romanesque carvings of female figures exposing their genitals, found mainly in Ireland, with some in England, Wales and Scotland. They are at present 'empty' images: it is not known who made them, what they represent conceptually or spiritually, what the name originally meant, nor how they functioned or were used (Kelly 1996). There is not even (and this seems extraordinary given Ireland's wealth of written and oral storytelling) any oral tradition about them which can supply clues. Consequently it would be easy to produce a construct of them as 'Other', primitive and ahistorical. This makes it imperative that their visual specificities are recognised. Síle na gigs have no perceptible visual patriarchal overlay. Their heads and their genitals are usually prominent; often they are holding the genitals open. They usually have no hair represented. They are not sexual fantasy figures, nor are they demons; some may grimace, but others grin, while many have no particular facial expression. They are not mother figures or nurturers: their breasts are usually not depicted or only in a sketchy fashion (although their ribs may be). Their stomachs or wombs are not made particularly visible. Despite this, mis-readings of them as 'primitive fertility symbols' have been recorded (Mullin 1991: 31) while one academic has presented them even more wildly and erroneously as 'the mother-goddess [...] of fertility in Celtic mythology' (Balzano 1996: 95). Both of these readings – which are not based upon the visual or historical evidence – once again reduce a female image to one of mothering; they structure it in a romantic 'primitivism', a misleading and ahistorical notion of Celtic myth, in order to produce a signifier of fertility.

Diana Fuss indicates that the important question for critics 'is not "is this text essentialist (and therefore 'bad')?" but rather "if this text is essentialist, *what motivates its deployment*?" How does the sign "essence" circulate in various contemporary critical debates? Where, how, and why is it invoked? What are its political and textual effects?' (Fuss 1990: xi). Her position is that the risk of essentialism is not necessarily one that has to be avoided at all costs. Gayatri

Chakravorty Spivak suggests that the volubility of the anti-essentialist argument is a symptom of displacement: 'The critique of essentialism should not be seen as being critical in the colloquial, Anglo-American sense of being adversely inclined, but as a critique in the very strong European philosophical sense, that is to say, as an acknowledgement of its usefulness' (Spivak and Rooney 1994: 157). Spivak is not much interested in producing a theory of essentialism, but rather seeks to acknowledge and use what she calls a 'strategic essentialism'. The emphasis here is on producing strategies rather than on anxiety about whether or not a particular strategy is essentialist:

> I think the way in which the awareness of strategy works here is through a persistent critique. The critical moment does not come only at a certain stage when one sees one's effort, in terms of an essence that has been used for political mobilization, succeeding. [...] It seems to me that the awareness of strategy – the strategic use of an essence as a mobilising slogan or masterword like *woman* or *worker* or the name of any nation that you would like – it seems to me that this critique has to be persistent all along the way, even when it seems that to remind oneself of it is counterproductive. Unfortunately, that crisis must be with us, otherwise that strategy freezes into something like what you call an essentialist position. [...] A strategy suits a situation; a strategy is not a theory. (Spivak and Rooney 1994: 153–154)

This 'persistent critique' is what we can see happening in Irigaray's work. When she uses the term 'woman' to refer to what I have called 'the representation, woman' then she is being essentialist in the bluntest sense, in that she is using the term in a practice of mimesis to expose its construction as an essentialising category within patriarchy. She mimeticises essentialism. On the other hand, when she uses the term 'woman' to refer to what has not yet become – the subjects, women – she is naming strategically a space of potentiality rather than a pre-existing ontological category.

Fuss suggests that to an extent such an act of naming can itself be an essentialising move. To announce oneself as anti-essentialist names a place for essentialism; and the most ardent anti-essentialist, in breaking supposed universals down into named categories, can by default be in that hazy space between identity and essence as a result of the act of naming (Fuss 1990: 20). This, however, appears to be that moment Spivak identifies when the critique is no longer persistent, and the strategy freezes – a short cut where an individual's sex, sexuality, class, race, age group, physical ability... are all named and thus turn into a check-list of categories. In Irigaray's writings what we see in the potentiality of the subjects, women, is instead what Spivak describes as 'vigilance, what I call building for difference, rather than keeping ourselves clean by being whatever it is to be an anti-essentialist' (Spivak and Rooney 1994: 155). It is necessary to attend closely to Irigaray's acts of naming, her deployment of words and vigilance over terminology. 'Morphology' is crucial in this respect. If we recognise it as naming a place between body and language, and recognise that it is not anatomy, then we also have to acknowledge that a careless, non-strategic (apolitical) reading reduces it to anatomical determinism.

The questions then when looking at *Sounding the Depths* is not 'is this work essentialist?' but 'what are the strategies of the artists? What morphologies can we see at play here? What genealogies are being called upon, reinvested in a new syntax?' In short, what is the vigilance at work here, what 'building for difference'? I would argue that in its structures of representation and its modes of production, *Sounding the Depths* forms a morphological, rather than indexical, link with the síle na gigs, and thus moves towards (among other things) possibilities for an appropriate syntax. By this I mean that it is in a relationship of *différance* with the síle na gigs as a dynamic, developing and culturally appropriate indicator of a transcendent female genealogy, rather than a determinant or causal link. The artists have therefore produced a site where cultural memory, female genealogy and horizons of latent possibility coexist through a process which recalls Griselda Pollock's term 'inscriptions in the feminine': 'a kind of analytical reading of symptoms – pressures and signs from the other scene, the other registers of meaning, the scripts of desire' (Pollock 1996d: xvi). Similarly, when I point to morphological resonance between the images of Anne and Mary and the Labille-Guiard self-portrait I am looking at a structural resonance: for example, the passing of knowledge from a woman of one generation to younger women of the next generation, and the ways in which these images can be used as models of practice. Thus the word 'heritage' as used by Nancy Spero should not be used in the narrow sense of preserving the past – a maintenance mimesis that Spero refutes through her own work – but as a productive site for genealogy and syntax. As indicated earlier, images of Anne teaching Mary may have been used to indicate the significance – or simply the possibility – of teaching girls to read. Recalling Irigaray's suggestions of placing images of the mother–daughter couple in public and domestic spaces, maybe Adélaïde Labille-Guiard's painting of herself with two of her students, Marie Gabrielle Capet and Carreaux de Rosemond, is an image that could have greater prominence in today's art school studios and offices.

## PRODUCTIVE MIMESIS IN MOTHER–DAUGHTER GENEALOGIES: HANNAH WILKE, FRANCES HEGARTY

For Irigaray, as we have seen, the mother–daughter relationship is fundamental to the structuring of women's subjectivities. The experience of daughterhood marks a woman's relation to the divine, to language, to civil society, to herself and how she can represent herself. In recent decades the mother–daughter dyad has been proposed as a 'proper', if still marginal, subject for visual representation and exploration through public venues such as galleries or publishing houses, from quite tough exhibitions containing some difficult work, like *Mothers* (Ikon Gallery, Birmingham, 1990) through to more celebratory publications verging on the sentimental like *Our Mothers: Portraits by 72 Women Photographers* (Esders 1996). These public expressions have come on the back of an increasing amount of work by individual artists who have been representing their mothers and working towards ways of representing the mother–daughter relationship. In some cases, such as we have seen in the work of Louise Bourgeois, this relationship may become legible through the gestural codes of the artist, the syntax developed in her use of materials and space. For others, the relationship with the mother has become the overt focus

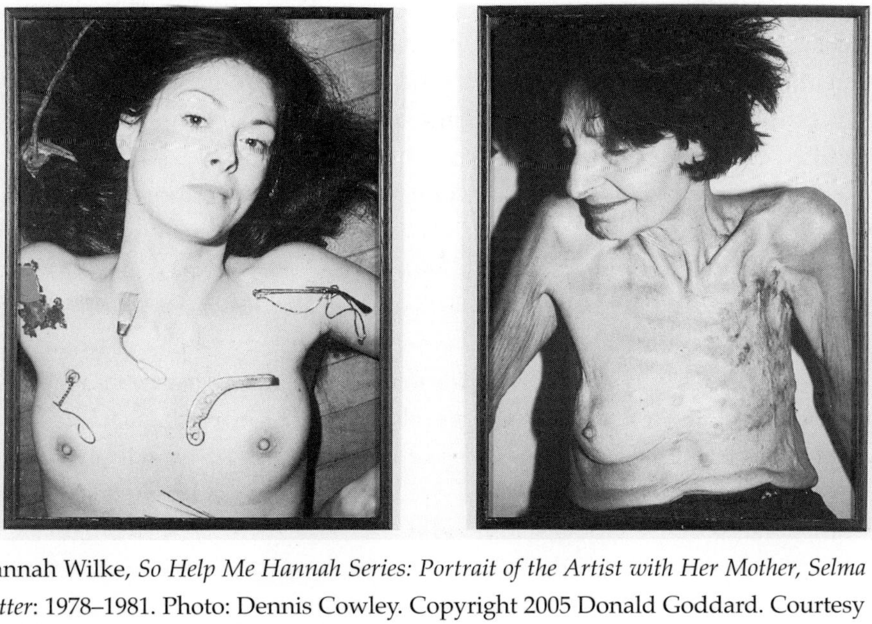

Hannah Wilke, *So Help Me Hannah Series: Portrait of the Artist with Her Mother, Selma Butter*: 1978–1981. Photo: Dennis Cowley. Copyright 2005 Donald Goddard. Courtesy Ronald Feldman Fine Arts, New York.

of the work, with also a concomitant redressing of the visual languages that can be used to articulate that relationship. While *Our Mothers* contains many moving tributes by women photographers in honour of their mothers, the images in the book for the most part comprise photographs that conform to relatively standard late twentieth-century portrait photography formats (notable exceptions would include such artists as Mari Mahr and Chila Burman). For every such example it seems that there can be found instances of women who are challenging the available visual languages, attempting to find a new syntax with which to articulate the intersubjective relationship.

It is instructive to look at the work of Hannah Wilke in this respect, and in particular three groups of works in conjunction with each other: her body works of the 1970s such as the *S.O.S. Starification Object* series (1974–1982); the series *So Help Me Hannah, Portrait of the Artist with Her Mother, Selma Butter* (1978–1981); and her final body of photographic work, *Intra-Venus* (1992–1993). Wilke's work of the 1970s came in for criticism from within feminism, most prominently from Lucy Lippard, who called her 'a glamour girl in her own right' who 'is considered a little too good to be true when she flaunts her body in parody of the role she actually plays in real life. [...] Her own confusion of her roles as beautiful woman and artist, as flirt and feminist, has resulted at times in politically ambiguous manifestations that have exposed her to criticism on a personal as well as artistic level' (Lippard 1990: 103). In the *Starification Object* series Wilke used chewing gum in particular, but also other materials such as clay and kneaded erasers to make small 'scars' or sculptures which were then sometimes placed over her body and the results photographed, and sometimes used in their own right. These objects consisted of the material being stretched or flattened, then given a simple single twist or folds. Usually referred to as vaginal in shape or like the keloid scarring used for beautification in some parts of Africa, these shapes are in fact more like the hood of the clitoris in their shape and morphology.

In the late 1970s–early 1980s Wilke produced a series of photographs of her mother, Selma Butter, showing her aging and ill body (she was dying from cancer) and the scar of the radical mastectomy she had undergone. Again, the critical reception was luke-warm, suggesting that Wilke was being exploitative of her mother or encouraging a voyeuristic gaze at her wounded body. However, the exhibition of Wilke's final body of work, *Intra-Venus*, shown posthumously at the Ronald Feldman Gallery in New York (8 January – 19 February 1994) suggested that there could be supplementary readings of the earlier works. Rather than revise the readings of the earlier work, the suggestion is that a development of particular concerns becomes discernible in the light of the late work. The bulk of the exhibition consisted of large photographs of Wilke, taken in collaboration with her husband, Donald Goddard. Wilke had died a year earlier, January 1993, of complications from lymphoma, and in this last series of works she uses her own body again, in its sick state, with the medical accessories that it required – in particular, drips, drains and bandages. Over the time of the production of the photographs, Wilke lost her hair, from head and body, as a result of chemotherapy, and this is evident. What is also evident though is that Wilke's confidence in her body as a means of mediating her subjectivity is still utterly in place. Dying as she is, there is nothing of the victim about her. As Amelia Jones has pointed out: 'even in the midst of her own physical disintegration Wilke insists upon her value (her beauty) as a subject and in so doing throws the very concept of body beautiful into question' (Jones 1996a: 29). Looking almost unrecognisable from the photographs she had taken 20 years earlier, swollen-faced, with belly, hips and thighs bloated, hair thin or gone, Wilke's subjectivity is intact: she has become beauty.

These photographs insist upon different readings of the earlier groups of work. It becomes impossible to look at the photographs imaging Wilke's younger body with the clitoral hood/'scars' and other accoutrements without seeing the morphology of the later images of the damaged body with pads and bandages. Likewise, the images representing Selma Butter when seen in

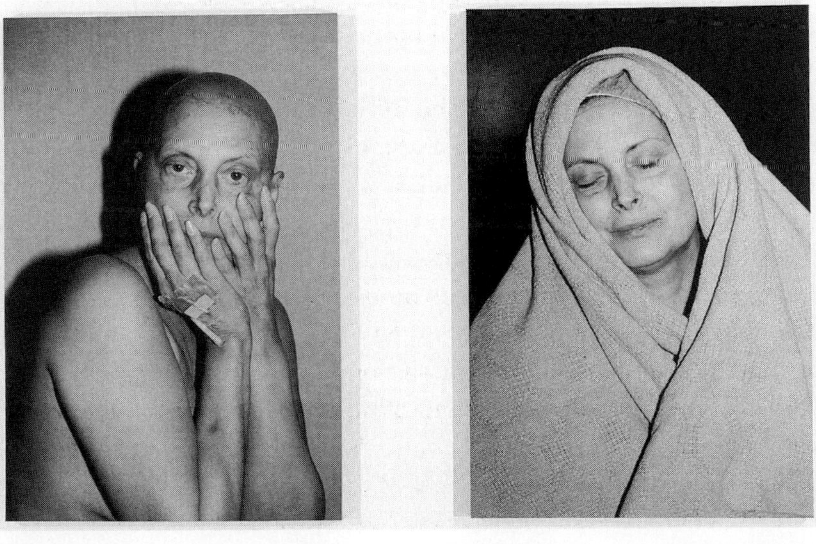

Hannah Wilke, *Intra-Venus Series #4: July 26, 1992/February 19, 1992*, 1992–1993. Photo: Dennis Cowley. Copyright 2005 David Goddard. Courtesy Ronald Feldman Fine Arts, New York.

conjunction with those from *Intra-Venus* begin to mean something different: a meditation upon the passing of experience of illness and dying from mother to daughter. Wilke worked in a long series over a number of years. What becomes evident is a life's project that works upon the mediation of a particular genealogy of body, beauty and illness. Wilke started making the photographs of her own body in 1970 – after her mother's mastectomy. As Joanna Freueh writes, 'As Wilke's mother was losing her body, Wilke wore her mother's wounds'(Freueh 2002: 579). The early works confront the representation, 'woman', through a process that works towards a productive mimesis. The artist explores the genealogy of her mother through exploration of the 'wholeness' of the body, the clitoral hood/'scar' on the representation, 'woman', that signifies the female sex and clitoral desire: a 'scar' that does not destroy beauty but is its mediator.

In the spring of 1996 in the Irish Museum of Modern Art, Frances Hegarty exhibited the final version of a video installation which had previously been exhibited in differing forms: *Turas* (Journey) (1991–1995). In a room to itself, *Turas* had two main elements. Down the middle of the floor were a series of light boxes with images of the surface of a river. This led to the far wall, on which was projected a video. A sequence of seven scenes were shown on a loop. On the left of the image sits an older woman, facing the camera; on the right, in profile, a woman approaching middle age. Each scene starts with a close-up of the hands of the younger woman touching the elder in a gesture which speaks of the possibility of communication from elder to younger: fingers touching the place of the elder woman's voice box; fingers touching a book in her hands; and so on. The camera pulls back to hold both women in frame; then finally the younger woman stands and leaves. We hear a voice speaking haltingly in Irish: 'An dtig leat cuidiú liom Gaeilge a labhairt arís?' The voice changes to that of an older woman saying 'Thiocfaidh liom cuidiú leat Gaeilge a labhairt, cinnte.' In the final sequence she collects the book from the elder woman's hands and leaves with it. Then the whole set of scenes repeat. The

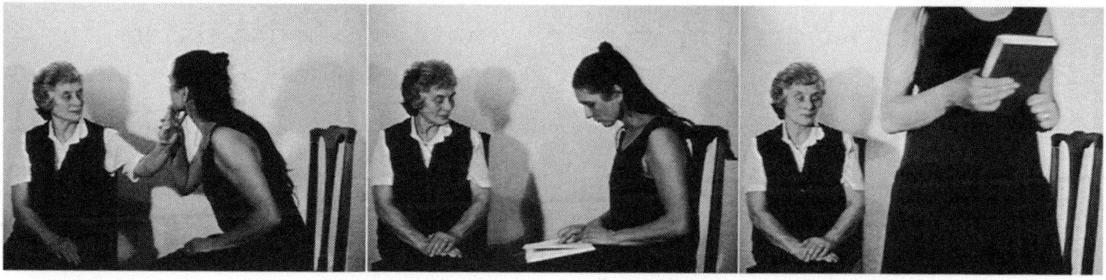

Frances Hegarty, *Turas*: 1987–1995. Still frames from film/video. Courtesy of the artist.

Irish cannot be exactly translated into English, but would be understood as 'Do you [think/believe/feel] you could [give/teach] me Irish again?' and 'I do [think/believe/feel] that I could [give/teach] you Irish, surely.'

I recognise the younger woman as the artist, and know the elder to be her mother; it is their voices on the tape. This is privileged information, not available to the majority who see the work; I mention it not to add 'authenticity' to any narrative reading into the work, but rather to demonstrate the morphological structures at different levels of it. In a letter responding to my request for the spelling of the Irish the artist told me

> you wouldn't believe the consternation it all caused back in Teelin [her family's home village in Co. Donegal] when I phoned some friends for the correct spelling. I was passed from house to house all week with no one agreeing on any word [...] The meaning of the words in brackets is more in the emphasis of the spoken maternal voice than its written form (Hegarty 1998).

Governmental rationalising of spelling (replacing certain letter combinations with accents) and centralising of Irish language teaching, combined with highly localised accents, word and sentence structure, ensure a tension between the mother's speech and its abstraction into writing. Her certainty that her speech can be transmitted is not shared by her daughter, and died with her. The answer for the daughter is in the gift-object of the old book from which the mother reads, and which remains a mediation of the mother tongue: a chance for its legibility, rather than unmediated authenticity. Maintenance mimesis is not possible; but what is at stake is the possible trauma of total loss of mother tongue. It is as if the representational trope of Anne teaching Mary to read has been reinvested with a very specific cultural and personal history. The video sequences have inscribed in them traces of histories that are common on the Irish west coast and that are particular to the artist and her family: traces of emigration, dispersal of culture and of language, shifting of culture through the diaspora and the impossibility of return to any 'authenticity'. All of these are granted extra poignancy through the death of this individual, Hegarty's mother, and with her the death of particular usage of Irish, and the end of possible mediation in a particular syntax between mother and daughter. The mother and daughter speak in this work not just of their relationship, nor just of Hegarty's trauma at the loss of her language, and their different historical processes, but of that possibility of mediation between them. Through repeated gestures of touching-upon and leaving, the daughter is struggling to realise the transcendent genealogy as mediated through her mother tongue, and thus the possibility of her own becoming. Hegarty has written of *Turas*:

> This [...] is where the Mothervoice offers itself as an alternative, a repository of knowledge and a fund of cultural energy with which to resist the effects of displacement. In *Turas,* the daughter's relationship the Mothertongue is not only gendered but predicated on a genealogical link with the maternal body. There is also an analogy between the separation from the mother and the emigrant's trauma of lost access to both language and the physical landscape. (Ziff 1995: 119)

Hegarty has produced a morphologically coherent space in which to speak of her mother, of her own history of being mothered, and finally of the loss and possibility of a transcendent genealogy. *Turas* speaks of the struggle to retrieve this loss through productive mimesis, and thus to become a woman.

# Conclusion

> But one apparently negative predicate still remains to [God]: that of invisibility. We keep invisible too, to a large extent, our sexual relation, our carnal act, especially through the mediation of woman. What birth takes place, is yet to come, between these two poles of invisibility? How can we discover and interpret its traces in discourse? How can we remodel existing languages [*langages*] so as to give place to a sexuate culture? That is what is at stake in my researches. (Translation modified; 1987g: 195–196, Irigaray 1991e: 152. )

The concept of 'becoming' offered by Irigaray can now be read in three ways: the 'becoming' qualities of the patriarchal masquerade, femininity; the aim of becoming subjects, women, shedding our being the representation, 'woman'; and the ongoing unfolding of being in a state of becoming as those subjects – becoming (as) beauty.

There are a number of things that Irigaray does not offer to women involved with art practice. She writes very little about visual art, and even less does she write about what art made by women might look like – either in its overall aesthetic, or its materiality or its overt imagery. To do so would be to offer a form of security, but a false security: it would be to set a fixity to that which has not yet developed its porousity, nor recognised the sites of its limits. The *parler-femme* and the witnessing-woman, enunciations in a syntax appropriate to women and through a morphologic that respects women's 'natural' and spiritual ontology, are as yet hardly realised. Irigaray's work is of strategic use for creative practices. In particular, it is of help in analysing how we might move from where we are now (in the spheres of the political, the philosophical and the performative) towards bringing this morphologic and its syntax in the Symbolic into being.

These strategic possibilities emerge primarily because of Irigaray's active practice of productive mimesis – as an anti-patriarchal position, rather than a binary oppositional, separatist or equal rights form of feminism. Her practice of mimesis (drawing together textual practices, civil rights and the empirical woman) in tandem with her practice within an appropriate morphologic (a structural relationship between the enunciation and the sexuate subject) provide patterns for art practices as a set of discourses (including its interrelation with criticism), rather than producing models for such practices. In particular, the attempt to engage with a productive mimesis and to develop an appropriate morphologic can make us aware of places of resistance – reserves – in extant syntaxes. In doing so, we can recognise that we, as the subjects, women, are always elsewhere from the patriarchal site of the representation, 'woman', and we can identify the sites we have to re-traverse in order to expose their blind spots and in order to signify women in the Symbolic.

What Irigaray provides for us, then, is a number of strategies, both pragmatic and philosophical, through which we can work as theoreticians and practitioners. These start from a recognition of the limits of the present Symbolic structures, in order to begin the development of appropriate syntaxes. This will inevitably involve a repossessing of images and a re-figuration of our sexuate subjectivity, rather than a trust in the abstract: 'The fact that this sort of language barely exists greatly restricts women's space for subjective freedom. It's possible to start to create it with everyday language' (Irigaray 1993i: 49; 1990a: 56). Crucially, it will develop discourses of representational economies which recognise sexuate subjectivity – economies which are, therefore, intersubjective, aware of the subject's limits and of *différance* rather than difference between the Same and its other.

This requires attention to be paid to the manner of mediation – its function in terms of subject–subject relations: in short, how artworks mediate between artist and audience. If women have existed in a state of immediacy with other subjects (if they have had no appropriate Symbolic for mediation) then one task – and this is a particular problem for artists – is to produce objects of mediation: gift-space/objects, the third term, which allow for mediated, intersubjective relation. These are not the capitalised objects of phallocentric discourse (familiar in the present mainstream art world), a discourse which closes down intersubjectivity by reducing the other subject to object status, to mirror status, to being nothing but the other of the same. Present phallocentric discourse, in capitalising art objects, does not require of them any more than the one-way mediation of the self of the artist. Mediation in intersubjectivity requests a two-way responsibility: it requires attentiveness from the subject audience. This suggests that there may be anti-patriarchal structures of looking at art, including gallery practices and the pre-writing aspects of criticism.

Finally, while Irigaray's writing does not tell artists what to say through their practice, it is clear that none of the above will be able to be worked upon without some concomitant – morphologically appropriate – sense of the transcendent and thus of the spiritual or divine and of women's genealogies. Here, Irigaray offers particular suggestions of representational practices: but they are pragmatically strategic, rooted in the knowledge of what is possible while working through the Symbolic presently available to us. They are concerned with creating gift-space/objects which mediate between women (including in domestic spaces and between mothers and daughters), which do not perform a maintenance mimesis of patriarchal languages, and particularly not of the representation, 'women' within those languages; which respect women as subjects, not reducing them to objects or to mothers; which recognise the subject's limits and her transcendental.

The question to be asked at this point is: What is to be done now? Given the above findings, what are the tasks for feminists concerned with progressing the theories of art, whether as artists or as writers? Most pressing, I would say, is the need to identify where Irigaray's analysis can be most productively juxtaposed with current feminist theories of art so they can, in Gayatri Spivak's dynamic term, 'critically "interrupt" each other, bring each other to crisis, in order to serve their constituencies' (Spivak 1988b: 241)[1] in order not only to make legible artworks of the past, but also in order to provide spaces of discourse capable of providing a background against which artists can work in the future. I would like to conclude by outlining briefly how this might happen.

In two important essays of the late 1990s, Griselda Pollock outlines the histories of feminist theories of and in art history, and identifies areas of possible development and tasks for feminist critical practices (Pollock 1996a, 1996c). These practices are ones that work antagonistically towards the present curatorial impulse of art history, with its categorisation according to dates and styles. Instead it looks for differently structured 'spaces of femininity':

> Yet the meanings of works produced by women will only become vivid to us when we can articulate what is particular to them, what makes them different from the existing norms, and when we define signifying temporalities quite other than those of styles, movements, avant-garde innovations and so forth. We are searching for ways to acknowledge the 'spaces of femininity' and its subjective temporalities in the rhythms of women's lived experience within and against the hierarchies of sexual difference as that is configured in complex social formations of class, race and sexuality. (Pollock 1996c: 8)

These 'spaces of femininity' are far from being the masquerading 'femininity' of Freudian terminology. Pollock identifies 'the feminine' as being a radical rupture of patriarchy, and denies the binary oppositional position of being the other to phallocentric man's same: 'feminism has needed to develop forms of analysis that can confront the difference of women as other than what is other to this masculine order while exposing the sexual politics of dominant discourses and institutions' (Pollock 1996c: 71). In order for the spaces of femininity to be legible as sites of mediation, we need to search for, and develop, what Pollock calls (drawing upon Mary Kelly's writing of the 1970s) 'inscriptions in the feminine':

> The phrase, 'inscriptions in the feminine', has an archaeological ring to it. As if deciphering an ancient culture whose language is lost while its strange monuments remain to puzzle and provoke our curiosity, we must assume that we do not yet know what is being traced upon the surface of culture by artists speaking in, from, or of the feminine. A feminist reading for the inscriptions of the feminine means listening for the traces of a subjectivity formed in the feminine within and in conflict with a phallocentric system. Beyond that, it implies figuring out what working from that place, however unconsciously, might be producing, as yet unarticulated, unrepresented, unsignified, unrecognized. (Pollock 1996c: 74)

Already we can begin to find a structural (if not terminological) rapport between Pollock's analysis of the present moment, and that of Irigaray. In the notion of 'the spaces of femininity' and 'artists speaking in, from, or of the feminine' there are echoes of the morphology appropriate to women as a site of mediation and productive of an appropriate syntax. There are echoes too of sites of Irigarayan 'reserve' as sites for re-entering as strategies of resistance and rupture.

This indicates one of the present points of tension: terminology. As of yet, although there may be areas of rapport between Irigaray's work and Pollock's theorising of the discourses of art, the use of terminology is far from agreed. In the short term this might be a problem, as differences of terminology (particularly across cultures and languages) can mean even further lack of legibility. In the longer term, however, this might prove more healthy: painstaking negotiation over terminology avoids the capitalisation of phrases, their reduction into mere translation (or maintenance mimesis) of extant terminology, their collapse into containable quasi-objects rather than dynamic processes aiding women becoming subjects. I am thinking here of terms such as 'difference' being mis-understood as 'other', and thus maintaining a phallic norm; or a 'feminine space' collapsing into celebration of the masquerade of femininity in Freudian terms; or the way in which 'écriture feminine' was dismissible as somehow both essentialist and something to do with surface style. For theoreticians to keep the spaces of terminology open through continual processes of resistance and open discourse can only rebuff assumptions and misreadings, and eventually do what is most difficult: help shift embedded ways of thinking. Such terms (including, of course, the ones I have identified in this book) may stretch structures of thinking and mark sites of intervention, but for them to become art-critical shorthand for style would be to miss the point. Neither the discussion of Pollock, nor the implications of that of Irigaray, indicate a prescription of style or of medium. However, as we have seen, for an artist to mimic technical means unthinkingly (including style in the use of media, composition, imagery, gesture, etc) can undermine absolutely any assumed feminist voice in the artwork. As Toril Moi says in criticising Jane Gallop on styles of writing:

> Jane Gallop is right to claim that to take up a style is to take up a position, but she is wrong to recommend a single stylistic move as uniquely feminist, just as she is wrong to assume that style can be analyzed without regard to contents and the specific historical space where it makes its intervention. (Moi 1988: 22)

Pollock outlines the theoretical work of artist and psychoanalyst Bracha Lichtenberg Ettinger and describes how it offers a potential articulation of the 'feminine':

> Lichtenberg Ettinger theorizes a way to imagine the Symbolic expanded to contain more than one symbol – more than one 'signifier of signifiers' for subjectivity. Neither replacing nor merely supplementing the phallus, itself the signifier for subjectivity based on the opposition of on/off, absence/presence, and all related binaries of assimilation versus rejection, she proposes the matrix, a symbol of coexisting and coemerging part-subjectivities that holds special promise for women, for whom this aspect has particular and profound resonance in allowing elements of their feminine but invisible bodily specificity and the fantasies to which it gives rise to filter into signification. (Pollock 1996a: 79)

Once again, there are structural resonances between aspects of this and aspects of Irigaray's thought. Lichtenberg Ettinger goes further than Irigaray in proposing 'more than one symbol'. Irigaray proposes the 'double syntax' and syntactical signification, produced through an appropriate morphology, while Lichtenberg Ettinger proposes the 'matrix' as a neutral term (alongside reasserting the phallus as a neutral term) productive of a space which relates to Irigaray's 'morphologic' in allowing mediation or a 'filtering' of subjectivity into signification.

The significance of an artist producing this work is of course profound, not least because of the very real knowledge she would have of the struggle to produce significations in the realm of the visual as well as through verbal language.[2] Pollock indicates the questions for art theory (including that produced by artists through their work) provoked by Lichtenberg Ettinger's writing:

> Lichtenberg Ettinger's suggestion that there may be more than one symbol (the one being the phallus that forces us to think of sex as the One and its Other, and thus in fact always and only as the One) opens up art criticism to ask: What is involved in a nonphallic, matrixial reading of an artistic text? What would be a matrixial exhibition? The matrix reveals the sexual difference at work in our forms of knowledge, interpretation, and curatorship and once acknowledged will change the politics of selection, viewing, and response. (Pollock 1996a: 81)

These questions can find a correlation in some that I have been attempting to ask in this book: What is a morphologically appropriate, nonphallic, reading of an artwork? If there is more than one syntax in the Symbolic, how does that syntax become legible? What are the processes of reading nonphallicly, intersubjectively? How, ultimately, can we shift the deeply phallocentric present discourses of the art world? While Irigaray's 'morphologic' and 'double syntax', Griselda Pollock's 'spaces of femininity', and Lichtenberg Ettinger's 'matrix' do not map exactly upon one another, it is in what I detect to be a fruitful tension between these terms that I feel the grounds for most optimism. It is here that I think we have the most likely space for the realisation, in the possibilities of their art, the becoming beauty of the subjects, women.

# Notes

## INTRODUCTION

1 In private conversation one American art historian told me in the late 1990s 'America always has room for one grand old lady in the art world. It used to be Georgia O'Keeffe, then it was Louise Nevelson; now it's Louise Bourgeois's turn'.

2 'It is refreshing to be interviewed without once being asked to explain my work in relation to where I come from. Most people who interview me seem to have this journalistic attitude that wants to explain or validate my work specifically in relation to my background'. Michael Archer, Guy Brett, and M. Catherine de Zegher (eds), *Mona. Hatoum* (London: Phaidon, 1997), p. 30.

3 As the title *The Art of Tracey Emin* indicates, the only substantial publication on Emin was produced explicitly to address this lack. Mandy Merck and Chris Townsend (eds), *The Art of Tracey Emin* (London: Thames & Hudson, 2002).

4 The major publications are: Carolyn Burke, Naomi Schor, and Margaret Whitford (eds), *Engaging with Irigaray: Feminist Philosophy and Modern European Thought* (New York: Columbia UP, 1994) vii, p. 428; Tina Chanter, *Ethics of Eros: Irigaray's Re-Writing of the Philosophers* (New York: Routledge, 1995) xvii, p. 345 ; Margaret Whitford, *Luce Irigaray: Philosophy in the Feminine* (London; New York: Routledge, 1991c) x, p. 241. Many other shorter works have been immensely important, but three that helped me rethink my whole approach to reading Irigaray are Christine Delphy, 'The Invention of French Feminism: An Essential Move'. *Yale French Studies*, 87 (1995), pp. 190–221; Henry Louis Gates, Jr, 'Significant Others', *Contemporary Literature*, 29 / 4 (Winter 1988), pp. 606–623; Cathryn Vasseleu, 'Illuminating Passion: Irigaray's Transfiguration of Night', in Theresa Brennan and Martin Jay (eds), *Vision in Context* (London: Routledge, 1996), pp. 127–137. I would also like to acknowledge the importance of writers such as Elizabeth Grosz and Gayatri Spivak for providing frameworks through which to approach aspects of Irigaray's work: Elizabeth Grosz, *Volatile Bodies: Toward a Corporeal Feminism* (Bloomington: Indiana University Press, 1994); Elizabeth Grosz, *Space, Time and Perversion: Essays on the Politics of Bodies* (London: Routledge, 1995); Gayatri Chakravorty Spivak and Ellen Rooney, 'In a Word. Interview', in Naomi Schor and Elizabeth Weed (eds), *The Essential Difference* (Bloomington: Indiana UP, 1994), pp. 151–185.

5 See for example, Gayatri Chakravorty Spivak, 'The Politics of Translation', in Michèle Barrett and Anne Phillips (eds), *Destabilizing Theory: Contemporary Feminist Debates* (Cambridge: Polity Press, 1992), pp. 177–200; Sherry Simon, *Gender in Translation: Cultural Identity and the Politics of Transmission* (London: Routledge, 1996), particularly

pp. 101–107 on the translation of Irigaray's work; and Carolyn Burke, 'Translation Modified: Irigaray in English', in Carolyn Burke, Naomi Schor, and Margaret Whitford (eds), *Engaging with Irigaray: Feminist Philosophy and Modern European Thought* (New York: Columbia UP, 1994), pp. 249–261.

6 Elizabeth Hirsh and Gary Olson, '"Je – Luce Irigaray": A Meeting with Luce Irigaray', in Gary A. Olson and Elizabeth Hirsh (eds), *Women Writing Culture* (Albany: SUNY, 1995), pp. 141–166. For other comments of hers upon translation in general and of her work in particular, see Luce Irigaray, *Je, tu, nous: pour une culture de la différence* (Paris: Grasset et Fasquelle, 1990a); Luce Irigaray, *Je, Tu, Nous: Toward a Culture of Difference*, trans. Alison Martin (New York: Routledge, 1993i), pp. 54, 58, 72; Luce Irigaray, *J'aime à toi: esquisse d'une félicité dans l'histoire* (Paris: B. Grasset, 1992b), pp. 102; Luce Irigaray, *I Love to You: Sketch for a Felicity within History*, trans. Alison Martin (New York: Routledge, 1996), p. 60; Luce Irigaray, *Le temps de la différence: pour une révolution pacifique* (Le livre de poche; Paris: Libr. générale française, 1989), p. 73; Luce Irigaray, *Thinking the Difference: For a Peaceful Revolution*, trans. Karin Montin (London: Athlone Press, 1994c), p. 58; Luce Irigaray, 'Questions to Emanuel Levinas', in Margaret Whitford (ed.), *The Irigaray Reader* (Oxford: Blackwell, 1991d), pp. 178–189. Marion Gentillehomme, who helped me with the translation of one article, exclaimed 'But she's not even writing French!'

## CHAPTER 1

1 According to Gebauer and Wulf, Derrida's interest in the mime artist is that 'what he [the mime; sic] represents does not exist outside of his representation [...] In the mime's representation, the distinction between fiction and reality also collapses.' Gunter Gebauer and Christoph Wulf, *Mimesis: Culture, Art, Society*, trans. Don Reneau (London: University of California Press, 1995), pp. 300–301.

2 Elizabeth Grosz, *Jacques Lacan: A Feminist Introduction* (London: Routledge, 1990), Jacqueline Rose, *Sexuality in the Field of Vision* (London: Verso, 1986).

3 One of the few substantive passages of Lacan that Irigaray quotes is this one, where Lacan relates the 'being' and 'having' of the phallus to the masquerade; she does so in order to demonstrate his closeness to Freud's castration theory. Luce Irigaray, *Ce sexe qui n'en est pas un* (Paris: Éditions de Minuit, 1977a), p. 58, Luce Irigaray, *This Sex Which Is Not One*, trans. Catherine Porter and Carolyn Burke (Ithaca, NY: Cornell University Press, 1985d), p. 62.

4 The word 'travestissement' carries the connotations of transvestism and of drag, thus emphasising that this disguise of 'femininity' is a masculine construction of femininity. Irigaray had earlier noted 'The fact that certain men want to "act like" women thus raises the question whether they thereby take back for themselves that "femininity" which was assigned to woman', Luce Irigaray, *Speculum de l'autre femme* (Paris: Éditions de Minuit, 1974), p. 55, Luce Irigaray, *Speculum of the Other Woman*, trans. Gillian C. Gill (Ithaca, NY: Cornell University Press, 1985c), p. 49. This could also apply to those aspects of 'femininity' deemed appropriate for male artists.

5 Surveys in the USA have shown a difference in attitude to body image between young white women and young black women, with a high percentage of the white women expressing a desire to lose weight and be thinner, while black women were expressing the importance of having 'thickness' on them and a physical presence. Elizabeth Nickson, 'Learning Curves', *The Guardian*, 8 April 1996, sec. G2 p. 7. Irigaray does not consider racial difference within hysteria; but neither does she mention anorexia in this context; it is Grosz's exemplar, which is, I think, valid in certain dominant Western contexts.

6 See Josephine Donovan, 'Everyday Use and Moments of Being: Toward a Nondominative Aesthetic', in Hilde Hein and Carolyn Korsmeyer (eds), (Bloomington: Indiana University Press, 1993), pp. 53–67. for a discussion of the dominative and the nondominative in aesthetic praxis

7 I would like to stress that here, and in all discussions of the reduction of women to mothers, I am not devalorising motherhood. Rather, I am indicating the destructive effects upon a woman's subjectivity if she is classified first of all by her relationship to mothering, rather than as a woman (one facet of whom is a relationship to mothering).

8 The exception to prove this rule is the pedagogically intended *I Love To You*, Luce Irigaray, *J'aime à toi: esquisse d'une félicité dans l'histoire* (Paris: B. Grasset, 1992b), pp. 29–31, Luce Irigaray, *I Love to You: Sketch for a Felicity within History*, trans. Alison Martin (New York: Routledge, 1996), pp. 24–25 where she does on occasion cite models of practice. This can be reflected back upon the pedagogical aspects of mimesis, but also requests reflection upon the model cited – notably, Buddha's fusion of mind and body in his contemplation of the flower, Irigaray, *J'aime à toi: esquisse d'une félicité dans l'histoire*, pp. 49–50, Irigaray, *I Love to You: Sketch for a Felicity within History*, pp. 24–25.

9 For example, Dianne Chisholm's wonderfully witty musings on whether Irigaray is a con-artist (con: Fr.: cunt, orifice, hole) or an 'ex'-centric – or even an 'ex-con' (as in an ex-convict) who has managed to escape, Dianne Chisholm, 'Irigaray's Hysteria', in Carolyn Burke, Naomi Schor, and Margaret Whitford (eds), *Engaging with Irigaray: Feminist Philosophy and Modern European Thought* (New York: Columbia UP, 1994), p. 264.

10 – taking our lead from Irigaray's use of the term 'morphology' in relation to bodies, not only as a metaphor as discussed in Margaret Whitford, 'Luce Irigaray', in Alice Jardine and Anne M. Menke (eds), *Shifting Scenes: Interviews on Women, Writing, and Politics in Post-68 France* (New York: Columbia UP, 1991d), pp. 58–59, but also in its sense within linguistics, referring to the formation of words. See Chapter 3.

## CHAPTER 2

1 I note that Martin Jay coins the term 'phallogocularcentrism' in the title of his chapter on Irigaray and Derrida – both less elegant and (for reasons which will become clear) less persuasively descriptive than the thread of 'phall-oculo-logo-centrism', Martin Jay, *Downcast Eyes: The Denigration of Vision in Twentieth Century French Thought* (Berkeley: University of California Press, 1993), p. 493.

2 Irigaray has re-enforced this with the analogy of the pictograph in a more recent interview: 'If the culture is founded on a certain repression of the graphic order, and if that which returns at night under the guise of the dream presents itself as a sort of pictograph, isn't there the trace of a much more generalizable pictographic order that had already been historically repressed [...] I know that cultures in which writing is more pictographic are generally more favourable to the feminine subject and to a culture of the feminine.' Irigaray in Elizabeth Hirsh and Gary Olson, ''Je – Luce Irigaray': A Meeting with Luce Irigaray', in Gary A. Olson and Elizabeth Hirsh (eds), *Women Writing Culture* (Albany: State U of New York P, 1995), p. 57.

3 Translation modified: *les yeux aurifés* was translated as gilded eyes, but in fact references gold tooth fillings. I take this not to be a reference to decorated gilt surfaces (she is talking about eyes, not the mirror's surface), but another confirmation of Irigaray's analysis that the amalgam of the exchange value of women in patriarchy and capitalism is essentially rotten.

4 As the title of this section of *Speculum* suggests ('Any Theory of the "Subject" Has Always Been Appropriated by the 'Masculine'), Irigaray places the term 'subject' in quotation marks when she is referring to the supposed universal subject which is, however, always already masculine – i.e., when she refers to that subjecthood granted men within a phallocentric economy.

5 Certainly, one might assume that she was aware of Lacan's reference to this painting during a discussion of anamorphosis in the publication of his 1964 seminar Jacques Lacan, *The Four Fundamental Concepts of Psycho-Analysis*, trans. Alan Sheridan (London: Penguin, 1994), pp. 85–89. During the course of this passage Lacan wonders 'How is it that nobody has ever thought of connecting this with... the effect of an erection? Imagine a tattoo traced on the sexual organ ad hoc in the state of repose and assuming its, if I may say so, developed form in another state', Lacan, *The Four Fundamental Concepts of Psycho-Analysis*, pp. 87–88.

6 Other critics, such as Francesco Bonami, have attempted to read Kapoor's work as indexically linked to his Indian-ness – something Kapoor steadfastly resisted. Francesco Bonami, 'Anish Kapoor: Jumping into the Void', *Flash Art*, 27/179 (November–December 1994), pp. 80–82. Thomas McEvilley has indicated that Kapoor has one Indian parent – his father – while his mother is Iraqi-Jewish, though he does not say if Jewish identification and religious practice was passed down the maternal line. Thomas McEvilley, 'The Darkness Inside a Stone', *Anish Kapoor* (London: The British Council, 1990), pp. 11–37. Paul Overy, after observing that Kapoor was in Israel aged 17–19, and that in criticism his Jewishness 'has been elided almost entirely in favour of his Indian-ness – which more dramatically connotes "otherness" in the '80s and '90s', points out that since then, Kapoor has lived in Britain. Commenting on his selection to represent Britain in the 1990 Venice Biennale, Overy traces British influences, including the holes and voids in work by Hepworth and Moore. Paul Overy, 'Lions & Unicorns: The Britishness of Postwar British Sculpture', *Art in America*, (September 1991), pp. 104–111, pp. 53–55.

7 See Griselda Pollock, *Vision and Difference: Femininity, Feminism and the Histories of Art* (London: Routledge, 1988), p. 81, for a discussion of *La Psyché* as an example of Morisot's 'concern with female subjectivity especially at critical turning-points of the feminine' and with 'spaces of femininity'.

8 Antoni has indicated her debt to feminist artists of the 1970s in particular, who she has said were 'more extreme' than those of the 1980s who 'used a language that was already respected and they put their content into it'. Laura Cottingham, 'Janine Antoni: Biting Sums up My Relationship to Art History', *Flash Art*, 171 (summer 1993), p. 104–105.

9 Amelia Jones investigates differing aspects of the relation between the art object, the subjectivity of the artist and photographic documentation in the context of performance in Amelia Jones, *Body Art: Performing the Subject* (Minneapolis: University of Minnesota Press, 1998), particularly in the introduction and in chapter 1.

10 R.H. Blyth comments closely on the difficulty of translation. I would like to draw out here just one phrase, which he translated as 'The Eye of the True Law', which, left without further comment could imply the worst excesses of phalloculologocentrism. He comments on the four Chinese symbols in the original: '[the first symbol] means absolute, beyond true and false and all other antitheses. [The second symbol] means things, the Buddhist Law. Here it means perhaps all existence. [The third symbol] means clear apprehension without any added intellectual deformation or emotional discoloration. [The fourth symbol] means that all is included, nothing omitted or wasted', R.H. Blyth (ed.), *Mumonkan*, ed. R.H. Blyth V vols (Zen and Zen Classics, IV; Tokyo: Hokuseido Press, 1996), p. 75. This gives a far more sympathetic reading in this context. While this is a standard English-language translation, it carries heavily the inflection of its time and its translator (Blyth was born 1898). More recently, Thomas Cleary has translated the phrase as 'treasury of the eye of truth' in Keizan, *Transmission of Light: Zen in the Art of Enlightenment*, trans. Thomas Cleary (San Francisco: North Point Press, 1990), p. 6. The meditation upon this problem forms the whole of section 6 of the book Luce Irigaray, *Passions élémentaires* (Paris: Minuit, 1982), pp. 37–44, Luce Irigaray, *Elemental Passions*, trans. Joanne Collie and Judith Still (London: Athlone Press, 1992a), pp. 31–36.

11 The meditation upon this problem forms the whole section 6 of the book (Irigaray, 1982 pp. 37–44; Irigaray 1992a pp. 31–36).

## CHAPTER 3

1 'l'entreouverture' (for example, Luce Irigaray, *Parler n'est jamais neutre* (Paris: Éditions de Minuit, 1985e), p. 300. Luce Irigaray, *Ethique de la différence sexuelle* (Paris: Éditions de Minuit, 1984), p. 108, can read as 'the inter-enter-opening'. It is usually translated (rather unsatisfactorily) as 'open'.

2 – to follow Irigaray's usage of the term in Luce Irigaray, 'La limite du transfert', *Parler n'est jamais neutre* (Paris: Éditions de Minuit, 1985a), p. 298 and Luce Irigaray, 'The Limits of the Transference', in Margaret Whitford (ed.), *The Irigaray Reader* (Oxford: Blackwell, 1991a), p. 110.

3 When asked in an interview if 'writing as a woman' [*écrire en tant que femme*] was 'valid' [*valable*] Irigaray responded to that particular question as if it were a tautology: 'I am a woman. I write with who I am. Why wouldn't that be valid, unless out of contempt for the value of women or from a denial of a culture in which the sexual is

a significant subjective and objective dimension', in Luce Irigaray, *Je, tu, nous: pour une culture de la différence* (Paris: Grasset et Fasquelle, 1990a), p. 61; Luce Irigaray, *Je, Tu, Nous: Toward a Culture of Difference*, trans. Alison Martin (New York: Routledge, 1993i), pp. 52–53. Later in the interview Irigaray queries the translation (from English to French) of the questions being put to her. In *This Sex, 'parler-femme'* is translated as 'speaking (as) woman', Luce Irigaray, *This Sex Which Is Not One*, trans. Catherine Porter and Carolyn Burke (Ithaca, NY: Cornell University Press, 1985d), p. 135.

4 This statement from Karibian, as a one-time editor of *Women Artists Magazine* raises what I would consider a questionable role for feminist criticism of protection and support. Additionally, it has a partial reading of what might constitute feminist practice in assuming that feminists have denied themselves interventions in particular areas.

5 Betterton also describes them as 'parodying [...] femininity [and] close to a strategy at work in Irigaray's writing, that is the idea of mimicry or mimesis'. As the implication here is of a maintenance mimesis with no possibility of a productive mimesis, this would again indicate a possible approach, but it is not at this point followed.

6 Conversation with Laura Godfrey-Isaacs in her London studio, summer 1997.

7 'For the anorectic, there is always excess matter deposited over the surface, the form of the body. The goal is to get rid of that surplus and to reveal the essential, core self – to get back to the original boundaries'. Lynda Nead, *The Female Nude: Art, Obscenity and Sexuality* (London: Routledge, 1992), pp. 10–11.

## CHAPTER 4

1 What Irigaray misses from this account is the practice as it can be read with a woman analyst assuming this position, though she does of course work towards different practices within psychoanalysis, as will be discussed.

2 'He was a boy. It is important to be faithful to the text. Not every substitution is possible, especially when sexual difference is involved. In Freud's text, then, the child is a boy. And Freud never wrote that it might have been a girl.' Luce Irigaray, 'Le geste en psychanalyse', *Sexes et parentés* (Paris: Éditions de Minuit, 1987e), p. 111; Luce Irigaray, 'Gesture in Psychoanalysis', *Sexes and Genealogies* (New York: Columbia University Press, 1993g), p. 97. Irigaray also discusses the story of little Ernst in an earlier lecture reprinted in the same volume of essays: Luce Irigaray, 'La croyance même', *sexes et parentés* (Paris: Éditions de Minuit, 1987b), pp. 35–65; Luce Irigaray, 'Belief Itself', *Sexes and Genealogies* (New York: Columbia University Press, 1993a), pp. 23–53.

3 It is noticeable that the concept of the fetishising of the art object and the construction of 'mastery' and 'genius', both mainstays of masculinist mainstream art discourses, have repeatedly come under fire from various feminist analyses. See for example the cumulative work of writers such as Lucy Lippard and Griselda Pollock.

4 Artists as diverse as Louise Bourgeois, Leonora Carrington, Geneviève Cadieux, Helen Chadwick, Mona Hatoum, Laura Godfrey-Isaacs, Jana Sterbak could be discussed in this context.

5 See Mary Kelly, 'Reviewing Modernist Criticism', *Screen*, 22/3 (1981), pp. 41–62, for a discussion of the economic investment in reading the gestural trace as authenticating

signature indicating both the presence and the commodification of the artist-subject. I would like to thank Griselda Pollock for reminding me of this.

6 This term is used by Freud to describe the child's interpretation and justificatory stories of his or her parent's behaviour, often including the 'relegation' of a biological parent into a hated step-parent, Sigmund Freud, 'Family Romances', *On Sexuality* (The Penguin Freud Library, VII; Harmondsworth: Penguin, 1991), pp. 221–225.

7 In this essay where this is quoted, Nixon offers a Kleinian reading of certain works by Bourgeois and other artists.

## CHAPTER 5

1 Irigaray's comments on race could prove contentious. As is frequent in her work, this analysis results from consideration of a 'usual' experience, and would certainly hold true for infants born into mixed-sex families (or similar social structures) as a member of the dominant race in a predominantly mono-racial society, no matter what that race is. How far this will break down where notions of the socially 'usual' are stretched is crucial. This structure may hold true for infants born into mixed sex families in minority racial communities. However, being born into a single-sex family or in a racially diverse family, for example, could well produce different chronologies.

2 It also accounts for patriarchy's (and patriarchal capitalism's) ability to exchange women through the structure of the representation, 'woman' – which is, after all, an abstraction. Luce Irigaray, *Ce sexe qui n'en est pas un* (Paris: Éditions de Minuit, 1977a), p. 171, Luce Irigaray, *This Sex Which Is Not One*, trans. Catherine Porter and Carolyn Burke (Ithaca, NY: Cornell University Press, 1985d), p. 175.

3 *Ce sexe* was first published in France in 1977, but other similar comments appeared in *Speculum* in France in 1974. I do not wish to suggest any direct influence one way or the other. Santoro's full text is reprinted in Hilary Robinson (ed.), *Feminism-Art-Theory 1968–2000* (Oxford: Blackwell, 2002), pp. 277–278.

4 See also Lynda Nead, *The Female Nude: Art, Obscenity and Sexuality* (London: Routledge, 1992), particularly pp. 25–33, on this definition.

5 Irigaray is meticulous in her usage of the two words for power: *le pouvoir* and *la puissance*. Here, the masculine *le pouvoir* re-enforces the patriarchal nature of power structures that must not be thoughtlessly reinstated.

6 I would like to note that there is an echo here of Lacan's 'mirror phase' and critiques of it; an echo which will recur through this section. To engage with this fully would be necessarily technical, lengthy and tangential to my aim, which is not to chart the differences between Irigaray and Jacques Lacan; such a project would be of more interest in a psychoanalytic-historical context, but is not really of interest here. So I will leave Lacan's work in the status of being symptomatic of the phallocentric structures that Irigaray is trying to undo, rather than present it as over-determinedly causal of her work.

7 Again, as laid down by the early Church. For example, Fortunatus (530–609), Bishop of Poitiers on pregnant women: 'When the belly swells from its wound and sensual dropsy grows, the woman's exhausted health hangs by a hair. The raised skin is so

distent and mis-shapen that even though the mother may be happy with her burden, she becomes ashamed… How describe the tears shed at the moment when the muscles relax to release the prisoner and procure relief for the viscera? A way is forced violently through the passage and a being, perhaps lifeless, brought to life. The mother painfully turns her dull glance towards him. What does she see? An infant stretched motionless… so that she no longer deserves to be called either mother or virgin' (quoted in O'Faolain and Martines, Laura, 1979), p. 151.

## CHAPTER 6

1 In other places Irigaray does tackle these constructions, for example, in her re-interpretation of the Annunciation, Luce Irigaray, *I Love to You: Sketch for a Felicity within History*, trans. Alison Martin (New York: Routledge, 1996), pp. 40–41.

2 In the St Anne Trinitarium woodcut from the *Heures à l'usage d'Angers* (sixteenth century) it could also be possible to read this matrilineal trinity as not only indicating the fertile womb of Anne, but also in the drawing of St Anne holding her cloak and the folds in her dress her figure evokes the morphology of the genitals.

3 One element only suggests otherwise. The size of the canvas depicted in the painting is a little smaller than it should properly be if it were this painting itself. However, there are good compositional reasons why Labille-Guiard might want this image to stop short of the upper limit of the painting: to do so ensures a visual stability that would otherwise be lost.

4 It is interesting that the attacks on Irigaray's 'essentialism' have come primarily from critics in the USA, where a need to counter reductive or racist identity politics may mean that some forms of difference – including European differences – are not recognised. See for example Christine Delphy, 'The Invention of French Feminism: As Essential Move', *Yale French Studies*, 87 (1995), pp. 190–221 for an analysis of 'New French Feminism' as a designation which has meaning only in Anglo-American academia, and none in France. Toril Moi, 'Feminism, Postmodernism and Style: Recent Feminist Criticism in the United States', *Cultural Critique*, (1988), pp. 3–22 and Gayatri Chakravorty Spivak, 'French Feminism in an International Frame (1981)', *In Other Worlds: Essays in Cultural Politics* (London: Routledge, 1988a), pp. 134–153. Both map out differences between developments in feminist theory in different geographical locations.

5 Gerardine Meaney, 'Sex and Nation' p 233. 'Mother Ireland' has multiple configurations. The most substantial source on the subject is Belinda Loftus, *Mirrors: William III and Mother Ireland* (Dundrum: Picture Press, 1990). See also a review of the book which adds further complexities, Joan Fowler, 'King Billy and Mother Ireland in Mirrors', *The Oxford Art Journal*, 14.2 (1991), pp. 104–107.

6 Exceptions to prove the rule are: Lynda Nead, *The Female Nude: Art, Obscenity and Sexuality* (London: Routledge, 1992), pp. 77–78, discusses work by Mary Duffy; Jo Anna Isaak, *Feminism and Contemporary Art: The Revolutionary Power of Women's Laughter* (London: Routledge, 1996) at 165–171, discusses work by Kathy Prendergast and mentions Dorothy Cross; and my own Hilary Robinson, 'Border Crossings: Womanliness, Body, Representation', in Katy Deepwell (ed.), *New Feminist Art Criticism:*

*Critical Strategies* (1995b), pp. 138–146, mentions briefly Mary Duffy, Anne Tallentire and a Pauline Cummins/Louise Walsh collaboration.

7 I have discussed in more depth elsewhere the relation between Irish visual culture, essentialism and work by Irish women. See Hilary Robinson, 'Irish/Woman/Artist: Selective Readings', *Feminist Review*, 50 (1995a), pp. 89–110, Hilary Robinson, 'Within the Pale in *From: Beyond the Pale*: The Construction of Femininity in the Curating of an Exhibition Season at the Irish Museum of Modern Art, Dublin', *Journal of Gender Studies*, 6/3 (1997), pp. 255–267, Hilary Robinson, 'Disruptive Women Artists: An Irigarayan Reading of Irish Visual Culture', *Irish Studies Review*, 8/1 (April 2000), pp. 57–72, Hilary Robinson, 'Becoming Women: Irigaray, Ireland and Visual Representation', in Sighle Cusack and Tricia Bhreathnach-Lynch (eds), *Art, Nation and Gender: Ethnic Landscapes, Myths and Mother-Figures* (Aldershot: Ashgate, 2003).

8 Pronounced 'sheela-na-gig'. One whose image has been used by Nancy Spero in various works in the 1980s such as *Sheela and Wilma* (1985) and *Chorus Line* (1885), is English, from Kilpeck, Hertfordshire.

## CONCLUSION

1 She was specifically referring to the historian and the teacher of literature, but this is a useful model for productive interdisciplinary engagement.

2 This is not to deny the obvious: that we all work with visual significations of gesture, clothing, etc, but rather to stress the particularities of producing artworks as signifiers.

# Bibliography

Archer, Michael, Brett, Guy, and de Zegher, M. Catherine (eds) (1997), *Mona Hatoum* (London: Phaidon).

Ashley, Kathleen and Sheingorn, Pamela (1990), 'Introduction', in Kathleen Ashley and Pamela Sheingorn (eds), *Interpreting Cultural Symbols: Saint Anne in Late Medieval Society* (Athens and London: The University of Georgia Press), pp. 1–68.

Bal, Mieke (2001), *Louise Bourgeois' Spider: The Archeology of Art-Writing* (Chicago: The University of Chicago Press).

Balzano, Wanda (1996), 'Irishness – Feminist and Post-Colonial', in Iain Chambers and Lidia Curti (eds), *The Post-Colonial Question: Common Skies, Divided Horizons* (London: Routledge), pp. 92–97.

Baruch, Elaine Hoffman, Serrano, Lucienne J., and Irigaray, Luce (1988), 'Luce Irigaray: Paris, Summer 1980', in Elaine Hoffman Baruch and Lucienne J. Serrano (eds), *Women Analyze Women: in France, England, and the United States* (New York: New York University Press), pp. 147–164.

Berg, Maggie (1991), 'Luce Irigaray's "Contradictions": Poststructuralism and Feminism', *Signs: Journal of Women in Culture and Society*, 17 (1), pp. 50–70.

Betterton, Rosemary (1996), *An Intimate Distance: Women, Artists and the Body* (London: Routledge).

Blyth, R.H. (ed.) (1996), *Mumonkan*, ed. R.H. Blyth V vols (Zen and Zen Classics, IV; Tokyo: Hokuseido Press).

Bonami, Francesco (1994), 'Anish Kapoor: Jumping into the Void', *Flash Art*, 27 (179), pp. 80–82.

Borzello, Frances (1998), *Seeing Ourselves: Women's Self-Portraits* (London: Thames & Hudson).

Braidotti, Rosi (1991), 'Body-Images and the Pornography of Representation', *Journal of Gender Studies*, 1 (2), pp. 137–151.

— (1992), 'On the Female Feminist Subject, or: From "She-self" to "She-other"', in Gisela Bock and Susan James (eds), *Beyond Equality and Difference: Citizenship, Feminist Politics and Female Subjectivity* (London: Routledge), pp. 177–192.

— (1994), 'Of Bugs and Women: Irigaray and Deleuze on the Becoming-Woman', in Carolyn Burke, Naomi Schor, and Margaret Whitford (eds), *Engaging with Irigaray: Feminist Philosophy and Modern European Thought* (New York: Columbia UP), pp. 111–137.

Burke, Carolyn (1994), 'Translation Modified: Irigaray in English', in Carolyn Burke, Naomi Schor, and Margaret Whitford (eds), *Engaging with Irigaray: Feminist Philosophy and Modern European Thought* (New York: Columbia UP), pp. 249–261.

Burke, Carolyn, Schor, Naomi, and Whitford, Margaret (eds) (1994), *Engaging with Irigaray: Feminist Philosophy and Modern European Thought* (New York: Columbia University Press).

Bush, Kate (2004), 'Animal Instinct', [web site], <http: / / www.frieze.com /

Butler, Judith (1990), *Gender Trouble* (London: Routledge).

Callois, Roger (1984), 'Mimicry and Legendary Psychasthenia', *October*, 31, pp. 17–32.

Celant, Germano (1998), 'Artist as Sacerdos', *Anish Kapoor* (Milan: Edizioni Charta).

Chanter, Tina (1995), *Ethics of Eros: Irigaray's Re-writing of the Philosophers* (New York: Routledge).

Chisholm, Dianne (1994), 'Irigaray's Hysteria', in Carolyn Burke, Naomi Schor, and Margaret Whitford (eds), *Engaging with Irigaray: Feminist Philosophy and Modern European Thought* (New York: Columbia UP), pp. 263–283.

Cixous, Hélène (1981), 'The Laugh of the Medusa', in Elaine Marks and Isabelle de Courtivron (eds), *New French Feminisms: An Anthology* (Brighton: Harvester Press), pp. 245–264.

Clarke, Kenneth (1956), *The Nude: A Study of Ideal Art* (London: John Murray).

Cottingham, Laura (1993), 'Janine Antoni: Biting Sums Up My Relationship to Art History', *Flash Art*, (171), pp. 104–105.

Coward, Rosalind (1984), *Female Desire: Women's Sexuality Today* (London: Paladin).

Curthoys, Jean (1997), *Feminist Amnesia: The Wake of Women's Liberation* (London: Routledge).

Datuin, Flaudette May V (2002), *Home, Body, Memory: Filipina Artists in the Visual Arts, 19th Century to the Present* (Quezon City: University of the Philippines Press).

de Zegher, Catherine (ed.), (1996), *Inside the Visible: An Elliptical Traverse of 20th Century Art, In Of and From the Feminine* (Cambridge, MA: MIT Press).

Delphy, Christine (1995), 'The Invention of French Feminism: An Essential Move', *Yale French Studies*, 87, pp. 190–221.

Derrida, Jacques (1981), *Positions*, trans. Alan Bass (Chicago: University of Chicago Press).

Donovan, Josephine (1993), 'Everyday Use and Moments of Being: Toward a Nondominative Aesthetic', in Hilde Hein and Carolyn Korsmeyer (eds), (Bloomington: Indiana University Press), pp. 53–67.

Dworkin, Andrea (1981), *Pornography: Men Possessing Women* (London: The Women's Press).

Eckman, Joanna (ed.) (1994), *Louise Bourgeois: Locus of Memory, Works 1982–1993* (New York: Abrams).

Ellis, John (1980), 'Photography / Pornography / Art / Pornography', *Screen*, 21 (1), pp. 81–108.

Esders, Viviane (ed.) (1996), *Our Mothers: Portraits by 72 Women Photographers* (New York: Sterart, Tabori & Chang).

Fletcher, John (1988), 'Versions of Masquerade', *Screen*, 29 (3), pp. 43–70.

Fowler, Joan (1991), 'King Billy and Mother Ireland in Mirrors', *The Oxford Art Journal*, 14 (2), pp. 104–107.

Freud, Sigmund (1991), 'Family Romances', *On Sexuality* (The Penguin Freud Library, VII; Harmondsworth: Penguin), pp. 221–225.

Freueh, Joanna (2002), '"Feminism" from *Hannah Wilke: A Retrospective* (1989)', in Hilary Robinson (ed.), *Feminism-Art-Theory 1968–2000* (Oxford: Blackwell), pp. 578–584.

Fuller, Diana Burgess and Salvioni, Daniella (eds) (2002), *Art/Women/California: Parallels and Intersections* (Berkeley and Los Angeles: University of California Press).

Fuss, Diana (1990), *Essentially Speaking: Feminism, Nature and Difference* (London: Routledge).

Gallop, Jane (1988), *Thinking Through the Body* (New York: Columbia University Press).

Gates, Henry Louis, Jr (1988), 'Significant Others', *Contemporary Literature*, 29 (4), pp. 606–623.

Gebauer, Gunter and Wulf, Christoph (1995), *Mimesis: Culture, Art, Society*, trans. Don Reneau (London: University of California Press).

Goldman, Shifra (1991), 'Contemporary Chicana Artists', in Arlene Raven, Cassandra Langer, and Joanna Freueh (eds), *Feminist Art Criticism: An Anthology* (New York: HarperCollins), pp. 187–205.

Greer, Germaine (1981), *The Obstacle Race: The Fortunes of Women Painters and their Work* (London: Pan Books).

Grosz, Elizabeth (1989), *Sexual Subversions: Three French Feminists* (Current books in women's studies; Sydney: Boston).

— (1990), *Jacques Lacan: A Feminist Introduction* (London: Routledge).

— (1994), *Volatile Bodies: Toward a Corporeal Feminism* (Bloomington: Indiana University Press).

— (1995), *Space, Time and Perversion: Essays on the Politics of Bodies* (London: Routledge).

Heath, Stephen (1986), 'Joan Riviere and the Masquerade', in Victor Burgin, James Donald, and Kora Kaplan (eds), *Formations of Fantasy* (London: Methuen), pp. 45–61.

Hegarty, Frances (1998), personal letter to Hilary Robinson.

Higonnet, Anne (1992), *Berthe Morisot's Images of Women* (Cambridge, MA: Harvard University Press).

Hirsh, Elizabeth and Olson, Gary (1995), '"Je – Luce Irigaray": A Meeting with Luce Irigaray', in Gary A. Olson and Elizabeth Hirsh (eds), *Women Writing Culture* (Albany: State U of New York P), pp. 141–166.

Huangfu, Binghui (ed.) (2000), *Text and Subtext: Contemporary Art and Asian Women* (Singapore: Earl Lu Gallery).

Hufton, Olwen (1995), *The Prospect Before Her: A History of Women in Western Europe* (1: 1500–1800; London: HarperCollins).

Irigaray, Luce (1973), *Le langage des dements* (Approaches to Semiotics; The Hague: Mouton).

— (1974), *Speculum de l'autre femme* (Paris: Éditions de Minuit).

— (1977a), *Ce sexe qui n'en est pas un* (Paris: Éditions de Minuit).

— (1977b), 'Women's Exile: Interview with Luce Irigaray. Interview by Dianna Adlam & Couze Venn', *Ideology and Consciousness*, 1, pp. 62–76.

— (1979), *Et l'une ne bouge pas sans l'autre* (Paris: Éditions de minuit).

— (1980), *Amante marine: de Friedrich Nietzsche* (Paris: Éditions de minuit).

— (1981), 'And the One Doesn't Stir Without the Other', *Signs: Journal of Women in Culture and Society*, 7 (1), pp. 60–67.

— (1982), *Passions élémentaires* (Paris: Éditions de Minuit).

— (1984), *Ethique de la différence sexuelle* (Paris: Éditions de Minuit).

— (1985a), 'La limite du transfert', *Parler n'est jamais neutre* (Paris: Éditions de Minuit), pp. 293–304.

— (1985b), 'Misère de la psychanalyse', *Parler n'est jamais neutre* (Paris: Éditions de Minuit), pp. 253–279.

— (1985c), *Speculum of the Other Woman*, trans. Gillian C. Gill (Ithaca, NY: Cornell University Press).

— (1985d), *This Sex Which Is Not One*, trans. Catherine Porter and Carolyn Burke (Ithaca, NY: Cornell University Press).

— (1985e), *Parler n'est jamais neutre* (Paris: Éditions de Minuit).

— (1987a), 'Les couleurs de la chair', *Sexes et parentés* (Paris: Éditions de Minuit), pp. 165–179.

— (1987b), 'La croyance même', *Sexes et parentés* (Paris: Éditions de Minuit), pp. 35–65.
— (1987c), 'Femmes divines', *Sexes et parentés* (Paris: Éditions de Minuit), pp. 67–85.
— (1987d), 'Le genre féminin', *Sexes et parentés* (Paris: Éditions de Minuit), pp. 119–138.
— (1987e), 'Le geste en psychanalyse', *Sexes et parentés* (Paris: Éditions de Minuit), pp. 103–118.
— (1987f), 'La nécessité de droits sexués', *Sexes et parentés* (Paris: Éditions de Minuit), pp. 13–18.
— (1987g), 'Les trois genres', *Sexes et parentés* (Paris: Éditions de Minuit), pp. 181–196.
— (1987h), 'L'universel comme médiation', *Sexes et parentés* (Paris: Éditions de Minuit), pp. 139–164.
— (1989), *Le temps de la différence: pour une révolution pacifique* (Le livre de poche; Paris: Libr. générale française).
— (1990a), *Je, tu, nous: pour une culture de la différence* (Paris: Grasset et Fasquelle).
— (1990b), 'Comment créer notre beauté?, *Je, tu, nous: pour une culture de la différence* (Paris: Grasset et Fasquelle), pp. 121–126.
— (1991a), 'The Limits of the Transference', in Margaret Whitford (ed.), *The Irigaray Reader* (Oxford: Blackwell), pp. 105–117
— (1991b), *Marine Lover of Friedrich Nietzsche*, trans. Gillian C. Gill (New York: Columbia University Press).
— (1991c), 'The Poverty of Psychoanalysis', in Margaret Whitford (ed.), *The Irigaray Reader* (Oxford: Blackwell), pp. 79–104.
— (1991d), 'Questions to Emanuel Levinas', in Margaret Whitford (ed.), *The Irigaray Reader* (Oxford: Blackwell), pp. 178–189.
— (1991e), 'The Three Genres', in Margaret Whitford (ed.), *The Irigaray Reader*, (Oxford: Blackwell), pp. 140–153.
— (1991f), 'Women-Mothers, the Silent Substratum of the Social Order', in Margaret Whitford (ed.), *The Irigaray Reader* (Cambridge, MA: Basil Blackwell), pp. 47–52.
— (1992a), *Elemental Passions*, trans. Joanne Collie and Judith Still (London: Athlone Press).
— (1992b), *J'aime à toi: esquisse d'une félicité dans l'histoire* (Paris: B. Grasset).
— (1993a), 'Belief Itself', *Sexes and Genealogies* (New York: Columbia University Press), pp. 23–53.
— (1993b), 'Divine Women', *Sexes and Genealogies* (New York: Columbia University Press), pp. 55–72.
— (1993c), 'Each Sex must Have its Own Rights', *Sexes and Genealogies* (New York: Columbia University Press), pp. 1–5.
— (1993d), *An Ethics of Sexual Difference*, trans. Carolyn Burke and Gillian C. Gill (London: Athlone Press) .
— (1993e), 'The Female Gender', *Sexes and Genealogies* (New York: Columbia University Press), pp. 105–123.
— (1993f), 'Flesh Colors', *Sexes and Genealogies* (New York: Columbia University Press), pp. 151–165.
— (1993g), 'Gesture in Psychoanalysis', *Sexes and Genealogies* (New York: Columbia University Press), pp. 89–104.
— (1993h), 'How Can We Create Our Beauty?' *Je, Tu, Nous: Toward a Culture of Difference* (New York: Routledge), pp. 107–111.
— (1993i), *Je, Tu, Nous: Toward a Culture of Difference*, trans. Alison Martin (New York: Routledge).
— (1993j), 'The Three Genders', *Sexes and Genealogies* (New York: Columbia University Press), pp. 167–181.

— (1993k), 'The Universal as Mediation', *Sexes and Genealogies* (New York: Columbia University Press), pp. 125–149.

— (1994a), 'Equal to Whom?', in Naomi Schor and Elizabeth Weed (ed.), *The Essential Difference* (Bloomington: Indiana UP), pp. 63–81.

— (1994b), 'A Natal Lacuna', *Women's Art Magazine,* (58), pp. 11–13.

— (1994c), *Thinking the Difference: For a Peaceful Revolution,* trans. Karin Montin (London: Athlone Press).

— (1996), *I Love to You: Sketch for a Felicity within History,* trans. Alison Martin (New York: Routledge).

— (1997), *Tra Orient e Occidente: Dalla Singolarità alla Comunità* (Rome: Manifestolibri).

— (1999a), *The Age of the Breath* (Rüsselsheim: Christel Göttert Verlag).

— (1999b), *Entre Orient et Occident: de la singularité à la communauté* (Paris: B. Grasset).

— (2002), *Between East and West: From Singularity to Community,* trans. Stephen Pluhácek (New York: Columbia University Press).

Irigaray, Luce and Lotringer, Sylvère (eds) (2000), *Why different? A Culture of Two Subjects: Interviews with Luce Irigaray* (New York: Semiotext(e)).

Isaak, Jo Anna (1996), *Feminism and Contemporary Art: The Revolutionary Power of Women's Laughter* (London: Routledge).

Jay, Martin (1993), *Downcast Eyes: The Denigration of Vision in Twentieth Century French Thought* (Berkeley: University of California Press).

Jones, Amelia (ed.) (1996a), *Sexual Politics: Judy Chicago's Dinner Party in Feminist Art History* (Los Angeles: UCLA in assn. with University of California Press).

— (1996b), 'Sexual Politics: Feminist Strategies, Feminist Conflicts, Feminist Histories', in Amelia Jones (ed.), *Sexual Politics: Judy Chicago's Dinner Party in Feminist Art History* (Los Angeles: UCLA in assn. with University of California Press), 20–38.

— (1998), *Body Art: Performing the Subject* (Minneapolis: University of Minnesota Press).

Jones, Serene (1995), 'Divining Women: Irigaray and Feminist Theologies', *Yale French Studies,* 87, pp. 42–68.

Kapoor, Anish (1990), 'Mostly Hidden: An Interview with Marjorie Althorpe-Guyton', *Anish Kapoor* (London: The British Council), pp. 43–51.

Karibian, Leah, Godfrey-Isaacs, Laura, and Johnston, Stephen (1994), *Laura Godfrey-Isaacs: The Alien and the Domestic* (Winchester: Winchester Gallery at Winchester School of Art).

Keizan (1990), *Transmission of Light: Zen in the Art of Enlightenment,* trans. Thomas Cleary (San Francisco: North Point Press).

Kelly, Eamonn P. (1996), *Sheela-na-Gigs: Origins and Functions* (Dublin: Country House in association with The National Museum of Ireland).

Kelly, Mary (1981), 'Reviewing Modernist Criticism', *Screen,* 22 (3), pp. 41–62.

Kelly, Mary and Pollock, Griselda (1992), 'Mary Kelly and Griselda Pollock in Conversation', in Kate Campbell (ed.), *Critical Feminism: Argument in the Disciplines* (Buckingham: Open University Press), pp. 182–216.

Kerr, Joan and Holder, Jo (eds) (1999), *Past Present: The National Women's Art Anthology* (Sydney: Craftsman House).

Key, Joan (1997), 'Unfold: Imprecations of Obscenity in the Fold', in Juliet Steyn (ed.), *Other Than Identity: The Subject, Politics and Art* (Manchester: Manchester University Press), pp. 185–197.

Kimmelman, Michael (1996), 'At the Met with Leon Golub and Nancy Spero', *The New York Times*, January 5th, sec. Weekend, pp. C1, C5.

Kirili, Alain (1986), 'The Passion for Sculpture: Conversation with Louise Bourgeois', *Arts Magazine*, (63), pp. 69–75.

Kuspit, Donald (1987), 'Louise Bourgeois: Where Angels Fear to Tread', *ArtForum*, (March), pp. 115–120.

Lacan, Jacques (1994), *The Four Fundamental Concepts of Psycho-Analysis*, trans. Alan Sheridan (London: Penguin).

Lippard, Lucy (1990), 'The Pains and Pleasures of Rebirth: European and American Women's Body Art', *The Pink Glass Swan: Selected Feminist Essays on Art* (New York: The New Press), pp. 99–113.

— (1995), 'The Women Artist's Movement: What Next?' *The Pink Glass Swan: Selected Feminist Essays on Art* (New York: New Press), pp. 80–83.

Loftus, Belinda (1990), *Mirrors: William III and Mother Ireland* (Dundrum: Picture-Press).

Lourde, Audre (1984), 'The Master's Tools will Never Dismantle the Master's House', *Sister Outsider: Essays and Speeches* (Freedom, CA: Crossing Press), pp. 110–113.

McEvilley, Thomas (1990), 'The Darkness Inside a Stone', *Anish Kapoor* (London: The British Council), pp. 11–37.

Meaney, Gerardine (1993), 'Sex and Nation: Women in Irish Culture and Politics', in Ailbhe Smyth (ed), *Irish Women's Studies Reader* (Dublin: Attic Press), pp. 230–244

Merck, Mandy and Townsend, Chris (eds) (2002), *The Art of Tracey Emin* (London: Thames & Hudson).

Meyer-Thoss, Christiane (1992), *Louise Bourgeois: Konstructionen für den Freien Fall/Designing for Free Fall* (Zurich: Amman).

Minsky, Rosalind (1996), *Psychoanalysis and Gender: An Introductory Reader* (London: Routledge).

Moi, Toril (1985), *Sexual/Textual Politics: Feminist Literary Theory* (London: Methuen).

— (1988), 'Feminism, Postmodernism and Style: Recent Feminist Criticism in the United States', *Cultural Critique*, (1), pp. 3–22.

Morgan, Stuart (1996), 'Louise Bourgeois', *Rites of Passage* (London: Tate Gallery), pp. 54–57.

Mullin, Molly (1991), 'Representations of History, Irish Feminism and the Politics of Difference', *Feminist Studies*, 17 (1), pp. 29–50.

Mulvey, Laura (1973), 'You Don't Know What is Happening, Do You, Mr Jones?' *Spare Rib*, (8), pp. 13–16, 30.

— (1975), 'Visual Pleasure and Narrative Cinema', *Screen*, 16 (3), pp. 6–18.

Nead, Lynda (1992), *The Female Nude: Art, Obscenity and Sexuality* (London: Routledge).

Nickson, Elizabeth (1996), 'Learning Curves', *The Guardian*, 8 April, sec. G2 p. 7.

Nixon, Mignon (1995), 'Bad Enough Mother', *October*, (71), pp. 71–92.

Overy, Paul (1991), 'Lions & Unicorns: The Britishness of Postwar British Sculpture', *Art in America*, pp. 53–55, 104–111.

O'Faolain, Julia and Martines, Lauro (1979), *Not in God's Image: Women in History* (London: Virago).

Parker, Rozsika (1977), 'Censored', *Spare Rib*, (54), pp. 43–45.

Parker, Rozsika and Pollock, Griselda (1981), *Old Mistresses: Women, Art and Ideology* (London: Routledge & Kegan Paul).

Phelan, Peggy (1993), *Unmarked: The Politics of Performance* (London: Routledge).

Pluhácek, Stephen, Bostic, Heidi, and Irigaray, Luce (1996), 'Thinking Life As Relation: An Interview with Luce Irigaray', *Man and World*, 29 (4), p. 343.

Pollock, Griselda (1988), *Vision and Difference: Femininity, Feminism and the Histories of Art* (London: Routledge).

— (1991), 'Missing Women: Rethinking Early Thoughts on Images of Women', in Carol Squiers (ed.), *The Critical Image: Essays on Contemporary Photography* (London: Lawrence & Wishart), pp. 202–219.

— (1992), 'Painting, Feminism, History', in Michèle Barrett and Anne Phillips (eds), *Destabilizing Theory: Contemporary Feminist Debates* (Cambridge: Polity Press), pp. 138–176.

— (1996a), 'Inscriptions in the Feminine', in de Zegher, Catherine (ed.), *Inside the Visible: An Elliptical Traverse of 20th Century Art, In Of and From the Feminine* (Cambridge, MA: MIT Press), pp. 67–87.

— (1996b), 'Killing Men and Dying Women', in Fred Orton and Griselda Pollock (eds), *Avant-Gardes and Partisans Reviewed* (Manchester: Manchester University Press), pp. 221–294.

— (1996c), 'The Politics of Theory: Generations and Geographies in Feminist Theory and the Histories of Art History', *Generations and Geographies in the Visual Arts: Feminist Readings* (London: Routledge), pp. 3–21.

— (1996d), 'Preface', *Generations and Geographies in the Visual Arts: Feminist Readings* (London: Routledge), pp. xii–xx.

— (1999), *Differencing the Canon: Feminist Desire and the Writing of Art's Histories* (London: Routledge).

Ragland-Sullivan, Ellie (1992), 'The Symbolic', in Elizabeth Wright (ed.), *Feminism and Psychoanalysis: A Critical Dictionary* (Oxford: Blackwell), pp. 420–423.

Reckitt, Helena and Phelan, Peggy (2001), *Art and Feminism* (London: Phaidon).

Ricoeur, Paul (1981), 'Mimesis and Representation', *Annals of Scholarship*, 2, pp. 15–32.

Riviere, Joan (1986), 'Womanliness as Masquerade', in Victor Burgin, James Donald, and Kora Kaplan (eds), *Formations of Fantasy* (London: Methuen), pp. 35–44.

Rose, Jacqueline (1982), 'Introduction II', in Juliet Mitchell and Jacqueline Rose (eds), *Feminine Sexuality: Jacques Lacan and the École Freudienne* (Houndmills: Macmillan), pp. 27–57.

— (1986), *Sexuality in the Field of Vision* (London: Verso).

Robinson, Hilary (1994), 'Irigaray's imaginings', *Women's Art Magazine*, (61), p. 20.

— (1995a), 'Irish/Woman/Artist: Selective Readings', *Feminist Review*, (50), pp. 89–110.

— (1995b), 'Border Crossings: Womanliness, Body, Representation', in Katy Deepwell (ed.), *New Feminist Art Criticism: Critical Strategies*, pp. 138–146.

— (1997), 'Within the Pale in *From: Beyond the Pale*: The Construction of Femininity in the Curating of an Exhibition Season at the Irish Museum of Modern Art, Dublin', *Journal of Gender Studies*, 6 (3), pp. 255–267.

— (2000), 'Disruptive Women Artists: An Irigarayan Reading of Irish Visual Culture', *Irish Studies Review*, 8 (1), pp. 57–72.

— (ed.) (2002), *Feminism-Art-Theory 1968–2000* (Oxford: Blackwell).

— (2003), 'Becoming Women: Irigaray, Ireland and Visual Representation', in Sighle Bhreathnach-Lynch and Tricia Cusack (eds), *Art, Nation and Gender: Ethnic Landscapes, Myths and Mother-Figures* (Aldershot: Ashgate).

Rowley, Alison (1996), 'On Viewing Three Paintings by Jenny Saville: Rethinking a Feminist Practice of Painting', in Griselda Pollock (ed.), *Generations and Geographies in the Visual Arts: Feminist Readings* (London: Routledge), pp. 88–109.

Santoro, Suzanne (1974), *Per una Espressione Nuova/Toward New Expression* (Rome: Rivolta Femminile).

Sasaki Roshi, Joshu (1974), *Buddha is the Center of Gravity* (San Cristobal).

Sautman, Francesca (1990), 'Saint Anne in Folk Tradition: Late Medieval France', in Kathleen Ashley and Pamela Sheinghorn (eds), *Interpreting Cultural Symbols: Saint Anne in Late Medieval Society* (Athens and London: The University of Georgia Press), pp. 69–94.

Schjeldahl, Peter (1992), 'The Documenta of the Dog', *ArtForum*, 80 (9), pp. 88–97.

Schor, Naomi (1994a), 'This Essentialism Which Is Not One: Coming to Grips with Irigaray', in Naomi Schor and Elizabeth Weed (eds), *The Essential Difference* (Bloomington: Indiana UP), pp. 40–62.

— (1994b), 'This Essentialism Which Is Not One: Coming to Grips with Irigaray', in Carolyn Burke, Naomi Schor, and Margaret Whitford (eds), *Engaging with Irigaray: Feminist Philosophy and Modern European Thought* (New York: Columbia UP), pp. 57–78.

Sheingorn, Pamela (1990), 'Appropriating the Holy Kinship: Gender and Family History', in Kathleen Ashley and Pamela Sheingorn (eds), *Interpreting Cultural Symbols: Saint Anne in Late Medieval Society* (Athens and London: The University of Georgia Press), pp. 167–198.

— (1993), '"The Wise Mother": The Image of St. Anne Teaching the Virgin Mary', *Gesta*, 32 (1), pp. 69–80.

Simon, Sherry (1996), *Gender in Translation: Cultural Identity and the Politics of Transmission* (London: Routledge).

Spence, Jo (1995), 'The Politics of Transformation', *Cultural Sniping: The Art of Transgression* (London: Routledge), pp. 147–166.

Spivak, Gayatri Chakravorty (1988a), 'French Feminism in an International Frame (1981)', *In Other Worlds: Essays in Cultural Politics* (London: Routledge), pp. 134–153.

— (1988b), 'A Literary Representation of the Subaltern: A Woman's Text From the Third World', *In Other Worlds: Essays in Cultural Politics* (London: Routledge), pp. 241–268.

— (1990), 'Criticism, Feminism and the Institution', in Sarah Harasym (ed.), *The Post-Colonial Critic: Interviews, Strategies, Dialogues* (London: Routledge), pp. 1–16.

— (1992), 'The Politics of Translation', in Michèle Barrett and Anne Phillips (eds), *Destabilizing Theory: Contemporary Feminist Debates* (Cambridge: Polity Press), pp. 177–200.

— and Rooney, Ellen (1994), 'In a Word. Interview', in Naomi Schor and Elizabeth Weed (eds), *The Essential Difference* (Bloomington: Indiana UP), pp. 151–185.

Storr, Robert (1995), 'The Discreet Charm of Louise Bourgeois', *Tate, The Art Magazine*, (6), pp. 24–31.

Sultan, Terrie (1994), 'Redefining the Terms of Engagement', in Joanna Eckman (ed.), *Louise Bourgeois: Locus of Memory, Works 1982–1993* (New York: Abrams), pp. 28–50.

Tickner, Lisa, (1978), 'The Body Politic: Female Sexuality and Women Artists since 1970', *Art History*, 1 (2), pp. 236–251.

Vasseleu, Cathryn (1996), 'Illuminating Passion: Irigaray's Transfiguration of Night', in Theresa Brennan and Martin Jay (eds), *Vision in Context* (London: Routledge), pp. 127–137.

Warner, Marina (1985), *Alone of All Her Sex: The Myth and Cult of the Virgin Mary* (London: Pan Books).

Watney, Simon (1995), *Laura Godfrey-Isaacs* (London & Exeter: John Jones Gallery & Spacex).

Weed, Elizabeth (1994), 'The Question of Style', in Carolyn Burke, Naomi Schor, and Margaret Whitford (eds), *Engaging with Irigaray: Feminist Philosophy and Modern European Thought* (New York: Columbia UP), pp. 79–109.

Weinbaum, Alys Eve (1994), 'Marx, Irigaray, and the Politics of Reproduction', *Differences: A Journal of Feminist Cultural Studies*, 6 (1), pp. 98–128.

White, Nicola and McParland, Brenda (eds) (1995), *Janine Antoni: Slip of the Tongue* (Glasgow & Dublin: CCA & IMMA).

Whitford, Margaret (1986), 'Luce Irigaray and the Female Imaginary: Speaking as a Woman', *Radical Philosophy*, (43), pp. 3–8.

— (1991a), 'Glossary', *The Irigaray Reader* (Cambridge, MA: Basil Blackwell), pp. 16–19.

— (1991b), 'Irigaray's Body Symbolic', *Hypatia*, 6 (3), pp. 97–110.

— (1991c), *Luce Irigaray: Philosophy in the Feminine* (London: Routledge).

— (1991d), 'Luce Irigaray', in Alice Jardine and Anne M. Menke (eds), *Shifting Scenes: Interviews on Women, Writing, and Politics in Post-68 France* (New York: Columbia UP), pp. 97–103.

— (1994a), 'Reading Irigaray in the Nineties', in Carolyn Burke, Naomi Schor, and Margaret Whitford (eds), *Engaging with Irigaray: Feminist Philosophy and Modern European Thought* (New York: Columbia University Press), pp. 15–33.

— (1994b), 'Woman with Attitude', *Women's Art Magazine*, (60), pp. 15–17.

Woolf, Virginia (1949), *A Room of One's Own* (London: Hogarth Press).

Wye, Deborah (1982), 'One and Others', in Deborah Wye (ed.), *Louise Bourgeois* (New York: Museum of Modern Art), pp. 13–33.

— (1994), 'The Drama of the Self: Louise Bourgeois as Printmaker', in Deborah Wye and Carol Smith (eds), *The Prints of Louise Bourgeois* (New York: The Museum of Modern Art), pp. 10–32.

Ziff, Tricia (ed.) (1995), *Distant Relations/Cercanias Distantes/Clann I gCéin: Chicano, Irish, Mexican Art and Critical Writing* (Santa Monica: Smart Art Press).

# Index